LIVING BRAVE LEADERSHIP

LIVING BRAVE
leadership

LEARN HOW:
Umbrella Beliefs, Trust, Accountability,
Bravery and Connection define you
and your organisation as Living Brave

GUY BLOOM

Further enquiries visit:
www.livingbrave.com

Living Brave UK Trademark UK00002527804

A CIP catalogue copy for this book
is available from the British Library

ISBN: 978-1-9160927-0-9

Cover   Israel Holtzhausen

Cartoons   Prasanta Biswas

Typsetting   Grzegorz Japoł

Proofing   Tara-Simone Mcleod

DEDICATED TO...

Milo and Hugo

I have made lots of mistakes, I hope this goes
some way to helping you to be the best you can be.
Without you, what would the point be? *

*That's rhetorical. There wouldn't be one.

Living Brave Leadership

Guy Bloom is the driving force behind Living Brave®, working with individuals and organisations to create truly trusted, accountable, brave and connected leaders. He has spent his working life investigating the human and organisational drivers that create long term systemic change.

A life-long martial artist he is an instructor in three martial art systems, a four-time Hall of Famer and an advocate of how fears can be overcome with proven technique, the correct mindset and the bit no one likes......
practice and feedback.

He spends most of his work life as an executive and team coach. In his spare time Guy judges leadership awards, has won a few of them, writes articles, is working on a second book.

This is all geared to ensure his two sons have a clear legacy of what leadership is for themselves and that those who truly want to define themselves as Living Brave have an approach that is deeply rooted in methodology and mindset.

His favourite quote is from the lawyer, politician and diplomat Adlai E. Stevenson, "It's hard to lead a cavalry charge if you think you look funny on a horse", as Guy says after sharing this, "I'll let that sit for a moment".

Testimonials

Over the years, Guy has become trusted counsel to the senior management team. He is authentic and has the ability to energise the room. He is motivational, inspirational and continues to make a positive value-add contribution to the success of our business. He has a fantastic ability to 'cut through the noise' and deal with the things that really matter. Guy is also insightful, bringing to life certain situations through management experience and with great stories that allow easier understanding of the subject matter. I could not recommend him highly enough.

- Anthony O'Keeffe - CEO, Link Asset Services

With your help we have come a very long way as a team - we all feel that we are well on our way from good to great as a result of working with you. The specific exercise we did yesterday will live with me well into the future, I have already witnessed the learning in action twice today! I have no hesitation in recommending you to any organisation that wants to invest in the development and success of their leaders.

- Dawn Marriott-Simms - Hg Capital – Partner

Guy has amazing insight, high integrity and has presence and impact on the group. He is working with. He strives for results and gets them and does so in a collaborative and compassionate way. He has a fearless ability to deal with the 'real' issue and won't shy away from tough but necessary conversations. Guy is a supportive and insightful coach too. I would highly recommend working with Guy.

- Julia Dell - HR Director at RFU (Rugby Football Union)

Very rarely in life do you come across someone who genuinely inspires you and your colleagues to greater leadership, gives you the tools to excel and is truly brilliant at what they do. Guy is outstanding in his ability to coach, mentor, communicate, inspire, present, motivate and above all he delivers the results that add true value to an organisation.

- Mark Taylor - Global CEO – InXpress

Guy has been a breath of fresh air to our business and instrumental in converting our hopes and aspirations into a reality through our management development/culture change program. I would have no hesitation in recommending Guy to anyone who is committed to change within their business and open to ideas.

- Colin Jellicoe - HR Director at VINCI Plc

His drive and energy to deliver to our management group has been inspirational, with very tangible results in engagement from the attendees and a clear positive change in their approach to the daily tasks and their people

- Richard Pollington - Global Customer Director
- Europe at Fletcher Building

Guy has given me a good listening to on many occasions! He is impartial but challenging, helps sets high goals and aspirations whilst being pragmatic. Top coach, top man.

- Kevin Robins - SVP Chief Technology Officer
- First Data Corporation

His presentations add tremendous value to people's thinking, many of whom base their subsequent thoughts on his delivery. He is very engaging and delivers with conviction and humour, challenging peoples' way of thinking.

- Jonathan Story, COO, Windsor Leadership Trust

The feedback from the team surpassed my expectations. Guys draws on a raft of experience's and really engages the team, but he challenges and holds them accountable for what they are going to do differently. I am looking forward to Guy working more of his magic!

- Julie Priestley, Human Resources Director, Agrial

His experience is clear to see, and there is no situation/ team dynamic he hasn't worked with before. As a first-time founder, I believe Guy is helping avoid a lot of the typical pitfalls young executives make when trying to build a high performing team, and all my guys have complete trust in his process.

- Simon Phelan, Founder, Hometree

Guy has high EQ which enables him to quickly assess the dynamic of any team in the most direct yet subtle way. He strips that team bare then rebuilds its collective strengths whilst being crystal clear on the challenges your company faces. Whichever company I lead, I always turn to Guy for help. Authentic and effective, he makes teams perform better.

– Dawn Airey, CEO, Getty Images

Guy is a fantastic coach. He has huge impact and creates an inertia of thinking that we have never done before, and I know we will be so much better as a result.

He has such vast experience that naturally shines through, there doesn't seem to be a team dynamic situation that Guy hasn't come across. And his delivery is powerful. He is knowledgeable, engaging, inspiring and firm in equal measure, the kind of leader any of us want to be.

His 'craft' combined with his humility make him an outstanding partner to any leadership team. So grateful to have Guy on this journey with our team!

– Elona Mortimer-Zhika, CEO, IRIS Software Group

WITH THANKS TO...

Interviewed*

- Dawn Airey, CEO, Getty Images
- Major General Paul Nanson, CBE, Commandant, Sandhurst
- Ian Ritchie, CEO, RFU (Rugby Football Union)
- Mark (Ted) O'Brien, Head of Learning & Development, Fire Service College

* roles correct at time of interview.

Special thanks to

- Anthony O'Keeffe, CEO, LINK Asset Services
  A leader who consistently steers his ship through waters that many would sink in, maintaining the balance between the commercials and the people. Someone I respect and see greatness in.
- Colin Jellicoe, HRD, Morrison Utility Services
  How every HRD should be: Impactful, human, trustworthy, genuine, highly commercial and pragmatic.
- Dawn Airey, CEO, Getty Images
  A fearless CEO who walks the walk.

My greatest admiration

- Marc Jantzen is just a special human being. One of those rare people who hold both commercial acumen and genuine care for others in a way that wins hearts and minds, he engenders a level of trust and discretionary effort that people imagine is unobtainable. For a decade he provided insight, education, feedback, more feedback and then feedback, all combined with a care that, frankly, I didn't always deserve. Most of all, he forgave.

Special thanks

- Kevin Green, who makes me realise I have a long way to go to be half as real as he is
- Matt Crund, a great human, who lets me talk to get my thoughts straight

Everyone else

So, it's like inviting people to a party: you invite X, then you have to invite Y, which is why I kept it pretty tight above. However, I have to say that everyone I know has taught me something. Every course attendee, every executive coached, every client served, and every colleague connected to.

CONTENTS

FOREWORD

By

Major General Paul Nanson, CBE

Commandant Royal Military Academy Sandhurst

I suspect many of you reading this book will remember your first signifi-cant leadership challenge. As a British Army officer, you will perhaps not be surprised to find that mine came with my first taste of combat. Where perhaps you may be a little more intrigued is in how much of my leadership journey and my resolution to develop and be the best leader I could be, reso-nates with the text of this book.

Not long after finishing basic training at the Royal Military Academy Sandhurst I found myself in Forming Up Place (FUP) GREEN on the border between Saudi Arabia and Iraq, in command of a Platoon of 24 men. FUP GREEN for us marked the beginning of the ground offensive stage of Operation GRANBY – more commonly known by its US title, DESERT STORM, the operation to liberate Kuwait. The definition of an 'FUP' is the place from which you launch an attack or an advance. It is the place where you wait for preparatory artillery or air fires to finish; it's a place where final orders are given, last minute kit checks are made, and bayonets are fixed. It's also a place where you have time to think!

For me and I suspect the rest of my platoon, these were thoughts that soldiers have had for centuries before being committed to combat for the first time. Thoughts of loved ones, of purpose, of those friends and comrades around you – but mostly fear! Fear of the unknown, of the unexpected and fear of failure. 'What happens if I am the one who, when the time comes, lets the rest down?' Perhaps these are just traditional fight or flight emotions, but for me, the Platoon Leader, there was another and perhaps stronger fear: that of failing as a leader. Leadership suddenly got very real; a poor judgement or a wrong decision and my men might die!

Fortunately, my training had prepared me well. For those of you who haven't been, Sandhurst is the home of the British Army Officer, situated in the town of Camberley, Surrey. All of us who hold the Queen's commission are trained there. It was constructed towards the end of the 18th Century and designed to educate potential Army officers for the leadership challenges ahead. And that is what it has done ever since.

The foundation of leadership taught at Sandhurst reflects the Army

Leadership Doctrine that has evolved over centuries. It is founded on a basic framework – who you are, what you know and what you do. At Sandhurst we are taught the enduring nature of leadership; the need to inspire your people, to be able to translate values into leadership behaviours, and to lead through the power of unselfish example – 'Serve to Lead' is the motto of the Academy.

But Sandhurst also teaches us that leadership is a journey of development and that we will need to adapt our leadership style and approach depending on the changing character of the challenge; be that on operations or due to a change of job or role.

As the operational environment becomes more complicated, as the characteristics of the generation of those we lead evolves, and as the rate and pace of change accelerates, so we need to constantly think about the way we lead. The Army teaches us to take time to think, to consider the context, to analyse our performance and how we want to develop and improve, to have an 'FUP' moment to consider how we might approach the next challenge.

That is where this book speaks so strongly to me – and I believe it will do to you. It encourages us to think about how we lead, providing a framework within which we can analyse our current position, identify a pathway to success and allows us to put in place plans to achieve these. It talks about 'trust' and the need to build that honest relationship with those in your team; a relationship built on belief. It deals with 'accountability' and the need for the leader to understand the consequences of his or her actions. It talks of 'bravery' and the need for moral courage when making tough decisions. And finally, it talks of the need for an emotional 'connection' with those who you are lucky enough to lead; servant leadership – 'Serve to Lead.'

Whilst I have been fortunate, and many will see my experiences as lying towards the more extreme end of some of the leadership challenges that we can face, the important thing is that every trial that we face is uniquely personal and special to each individual. Every one of us can be a better leader. Even those times where our team is small, or we are not "the boss", our ability to step forward, set the example, be brave and stand up for what is right is what, as part of a connected society brings results and reward. From the most junior supervisor to the top CEO, everyone is a leader – it is beholden on the individual to decide how successful they wish to be.

So, I have no hesitation in recommending this book to you. Guy makes us stop and think; allowing us the opportunity to reflect on our own style of leadership and how we might adapt and evolve to meet the challenges ahead – to face your own FUP moment. Enjoy!

LIVING BRAVE CREDO

Don't hide.
You are intrinsically valuable.
There is no permission required for you to have an opinion.
Curiosity is not challenge it's okay to ask a genuine question.
Offering your observations and counsel is not opinionated.
Ask yourself "who am I doing this for?" The answer will guide you.
Holding a position is not aggression.
Learning is the route to your future self.
Learning is knowledge and experience.
It's ok to be scared, we all are about something.
Help others, don't create a dependency for you or them.
Say yes if you want to.
Say no if you want to.
Say maybe if you want to.
Being an elegant version of yourself is the goal.
Hurting others because you are being yourself is bullying, don't be that person.
Not everything is a battle but recognise when you are in one.
The more you put yourself out there, the more successes and the more failures, it's not a paradox, it's supposed to be that way.
You have more impact than you think.
There is no 'being neutral'.
When all is said and done, stand for something, make some ripples, leave a positive imprint in people's lives.

INTRODUCTION

Start by doing what's necessary; then do what's possible;
and suddenly you are doing the impossible.

- Saint Francis of Assisi

Sometimes things creep up on you. A little thing that starts as an idea or turn of phrase grows into something you end up having tattooed on your back. That's how it's been for the thinking, the tools and ultimately, for me, the way of life that is symbolised by the concept of Living Brave.

Living Brave evolved out of three decades teaching martial arts and being constantly challenged to step up to the plate and deliver excellence on the mental, physical and emotional platforms that drive personal performance, enable new behaviours and add value to life.

Living Brave comes from two decades of service and delivery in commercial environments as an executive coach, speaker, director, award-winning training provider and team coach for leadership teams within national and global organisations.

It is the output of 20+ years of leadership development, executive coaching, team effectiveness and cultural transformation. It is the result of seeing the impact that the philosophies in this book have made to individuals, teams and entire cultures.

It's become clear that I don't have the right to NOT write this book.

If I am the person I profess to be and want to be, then Living Brave needed to be written and held out for others to engage with.

It came to a head when I was at a conference with Marc Jantzen, one of the best leaders I've had the privilege of working for. We were all given a book by the keynote speaker and that night I tried to read it. I say tried, as it was a terrible read. The next day I spoke to Marc and said, "I tried to read some of this last night, it's pretty rubbish". He paused, looked at me, smiled and said: "Yes I know. However, it's better than your book." I hadn't of course written a book at that time.

Ouch! That was like getting a punch in the solar plexus. It stopped me in my tracks and put me in my place. He had, with great elegance and craft, berated me, coached me and challenged me… the worst book in the world was better than the one I still hadn't written.

This was also why I trusted Marc implicitly. He gives direct feedback, calling this 'taking it to the source'; he'd been Accountable and challenged me to be; he'd been Brave enough, through his accountability, to tell me the truth. He challenged me to look in the mirror to see that. And he'd been fully Connected to the moment, not waiting, delaying or procrastinating. He challenged me there and then to get on with the writing of this book.

So here we are Living Brave. I hope to do more than explain my concept to you. My intent is to share my thinking, vocabulary, mindset and approach to a way of thinking that drives high performance in individuals, teams, and organisations. I am clear in my focus. I want you to feel that this book provides a framework for you to move towards and excel through a Living Brave mindset and, through this mindset, enable others.

My experience with Living Brave is organic. Every day I discover increasingly elegant ways to approach the idea of truly Living Brave. As I coach, train and give keynote speeches the feedback continues to grow, and the calibrations get ever-more refined. I hope it never stops.

Living Brave is both a question and a statement.

Consider it as a way of challenging yourself with the question "Living Brave?"As an individual, a team member or team leader, you will recognise those moments where the question "Am I/are we Living Brave?" is the trigger for recognising the reality of the moment and the need for Trust, Accountability, Bravery and Connection.

Think about it as a method of self-reinforcement. The statement "Living Brave!" is a way of affirming the reality of your bravery. If a team asks itself whether it is "Living Brave?" in order to make the decisions it has to make, being able to then declare it is "Living Brave!" acts as a call to arms, a catalyst and reinforcement.

Your life is a journey and within that, there is the overall mindset of what Living Brave will mean to both you and to those who surround you either socially or at work. The idea of Living Brave is an overall approach, a commitment to striving to own your space and to hold strong in situations where your identity is threatened.

Living Brave has the capacity to make a great impact within an organisation. When individuals with a Living Brave attitude comprise of the teams, that are the organisation, that make up the senior levels that represent the culture, then this cohesive approach is unstoppable.

Living Brave changes the conversations, that change the culture. Is Living Brave a panacea for all ills and woes? The answer is 'that is the wrong question', the question is 'can it help me/us navigate complexity, ambiguity and enable our resilience?'.... then the answer is 'yes'.

This isn't a panacea, a quick fix, a cure-all; in fact, it is far from that. Living Brave doesn't offer to make you the caricature of successful, a millionaire or to be walking around in joy, it doesn't offer a business of everybody being at one with the universe.

Living Brave is a vehicle to enable individuals, teams and cultures to make the decisions that need to be made, to own them, to adjust as required and to 'Face Into' the issues at hand.

In fact I'd go as far as to say that most of the feedback I receive from those that take the course of action in their lives to be Living Brave is that the more they take on board the mindset and the methodology then the greater their resilience, willingness to adjust to the reality of the situation and thus the more agile they and the team are as they have created Trust, taken Accountability, been Brave and stayed Connected to their true self, the team vision and the overall organisational drivers.

WHAT IS LIVING BRAVE?

Living Brave represents a way of 'thinking and being' that operates across one's whole life: personal, social and commercial that I firmly believe holds the key to wellbeing, resilience, mental health and pride in the actions of oneself and those around us.

Living Brave is a way of thinking, a way of feeling and most importantly a way of being, a way of being that I believe doesn't just impact but will in the most positive way affect the way you consider yourself and interact with others.

It is an enabler for the individual and an enabler for the organisation, an enabler that I fundamentally believe can be the differentiation that embodies the ideas, models and thinking that is contained within this book.

It is asking you to consider your actions as an individual and as a collective, as they have been, as they are today, how they are likely to be in the future as indicated by all the evidence to date, compare this against the vision you have for yourself, the team, the organisation and head towards it.

To have a personal and collective view that does not look for validation from others yet uses others as a calibrator for behaviour. To have a voice that is balanced between the need to contribute, the need to respect the opinion and value of others, the willingness to be led when others take the lead role and to lead when others wish to follow.

Living Brave sets out a way of framing your own and others existence in the world that creates a balance that once understood, practised and embedded in one's own behaviour becomes a catalyst and enabler for the behaviour of others.

AM I DOING ANY OF THIS NOW?

Some of us are already Living Brave and some of us are not, for some Living Brave will:

- Confirm what is already being done, reinforce it and give Living Brave a vocabulary and focus that will enable you to guide others to be Living Brave
- For others Living Brave will enable the steps that will create a new way of living in the world

One thing is clear, that Living Brave is liberation, it comes with many routes to the final reality of making this part of an individual's life, a team's practice and an organisation's culture.

Simply said, Living Brave works if you embrace the process intelligently. If you read this book, whilst thinking 'I bet this won't work' then you'd be right. Well done for validating your own reality. By the same token neither will it help you to go full cult member and become an evangelist, with a T-Shirt that states, "I'm Living Brave, are you?" or "Ask me about Living Brave". It needs elegant balance, common sense and hard work alongside the moments of easy successes.

And finally, while I am on a roll, I haven't aimed this book at any one person, team or culture in any particular phase of their life cycle. The idea for Living Brave is an encompassing philosophy that is large enough for you to take it and work it into your life whatever it is, whoever you are and wherever you are in time, geography and life.

And that's important, because Living Brave is not trying to fit a niche; I have over the years talked to people about the ideas and the concepts and I'd say for nearly every person I have come across it seems to resonate at some level, that either enables the individual in the moment or serves to aid their thinking or the thinking of others they pass it onto at some point in the future.

QUACK, QUACK

Ever heard the saying, "if it walks like a duck, looks like a duck and quacks like a duck…. it's a duck!" I can't recall when I first heard that, but it just rang true with me.

So I say, "if it feels like it'll work, looks like it works, and it feels like it works then….do you know….it probably works!" (Quack, quack!)

ONE

SETTING THE CONTEXT FOR LIVING BRAVE

This is where we look at

Setting the context with a historical timeline |
The impact of social media, the internet, IT and mobile phones | What
Living Brave is for you, the team and organisation | How society feels
right now | The fears to be overcome

CHAPTER ONE

SETTING THE CONTEXT FOR LIVING BRAVE

"The bravest are surely those who have the clearest vision
of what is before them, glory and danger alike,
and yet go out to meet it."

- Thucydides

LIVING BRAVE AND YOU

Living Brave is for everyone, in every context. It is for those who want to be true to themselves instead of being scared to agree or disagree. It is for those who sometimes want to say, 'I need time to think about that' or 'I've changed my mind'. It is for those who want to contribute without fear of a put-down or a negative response. It is for those who want to step up, take space, or step back.

Living Brave says, 'I take ownership of myself and my own personal space to which no-one else has rights unless I give them permission'. It says, when you look in the mirror, 'you own your own image and you are not beholden to some else's ideas of who you should be'.

Living Brave is the decision to be the author of your own life story. While things will happen to you that you have no control or influence over, the response that you decide upon is not only your choice but actually your responsibility. It is an exercise of your free will which is, in fact, the only thing in life that you truly own.

Living Brave is a way of being, whether you work, or you don't, whether you manage others, your family or yourself, whether you are in a place of positional power or you are not. It is about addressing old patterns of behaviour that hamper and impede your progress, your confidence and your quality of life. It is about identifying your fears, analysing them and figuring out the best way forward for you.

It is not about bulldozing others or steamrollering over their ideas or sensitivities, but about being honest, open, genuine and clear while working for the greater good of those you work with or live alongside, your organisation, your family, your society, your community.

Living Brave is about the ultimate clarity of choice that resides in all of us and must be faced every moment of every day. It lies at the core of every decision you make on every subject. It is about maintaining a balance between the need to contribute, the need to respect the opinion and value of others, the willingness to be led, to lead, or to step up when no one else will.

It is the power of personal choice and free will, it is the conscious choice and the manner in which we sit with it, that is the pivotal point of Living Brave. Living Brave says that if we act from the heart then the 'why' of our intent will be easier to connect to.

Now that's a push for many of us, but it will ring true as we walk the road of elegant choice. Be clear, we are not talking about the aggressive, distasteful choice of 'well it's just me being honest'; that's an inelegant way of voicing a decision to cocoon one's feelings behind a shield of individual bias whilst rejecting the world for not sharing our outlook.

No, Living Brave is the belief that honest thinking, authentic reactions and personal insight mixed with intelligent, heartfelt words and sincere human emotion enable you instead to interact with yourself and others from a platform of personal integrity and truthful interaction.

When I look into the eyes of a person that I trust, respect or love and I know that that connection, at whatever level, is returned to me, then I don't have to consider their internal politic and can accept the interaction at an honest level.

The same goes for your internal dialogue. When you or your team are able to hold an honest interaction, with no filters to mislead you into a dialogue that isn't the essence of who you are, then you are free to be

Living Brave. Open dialogue, a Living Brave mindset and careful fore-thought enable the acceptance of whatever the outcome may be.

Living Brave enables individuals and teams to be themselves in a manner that doesn't require command or control.

You want to be Living Brave because just the thought of saying, with real meaning, "I am Living Brave" does something to your state; it empowers you. And when you can counsel friends/your team/your organisation to be Living Brave you will feel something start to stir.

Let's start by giving ourselves some real context as to where we are in the world and the time in history, in which we inhabit. This is a key stepping stone to recognising our place in the world and our place in its history.

All in all, we should be in great cheer, yet a recent World Happiness Report[1] notes we are at the lowest level of perceived happiness in the history of the survey. So, what's happening?

The world is at one of the most complex moments in its history. We are, on the one hand, living in the best of times. At the same time, we are living in the worst of times. With life expectancy the highest, it has ever been and with disease and wars on the decrease, we should, as a society, be moving towards a time of greater calm and contentment. Yet the opposite is true. We have the greatest levels of distrust, numerous work-days lost to stress and a pervading unease.

WHAT A DIFFERENCE A DAY MAKES

We have seen a huge decrease in our tolerance for waiting. Someone types, "What is a unicorn?" into a phone's browser, and if the answer doesn't come back in literally 1 second, that person is going, "come on dagnabit". The fact that the question, "What is a unicorn?" has been typed into a phone, in a coffee shop, using free Wi-Fi, has left that phone, has 'wirelessly' gone into the 'cloud' then has found its way to a server in another part of the world and is sorting through basically all human knowledge on the subject and is on its way back, doesn't seem to come into it, because we want the answer now.

Of course, there lies the rub, 'expectation', when we have exposure to something, we quickly acclimatise and expect all things to operate at that pace and quality level, we know what we want and we want it now.....
and so does the organisation.

We are in a fascinating moment of overlap where we have generations in the world and the workplace who both grew up with barely any technology and those who have been immersed in it. I am quite fascinated by the blindness that this can bring to some and the insights it brings to others.

I have sat with a FTSE MD and asked, "Do you have a PC?" They replied, "No, why would I need one? I have two PA's, one for business and for personal". His relationship with social media and the internet was zero and thus his ability to feel the pulse of the world outside of his domain was negligible.

Also watching a new MD completely embrace social media, with a big red sofa, live webcasting and him talking about what's going on in the business was indicative of someone wanting interaction and connection.

In the same way, I see parents who fear the technology that their children are using, hearing "oh it is all a mystery to me", "they are probably hacking into NASA" and "they'll be all right". This self-imposed embargo on technology not only alienates both parties, it creates a sense of 'ignorance' from both. The parent feels ignorant and the child perceives ignorance, this doesn't create understanding or connection, and that "it's all a mystery to me" is also a mindset that I see in senior managers, who want the people that report into them to understand it, but aren't prepared to engage with it themselves.

We are also seeing a move of some parts of society to an almost wilful or at least misled immaturity as new generations are framing reality through a lens of their relationship with social media and digital applications. The digital world often portrays itself as better than reality, with digital you can communicate immediately, research instantly, contribute without frontiers, and comment without repercussions. This often distorts people's relationship with both commercial and personal relationships, the promise of speed, sharing and transparency often isn't played out in real life.

Technology was the golden future, giving more time to do what you want to do, as everything will be easier with technology. What has happened is a combination of two truths, we have unprecedented access to knowledge, wisdom and insights on a global scale. We also have a very invasive set of tools that create an expectation of immediacy with little contingency for personal space.

It used to be that to get the news you had to leave your house. Go back centuries and communication happened at the campfire, with a mixture of truths and tall tales. Decades ago, you would go to a social gathering, watch a newsreel at the cinema, buy a newspaper or go to a library. Then it moved to listening to the radio with TV news first thing in the morning or last thing at night. Now we have 24-hour news both on TV and streamed to a smartphone, so it's almost impossible to separate or distance ourselves from it. I am sure I am not the only one that uses their phone on the loo.

I think about this in terms of 'experiential proximity', meaning the closer the experience, then the greater the personal impact. This has dramatically increased due to the digital age. I am inclined to think that it necessitates a far greater sense of personal and self-calibration than was required previously. Many receive immediate positive feedback from social media and that increases our anxiety to not be parted from it or to miss out. With all that connection and feedback sitting in the palm of our hand, we have a breach of our once safe spaces. We now are exposed to other people's commentary 24/7, be they radical or reasonable.

Social media algorithms feed us the news we enjoy, reinforcing our confirmation bias and delivering just one perspective of the world, so it becomes difficult to spot the real, the biased, the distorted and the fake. It takes conscious competence to develop the insight required to work out if something is true.

This digital delivery has had a huge impact on our ability to maintain a safe space, to recuperate, to refresh and to calibrate. We now receive the world's realities in their glorious accuracy and horrid distortions, the news of amazing truths and alarming realities straight into our homes, even when we are desperate to have a moment to ourselves.

WHERE HAS THE TRUST GONE?

The opening up of the internet, coupled with the depth and immediacy of the information we can access has had a profound impact on our trust levels across all parts of society.

Day after day we discover reasons not to trust any form of positional power.

- In the UK in 2010 we had the expense scandals [2] with the revelations of abuse by some MPs and eye-watering details of fraud, fake receipts and claims for ornamental duck houses and moat-cleaning

- The Libor Scandal [3] led to individual prosecutions and Citigroup, J.P. Morgan, Barclays, RBS and UBS [4] pleading guilty to criminal charges
- A constant stream of sexual abuse allegations against celebrities, such as Jimmy Saville [5], Kevin Spacey [6] and Harvey Weinstein [7]
- Shocking revelations about Oxfam aid workers in Haiti [8]. Those at the most senior levels sexually exploiting those in their care who were at their most vulnerable
- Key consumer brands such as Apple throttling battery life [9] and trusted brands such as Volkswagen falsifying emission data [10]

The message seems to be a never-ending 'don't trust them, they don't care about you'. We do hear good news stories, but they seem to receive little space in the media [11] or in our conversations, compared to the negative.

The negative tales are often indicative of systemic issues and, at their most dangerous, give unwritten permission to step off the straight line, corrupt fresh incomers and pressure good people to do the wrong thing.

In 2017 the Edelman Trust Barometer [12], a survey that measures trust globally, stated that trust in the four major institutions of government, organisation, media and not-for-profits was at an all-time low. Those are the subject headers; come down a level and you are talking about politics, organisations, media and even charities.

In 2019 [13] the report stated, "Globally, 'my employer' (75%) is significantly more trusted than NGOs (57%), organisation (56%), government (48%) and media (47%)". Richard Edelman, president and CEO of Edelman, says: "The last decade has seen a loss of faith in traditional authority figures and institutions. More recently, people have lost confidence in the social platforms that fostered peer-to-peer trust. These forces have led people to shift their trust to the relationships within their control, most notably with their employers."

This impacts on us on two levels, on the 'you and me' level, how it feels in the reality of our everyday life and on the 'world' level, where there's a lot of noise that has huge repercussions for us in the way we feel about the greater good and our sense of connection or dislocation.

LIVING BRAVE AND THE ORGANISATION

Many organisations are struggling with their identity as they try to balance the drive for commercial success with society's demand that they acknowledge not just Corporate Social Responsibility but direct Social Responsibility.

Living Brave offers a mindset, an approach and a methodology to individuals, teams and organisations to face the anxiety, doubts and fears that can subtly and aggressively affect and infect us causing a shift in our behaviour in order to not rock the boat. Living Brave is a focal point for leadership to hold itself to account not just for the commercial, strategic outputs, but to examine what it means to enable, nurture and engender an environment that realises the true potential of its people. We're not talking about an esoteric lovefest, but a genuine demonstration of mutual engagement around the belief of a shared context that engenders Trust, Accountability, Bravery and Connection.

Living Brave is a mindset for those who want to be leaders of themselves in all the contexts faced. It is for teams that want to be leaders of their own outcomes and organisation leaders that seek the creation of a compelling story, a frame of reference that engages, and behaviours that demand Accountability. The story created should free people to design a workplace that has a positive impact on commercial imperatives, innovation and engagement and that attracts customers to the product, the service and the people.

The key to Living Brave is its capacity to be utilised by both individuals and teams as a vehicle for freeing themselves from a position of doubt, anxiety or fear and, in doing so, creating a resilient and mentally healthy environment. This includes being free from the fear of saying the wrong thing, of living a life half-lived, of being punished by a boss, peer, team member or line report or, worse, the punishment we often mete out to ourselves. The hub of the matter is the individual's relationship with the need to align and/or change and whether they are willing to engage. People can be excited and motivated, or they can be unsure, dubious, fearful and fatigued, depending on their workload, place in life and or past experiences. A culture that is Living Brave engenders a culture that can have the conversations that change both the narrative and the outcomes of engagement.

YOUR PERSONAL REALITY AND WHY IT MATTERS

There is a spectrum of reality that is unique to and set at a different level for each of us throughout our lives. It's like a volume control that at times is set low so everything is clear and you know where you are while at other times it is set higher. With that higher setting comes uncertainty, hesitation, doubt and even fear. Often the volume keeps going up and if you don't have control over it that's where damaging pressure and stress kick in.

At a low level, it might be that the environment you are working in requires you to be smartly dressed so you need to wear a tie, something that bears no relation to competence but seems to be of importance. So, although you're not keen you do it, why wouldn't you? At another level, you might be unhappy with your career or your relationship with someone at work or feel overwhelmed by a situation you are in. Perhaps you are asked to do things that don't feel right, or perhaps you are bullied by someone in the workplace. Maybe you are suffering mental or physical abuse. The volume is different for all of us and only you can feel the effect on you. Part of our life journey is managing the feelings the various levels of volume provoke. Sometimes you feel you have life in the palm of your hand, sometimes it feels as if it holds you in its.

Fig 1: Real You/Fake You

FAKE YOU
Each time you behave according to the needs of others to protect against your own fears. There is less room and evidence of the REAL YOU.

YOUR FEARS
The things that give you doubt, concern and fear. Real or not they take from you if not managed.

conscious choice

REAL YOU
Person you want to be, your genuine, authentic self. Often lacking in skill if ignored for more caricatured behaviour

conscious choice

© 2018 LivingBrave-Guy Bloom

While you are coping with your own stresses you are also exposed to the extremes of other people's lives. The crazy joy you can feel, for example, at babies being born at one end is counterbalanced by the grim stuff of life thrown at us. In mere minutes in our digital world, we can go from feeling elated to appalled. Our constant inter-connectedness can both strengthen or erode our buffers. The boundaries of personal privacy, time and space are breached so often we can lose the ability to process incoming news properly. All this eats away at our resilience and at our confidence in our ability to make sense of the world, to be sure that we are doing things the right way. With this can come a decrease in personal, corporate and social bravery. There is a sense that we may not say the right thing, that our view may not chime with others, and we may become less real about who we want to be. We may shudder when we see others who step out of line and are branded as an oddball, an outsider, a whistleblower, a non-conformist.

THE COVENANT THAT NEVER REALLY EXISTED

The truth that many people suspect is that at any time they could be called into a room and hear: "Personally I'd like to keep you on, but the numbers are down… I know you do a great job, so it's not your competence or dedication, but we have to let you go."

Not so many years ago there was a culture of 'jobs for life', i.e. 'don't do anything illegal, work hard and you can stay until retirement'. The prevailing view was that you must not be very competent if you had more than two to three jobs in a 20-year period. The perspective now is almost that potential employers are suspicious of someone who has hung around for too long when others have moved every two to five years to gain greater competence and experience.

Of course, staying somewhere for 20 years can hide incompetence just as easily as moving at key moments, however, the point is, back in the day, you got a job and you were most likely to keep it. The idea of a mobile gig economy workforce with a culture of constantly moving for experience, satisfaction and personal fulfilment would have been anathema.

Now we all need to hold on to the multiple truths of long-term institutional service, the gig economy and 'zero-hour' contracts.

WHAT THE WORLD FEELS LIKE RIGHT NOW

There is a definite sense of increasing anxiety. People have a sense of being pushed harder in most areas, to do more with less and to do it faster. Stories abound of painful experiences at a local and global level which fuel the fire of life getting increasingly hard.

Some years ago, I heard the then Financial Director of Capita PLC deliver a message of 'focus and challenge'. "It's not about grinding the numbers once a year as the financial year-end approaches in order to reduce cost," he warned. "It's about grinding the numbers every day, every day tirelessly, driving the cost out, there's no room for niceties, it's about the figures."

Technically he was right: work on cost reduction in your organisation all the time. No real argument there. However, it's not the intellectual position that's the issue per se, it's the manner of the delivery, the focus on behaviours. This isn't about cultural niceties or innovation. It's not about personal development or the courage to push into new areas. It's about grinding day-in, day-out with one main focus – cost reduction.

I often see people completely unsure about what they are supposed to be doing, other than keep going. I don't think that will come as a surprise to you. And often the truth, as I see it, is that many keep a societal veneer maintaining 'everything is all right', while internally they believe that things are pretty far from all right.

For many, there is a sense of disconnection from their true self. There is also a disconnection from the team, culture and thus the organisation.

It isn't that people walk around fatally flawed and empty, though that can be true; it is more that even with all the good things that exist there are areas that are not satisfied, and this takes the edge off what good might look like.

Having worked with many organisations, having thousands of conversations and doing hundreds of diagnostics, I've witnessed many times when things are just not as good as they should be. And I've seen that when this is so, it creates more anxiety than when things are fundamentally broken.

When things are actually flawed and broken there is an almost resigned fatalistic, "Well, what can you do?". Whereas when things are ok to good, but 'could' be so much better, then it appears to create a sense of dissatisfaction based on "We are so close to something better". An analogy is looking through a toyshop window as a child and being short of money by the smallest amount. And you're short because someone promised they'd pay you the money you needed for mowing their lawn, but then only gave you half. That leaves you feeling downright cheated.

It is this sense of being cheated that I see played out again and again. We have it at a societal level where if a neighbour turns out to be a menace, then we feel cheated by the fact we just paid a lot of money to live in a nice house but next to someone we're finding intolerable. Or a great new job where the culture doesn't match the sales pitch. Or when the marketing of a product promises a certain experience, but on purchasing it you find that it doesn't deliver on its promise.

When I coach or work with teams, an overarching anxiety is a sense of knowing what good looks like and not wanting to be cheated of the potential of achieving it.

FEAR IS THE MIND KILLER

We all have our own fears. Individuals, teams and thus organisations have fears. The same goes for confidence. We all have varying levels of it. Individuals and Teams have confidence and organisations have collective confidence.

Fear makes things particularly volatile for organisational leaders and senior teams. Organisations have individuals with their unique fears and confidence issues, they have teams with issues, they have senior leaders who are often holding the duality of their own span of control alongside the organisation's need for them to contribute to areas they don't directly control.

Mostly we have our personal fears under control and coping mechanisms for dealing with them, but people rarely transcend all earthly anxiety; we all have things that worry us and feeds our doubts and insecurities.

Living Brave is an antidote to fear and like penicillin, it's best if you take the full course. If you, your team and your organisation function through a rallying cry of Living Brave it can be infectious in its power of story, metaphor and content and can be brought to play in any given situation.

Fear is a biological response. Living Brave is its nemesis. Simply put, fear is the release of chemicals due to a stimulus response to a given situation. I'm not referring to terror, like if you walked into your bedroom and there was a lion sitting on your bed, I'm talking about the type of fear that exists in modern-day society, the kind that, for most of us, comes from a gnawing doubt from a list of possible sources and which releases adrenalin, both in large dumps and as a slow drip-feed. It increases aggression, makes it hard to focus, affects our moods, makes us irritable, and affects sleep patterns and motivation. It is the kind of fear that leads us to protect ourselves at work by pulling our contribution or, conversely, by over-involving ourselves.

Though different for everyone, it often manifests as:

- Not telling your boss they are selfish, thoughtless or bullying
- Not asking for a pay rise
- Not leaving a job you have had for years as it's safe
- Not telling your peers they don't treat you or others correctly
- Not taking a position that's unpopular
- Not pointing out negative behaviour
- Not challenging unrealistic timelines
- Not being curious as to the 'why?' of an issue
- Not self-analysing
- Not changing one's own behaviour for fear of the impact that will have on others

Fear gnaws away at us and disguises itself in ways that trick us into behaving in a manner that creates in us a shadow of our real self. This 'shadow self', over a period of time, eats away at our ability to access our 'true self'. Thus we often present an aspect of ourselves to the world that is significantly less than the person we really are. This is how it can be for the individual, for the team and even for a culture.

This 'shadow self' or 'shadow culture' is something that most of us can recognise in ourselves and others around us at various times.

EXAMPLE 1 - JONATHAN

Jonathan works in a bank. He's a senior executive, mid-50s, and has had, for all intents and purposes, a very successful career. When talking to Jonathan it soon became apparent that he had a wide spectrum around which he felt, in his words, 'weak and strong'. In the words of Living Brave, that's 'fearful and brave'.

At home, he felt he and his wife had a good, long-term partnership, and that his family unit sustained him in the parts of his life where he felt challenged. At work, within his span of control, direct reports and financial control there was also a sense of managing well that engendered a sense of calm.

Then there was the executive board and the relationship that he had with the CEO, an entrepreneur who'd started and dominated the organisation.

In this area Jonathan felt weak, disempowered and very much the 'little boy' waiting to be given instruction before being judged as to whether he had done a good job. In Jonathan's own words: "For heaven's sake, I'm a grown man and I walk in there as a board member yet I'm really not an equal or peer in any way. I want to be treated as an adult."

EXAMPLE 2 - SUSANNAH

Susannah is an HR professional in a global organisation. She has two children, a husband and a demanding job that takes no quarter, leaving little leeway for her desire to have a healthy work/life balance, despite the organisation's verbiage about caring for its people.

But this is ok for Susannah. She and her husband have negotiated a powerful working coalition. They are true friends and partners, supporting each other and enabling Susannah to handle the pressures and, in her words, "the crap that comes with the territory".

However, Susannah volunteered that one area in her family life triggered deep anxiety. When it came to her relationship with her mother and sisters, there was a complete change in her outlook. Here Susannah had the experience of being the sounding board and go-between for the family's warring factions and felt burdened by the emotional load they gave to her to hold. In Susannah's words: "They ring me and could be on the phone for hours. They seem to unburden themselves and it then sits with me. I'm left with it and just feel overwhelmed, and it leaves me with less to give to my family."

EXAMPLE 3: SIMON

Simon, husband, father, son, middle manager in a well-known international organisation. Simon's father died at an early age. His mother had then raised him and had, for a multitude of reasons, become not just a mentor but also a dominant force in Simon's life. Simon wanted to please people by doing the right thing. He wanted to please his wife, friends and children, he also wanted to please his colleagues, direct reports and, most importantly, his boss.

This desire to please meant committing to buying a big house, paying private school fees and providing wonderful holidays. It meant working late and taking on all the projects that would ensure he stayed the boss's favourite. By his mid-40s Simon had reached a point in his life where he wasn't sure who he was anymore. His identity revolved around 'giving and pleasing' had left him in a place where he had, over a period of time, slowly subjugated his own personality and character until he admitted: "Now I find it difficult to stand up for myself in any identifiable way."

WHAT FEARS MUST BE OVERCOME?

In the first two examples, we have a spectrum of 'strengths and weaknesses' as perceived by each individual that probably resonates with many of us to some degree.

There is often a delicate balance between what we can stand strong on and the things that nudge us into the shadows and mean that we function from a place of doubt and fear, with all the problems that manifest with living in that place:

- Anxiety
- Self-doubt
- Incongruent and fearful behaviour
- Lack of trust
- Self-protection
- Aggression

- Tension
- Pressure

Then there's the third example, where Simon became so fearful of his own identity that he validated not from within but from without. As he sought to call upon the foundational strength that used to exist in his character, he failed to find the sustaining reserve. At this stage, people encounter an emptiness that dominates their lives often leading to states of:

- Instability
- Panic
- Fear
- Neurosis
- Illness

That end-state can overwhelm lives in a manner that undoes our 'true self' to a point of:

- Resignation from role (work and/or family)
- Breakdown
- Aberrant behaviour
- Sabotage of self, others and/or work

Living Brave is designed to help every individual generate Trust in themselves and from others. It helps create personal Accountability, establishes a level of personal Bravery and facilitates a level of Connection to one's own and others' needs and visions.

Do you know anyone at work who:

- Says one thing and then does another?
- Speaks ill of others when they are not present?
- Isolates his or herself and doesn't contribute?
- Spreads general rumour without any real facts?
- Seems to enjoy the failure of others?
- Finds the bosses' jokes funnier than they really are?
- Talks about how 'rubbish' it is to work here but doesn't leave or try to change things?

Ever done any of these?

Workplaces, where these kinds of behaviours exist, are 'affected' and at worst 'infected' with fear which, unless addressed, will undermine and damage any initiative aimed at adding value. It won't be that things don't get done, although that's probable, but that the value of any intervention is likely to decrease due to this negative mindset.

WHAT HAPPENS WHEN YOU DECIDE TO BEGIN LIVING BRAVE?

Whether at home or at work, when you start Living Brave, some highly beneficial behaviours play out. These include:

- Having fully open conversations
- Handling conflict in real time
- Taking ownership of your feelings
- Being able to express curiosity or to challenge regardless of rank or status
- Listening regardless of rank
- Being fully connected and present in all interactions

Imagine an environment where there are no whisper campaigns, a place where people self-police and where there is constant communication and conversation between tiers.

Imagine what it would be like to join an organisation that, during the interview process, actively talks about the value of Living Brave, that says, regardless of role, rank and responsibility, one overriding behaviour/output is required, and that is to be Living Brave.

Consider an environment that both nurtures and rewards this concept through vision, mission statements, values and behaviours that all align with the single concept of Living Brave on individual, team and cultural platforms.

An environment in which individuals contribute from a sense of personal identity and the presence of their full character, rather than from the partial presence of a subjugated personality.

An environment where team members contribute fully as individuals, thus enabling the team to contribute to its maximum ability to a sense of community which has a positive impact on the organisation and the culture.

An environment that enables a culture of Living Brave and so represents a commitment to honest conversation and the respect and development of the individual.

This starts to look like the following, where:

The individual can say:

- I accept who I am, regardless of imperfections, while I try to develop
- I accept others, regardless of imperfections, as long as these aren't used as excuses
- I have a right to own my own space, physically, intellectually and emotionally in any context be it at home, work, social
- I define myself as I am, not how others see me
- I am a product of my own design
- I choose to be like this
- I am not defined by my past, but by what I do now
- I don't pretend to be what I'm not
- I'm not fooled by the fantasy of what could be
- I aspire to achieve both measurable and attainable goals
- I validate myself internally (I, not others, decide my value)
- I calibrate myself externally (others provide feedback)
- I select my counsel, seeking the truth
- I am willing to give and receive feedback, in all forms
- I try to connect with the moment
- I can acknowledge my own value
- I can acknowledge the value of others
- I value myself as an unfinished article
- I strive for growth, emotional, intellectual and physical
- I am accountable for my actions
- I am curious about the world
- I have transparent intentions
- I will not intentionally do harm
- I offer trust, intelligently
- I experience challenges, I Face Into them, I am brave

The team can say:

- We accept who we are, regardless of imperfections, while we try to develop
- We accept others, regardless of imperfections, as long as these aren't used as excuses
- We have a right to our own space in the world, physically, intellectually and emotionally in any context
- We define ourselves as we see ourselves, not as others see us
- We are a product of our own design.
- We choose to be this way.
- We are not defined by our past but by what we do now
- We don't pretend to be what we're not.
- We are not fooled by the fantasy of what could be
- We aspire to achieve the possible, even when others doubt us
- We validate ourselves internally and we decide our value, not others
- We calibrate ourselves externally (others provide feedback)
- We select our counsel, seeking the truth
- We are willing to give and receive feedback, in all forms
- We try to connect with the moment
- We are able to acknowledge our value
- We are able to acknowledge the value of others
- We value ourselves as unfinished articles
- We strive for growth, emotional, intellectual and physical
- We are accountable for our actions
- We are curious about the world
- We have transparent intentions
- We will not intentionally do harm
- We offer trust, intelligently
- We experience challenges, we Face Into them, we are brave

The organisation can say:

- We want individuals and teams to accept who they are, regardless of imperfections

- We expect people to be dedicated to development
- We realise people are different and believe that adds to our organisation.
- We value difference unless it is used to excuse bad behaviour, low competence levels or lack of motivation
- We recognise people have the right to their own space (home, work, socially).
- We believe that the more we respect that, the more we get back
- It's not up to the organisation to define who people are. We want individuals and teams to define themselves. The job is the job and people should be themselves while doing it
- We believe people are a product of their own design. They choose to be as they are and are not defined by their past. We allow people to redefine themselves rather than pigeon-holing them. Individuals are defined by what they do now
- We don't want people to pretend to be what they are not; we are not fooled by promises or rhetoric.
- As a culture, we recognise the struggle of maintaining (or trying to achieve) excellence whilst pushing forward
- We want individuals and teams to validate internally (they decide their value, not others)
- We expect individuals and teams to calibrate externally (seeking feedback)
- We expect people to select counsel, with the intent to seek the truth
- As a community, we are willing to give and receive feedback in all forms without using hierarchy to avoid the truth
- Our culture is striving to be connected with the moment rather than bewitched by our own needs
- We want people to feel they add value and are valued in terms of their character and competence
- Our organisation seeks to acknowledge the value of others
- We expect, at all levels, to recognise we are unfinished articles
- As an organisation, we need our people to strive for growth, emotional, intellectual and physical
- This is a culture where we are accountable for our actions

- We encourage curiosity in all aspects of what we do
- We aim to have transparent intentions at all levels
- No one should intentionally do harm
- Trust should be given, intelligently
- As we experience challenges, we need to Face Into them, we are brave

The overarching behaviours of Living Brave manifest in the following way:

- Having fully open conversations
- Handling conflict in real time
- Taking ownership of one's feelings
- Being curious and challenging, regardless of rank or status
- Listening, regardless of rank
- Being fully connected and present during interactions
- Customer and supplier relations thriving through honest, human and connected interaction

LIVING BRAVE FOSTERS OPENNESS

Working for more than two decades in organisations where people are dedicated to the development of other individuals, teams and cultures has allowed me to build a large set of cumulative observations. The theme that comes up consistently is the need for greater openness.

The Living Brave Mindsets in Chapter 8 focuses on the creation of greater openness, both with oneself, others and on building a culture that encourages openness in conversation, action and intent.

The key to openness is creating an environment that rewards and encourages people who operate in the light, not in the shadow, and whose focus is contribution, not self-preservation.

It is evident when people operate to protect themselves rather than to enable others. This is often done not from an innate meanness or desire to hurt or harm, but because someone has a mortgage to pay and their own personal confidence is overshadowed by the momentum and might of the corporate commercial world. These people are infected by peer pressure and often become focused on distorted needs instilled by a society that values the superficial and the fleeting over sustainable and legacy-driven behaviours. When people have a big mortgage, expensive car, designer watch, they may feel validated to the world. But they've created a self-imposed yoke that requires earning a certain income and enslaving themselves.

It is hard for many people to be open if they fear repercussions that threaten their finances, career and status. It might be as simple as being seen as too challenging, or as a threat to someone else's ego. Reality is often irrelevant when it comes to how an individual perceives something.

Openness means doing away with:

- What's in it for ME?
- Why should I help YOU?
- I don't even know THEM!

Openness means moving towards:

- I want to be more than I am
- I want to contribute
- I want to help YOU
- 'They' are also US!
- I am US

I am talking about clear and transparent motives for all, about the willingness to contribute to others' success, about enthusiasm for Facing Into the conversations that flow between us.

YOU MUST CARE PAST YOUR OWN NEED

Living Brave is a vehicle for organisations that intend to thrive in a sustainable and legacy-driven way. Living Brave is, I believe, a key factor if an organisation is to foster a healthy culture and community that goes deeper than the balance sheet.

As the 2008/9 Credit Crunch demonstrated, the bankers who drove it were in positions of such power that they had, over decades, disabled the capacity of both government and other people within their organisations to be 'Living Brave' and to challenge their behaviour.

We now know that within such organisations any form of curiosity or challenge was often met with some form of overt or covert punishment. Thus chastised, employees lost their capacity for Living Brave in case it led to losing credibility or their job.

The concept of Living Brave, therefore, must be underpinned with a level of governance and external jurisdiction that enables it to exist.

The issue, at a systemic level, is the constant drive for the bottom line versus the human element.

I developed Living Brave as a top-down intervention. I am convinced that any form of cultural change starts with the drive, belief and commitment of the Chief Executive, MD, CEO or most senior team member, and is brought to life through the work of those at the coal-face. I have yet to see a fully-fledged cultural change programme work when this is not the case. Don't get me wrong, I've seen situations where all the boxes are ticked and the whole project signed off as completed, but it's only really working through the benevolence and daily actions of an engaged executive.

Another thing I'm convinced of is that individuals infect (which is bad) and affect (which is influence) teams and that those teams then infect/affect cultures. For Living Brave to really work, it has to enter the hearts, minds and behaviour of the individual, as it is there that true change happens. Personal insight allows the lowest-ranking person in an organisation to impact on the highest, for once you give another human being a personal insight that challenges and changes behaviour, then there is no hierarchy to get in the way of the relationship.

However, and this is the key, you must want what you are asking for.

Living Brave can, if done badly, behave like a herd of wild horses. It takes someone who knows what they're doing to harness the energy.

Questions to reflect on:

1. How trusting are you of leaders in politics, organisations, charities, religions?
2. What impact do you think you can have in the world?
3. What role do you think organisations have to play in adding value to the world?
4. What's the balance between your commitment to your own success and to the success of others?
5. When it comes to Living Brave, in your context how brave do you feel?
6. How much faith do you have in those around you, especially leaders?
7. What do you admire in your leaders?
8. What do you not admire in your leaders?

TWO

THE LIVING BRAVE MINDSET

This is where we look at

Introducing the Stuckness Equation | Elegant aspiration
to drive energy | Getting unstuck with Elvis Presley

CHAPTER TWO

THE LIVING BRAVE MINDSET

> "There are two kinds of people. One kind, you can tell just by looking at them at what point they evolved into their final self. It might be a very nice self, but you know you can expect no further surprises from it. The other kind keep changing... They are fluid. They keep moving forward and making new trysts with life, and the motion of it keeps them young. In my opinion, they are the only people who are still alive. You must be constantly on your guard against congealing."
>
> *- Gail Godwin, novelist*

The question that interests me is:

"Have you ever been stuck about making a decision?"

We have all seen individuals, teams, groups even entire organisations stuck, unsure, scared, even paralysed by the fear of the unknown output of a decision.

At this point what is usually feared is the loss of:

- Standing
- Success
- Credibility

For others, it can be:

- Income
- Promotion
- Self-worth

At the most extreme:

- Safety
- Well-being
- Mental Health

Don't for one moment read the bullets above and relate them only to an individual person. They also relate to teams, organisations and cultures because, if it's going on for one person, you can be sure it's going on for everyone else. Layered upon that is the fact that those in charge have their own individual fears and these accumulate as a set of behaviours that affect and infect those around them, such as:

- Short-term decision making
- Dismissiveness
- Micro-management
- Bullish to bullying behaviour
- Not listening
- 'We are right' syndrome
- Lack of focus on talent
- Distraction from innovation

The behaviours above are ones I'll bet you have experienced or witnessed as I have never met anyone who hasn't, at some time in their life, been able to recognise what not Living Brave looks and feels like.

THE STUCKNESS EQUATION

I said at the start,' have you ever been stuck?', 'Stuckness' may not be the most grown-up term you'll come across, but it seems to fit the bill as a way of describing not being in the flow of 'intelligent action'. 'Stuckness' is when we find ourselves fearful of 'blind action' as we can't, with any certainty, see what to do, or we fear the reality of the process.

Rittel and Webber contrasted 'wicked': we don't immediately have the answer to hand problems with 'tame': the answer is known to us, solvable problems. This serves very well as a root cause of how we become stuck, we aren't stuck on the 'tame' problems, we are stuck on the 'wicked' ones.

What do I mean by being stuck, paralysed or scared about making a decision? I see 'stuck' as being made up of the following components:

- Knowledge Gap (KG)
- Barrier to Action (BA)
- Uncertainty Factors (UF)
- Motivational Drivers (MD)

This cocktail can be seen all around you; think about anything that you or someone around you is not moving forward on and I'll bet it's a single or shared set of factors from the above 'stuck enablers'.

Fig 2: Stuckness Equation

$$\text{Level of Stuckness (LOS)} = \frac{\text{Knowledge Gap (KG)} + \text{Barrier To Action (BA)} + \text{Uncertainty Factors (UF)}}{\underset{\text{Motivational Drivers (MD)}}{\overline{\text{CONSCIOUS CHOICE}}}}$$

© 2018 LivingBrave-Guy Bloom

In terms of Knowledge Gap (KG), this means data is missing, you don't know or understand something:

- Perhaps it's being withheld, and you need help to access it
- Perhaps you can't see the wood for the trees and need counsel
- Perhaps you've been lazy and need to actively learn
- Perhaps you need help to make sense of what you do know
- Perhaps the picture is constantly shifting and there is no definitive answer

When there is a Barrier to Action (BA), there is something emotionally, intellectually or physically blocking you:

- Someone in power saying "No" to your need for access, resource, budget, help, time or care
- Your own uncertainty, doubt or even fear stopping you from acting, which can create a flight (run), fight (defend), freeze (inaction), fawn (submit) response in individuals, teams and whole organisational cultures

Uncertainty Factors (UF) are where we have facts and data, we know what we know, but we cannot be sure:

- The lack of certainty is weighing the scales of decision making in favour of either needing more data or needing to wait and see; someone else needs to tell you or someone else needs to go first
- What we know about uncertainty is that it can trick us into overly reflecting or pausing and even complete inaction

Motivational Drivers (MD) are the key components of what moves us forward. When Motivational Drivers are lacking, they hamstring us:

- 'I want' and/or 'I don't want'. These two statements are the nub of any action we take.
- This is true for both individual and collective ('we want' and/or 'we don't want')
- Not being stuck is at the very source of success or failure
- The question of 'how motivated are you?' is simple to ask but the answer requires genuine reflection, not just a superficial response

The motivational drivers of the individual, team and organisation are the main vehicle for working through the Knowledge Gaps (KG), Barriers to Action (BA) and Uncertainty Factors (UF). A key set of Motivational Drivers (MD) is crucial for perseverance.

When seeking clarity on what 'stuck' looks like consider the following questions and ask yourself if any of them resonate:

Individual or Team

- Dare I/we leave this job?
- Can I/we stand up to her/him/them?
- How do I/we approach them about this?
- Am I/are we good enough?
- Can I/we do better?
- What will happen if I/we volunteer an opinion?
- What happens if they say no?
- How will I/we cope if our actions go wrong?
- What happens if I/we are not as good as the image I/we portray?
- What are the repercussions, of getting this wrong?

- Why can't I/we be myself/ourselves in this situation?
- Why am/are I/we scared?
- Can I/we make the decisions we need to?
- Can I/we re-invent myself/ourselves?
- Why don't I/we feel safe to make decisions?

If any of these resonate, then consider the following:

As an individual:

- Where do I hold doubts?
- Where do I feel unsure?
- What makes me hesitate?
- Where do I navigate carefully?
- When do I appease?
- When do I worry?
- Who/what puts me on the back foot?

What is the output of this?

- What does this look like?
- What do I do?
- How does it make me feel?
- What does it do to my sense of self?
- What is the impact on me?
- What is the impact on others around me?

As a team:

- Where do we hold doubts?
- Where do we feel unsure?
- What makes us hesitate?
- Where do we navigate carefully?
- When do we appease?
- When do we worry?
- Who/what puts us on the back foot?

What is the output of this?

- What does this look like?

- What do we do?
- How does it make us feel?
- What does it do to our sense of self?
- What is the impact on us?
- What is the impact on others around us?

I'd advise finding the time to really think about them. It adds great value to do so as personal reflection, with trusted counsel and as a team. If you come at this honestly and with genuine reflection, there is an opportunity to gain absolute clarity on what is preventing you from operating in a Living Brave space.

Remember here that 'stuck' includes both major and minor barriers. Being 'stuck' refers to anything that is stopping you or the team from Living Brave in any particular context.

As with all things in life, it isn't 'what the issue is' that will be the issue, it will be the reaction to it, the 'how it makes you feel' and the collective impact of that when it's felt by more than one person.

KNOWING IS BETTER THAN NOT

The act of identification is the start of any process. All evidence demonstrates that 'knowing' is better than not. People who have an illness often say the uncertainty of not knowing was even worse than hearing something they didn't want to hear.

Clarity and knowledge, even when it hurts, is good. We human beings aren't good with not knowing. We imagine demons that are far darker than the reality; our minds seem pre-disposed to see the worst. It's partly a safety mechanism from our evolutionary start, where being cautious generally ensured you lived longer: 'That might be dangerous' generally paid off as a safety strategy. 'I'm sure it will be fine' probably worked less well when it came to survival.

We have as much to lose nowadays as we ever did. But now, as well as carrying residual hot-wiring aimed to ensure our physical survival, we also need to be on the alert when it comes to protecting our status and our financial and emotional wellbeing.

Unsurprisingly for many, the reality isn't Living Brave but Living Cautiously.

Think back to the questions on pages 35-37 and you'll understand why we all have times when we're wrestling with some, if not all, of them.

What differs for each individual is the level of impact the questions have. For some both the questions and the doubts are transitory, while others live with them for a lifetime, stuck, paralysed or fearful their entire life. What a waste of a life that is!

Answer those questions honestly as an individual, as a team......acknowledge your truth.

REASSESSING WHAT'S POSSIBLE TO BECOME UNSTUCK

The key to moving forward is to acknowledge that you're stuck and then explore the possibilities. Here I like to remind people of the Roger Bannister story. It's an oldie but a goodie.

- On the 6th May 1954, runner Roger Bannister broke the four-minute mile record. Just 46 days later Bannister's record was broken. By 1957, 16 other people had broken his record.

What this tells us is that something we perceive as impossible is another person's current or future reality. Whether we believe something to be possible or impossible is often dictated purely by the nature of the boundaries we've created for ourselves. And these are usually set by what we've been told through stories or via observation of established facts. It's the same with bravery: we often see bravery through the lens not of what is possible, but of what others define as possible. Living Brave is often a re-defining of the possible, not the impossible. It's about shifting the reality in which you currently exist. Living Brave is first daring to imagine, and then Facing Into the reality of the hard work.

So, don't underestimate what is possible when trying to discern what's within your grasp and within your creational powers. Next, be expansive when considering what you're prepared to do to achieve your goal. If you're thinking about this from a team perspective, encourage the team to be expansive and ambitious in its imaginings.

This is the key, it's understanding what your context is, what is within your grasp, what is within your creation, what is within your motivational spectrum, what is it you are prepared to do to achieve it. The question just gets added to, 'what is within my grasp and what is within our grasp?' We don't get rid of the personal pronoun we add one.

For an individual, Living Brave is very much about understanding the answers to the questions: "What and where are my boundaries?" and "Are these boundaries real or self-imposed?" It doesn't matter whether your goal is selling more, getting promoted, redefining a brand, engaging the hearts and minds of an entire organisation, team or client, capturing market position, holding your ground, avoiding being bullied, allowing yourself to go home on time, not joining in with gossip, requesting a pay rise, making time for people or simply being authentic. You don't need permission to explore and test, with integrity and enthusiasm, how to grow your own span of self-permission of personal license giving.

What I see repeatedly are people trapped by their own belief system. This is primarily linked to the phrases:

- I can't
- They won't
- It's not possible
- How would I?
- It's too risky

ELEGANT ASPIRATION AND A PLAN

It's very important not to waste time chasing unattainable dreams. However, it's equally important to recognise that the so-called 'impossible' is, with a plan, a lot of hard work through the Living Brave lens, often possible.

"an idiot with a plan can beat a genius without one"

- Warren Buffet

Elon Musk is a classic example of a person who personifies, 'dare to imagine, be brave in action'. This is a person who wants to single hand-edly abolish combustion engines in cars by leading the charge with Tesla and battery cars. He wants to create Hyperloop trains that can go 800 mph, that's faster than the speed of sound and has launched SpaceX with the intent of going to Mars. That's right Mars! Let me just say that again…Mars. Holy mackerel.

So, Elon Musk, well he's definitely a genius with a plan. Is that the bench-mark? Yes and No. What we have to do is create a reality for ourselves at an individual and cultural level. Living Brave has to sit in the context of our own making. You can't make a thing true just by wishing. That's obvious but pretty important. Whilst Living Brave is the context of your own environment let's not pretend that reinventing the world is within everyone's grasp, however, it is Elon Musk's version of Living Brave.

"If something is important enough, you should try.
Even if the probable outcome is failure"

- Elon Musk.

While you believe something to be true, another person may be oper-ating with a completely different frame of reference. And, if your own reality is challenged by their new data, you are free to achieve the previ-ously unthinkable.

Take Tyrone Curtis "Muggsy" Bogues as a brilliant example, at 5ft 3ins he was the shortest basketball player ever in the NBA (National Basketball Association), he was there for 14 seasons, which is no mean feat. The average height of an NBA basketball player is 6ft 7ins, yep 6ft 7ins have you ever stood next to someone who's that large? I'm 5ft 10ins so Muggsy at 5ft 3ins would be noticeably smaller than me and there is no way I'd think, right I'm going to be an NBA player, I'd think, "I have no chance, I'm 5ft 10ins, I am way too small to play"……and….. drum roll…..I'd be wrong. I might be right in terms of my compe-tence (which I could learn if so motivated), but I'd be wrong…..and that would be 'stuck thinking' in the sense of my boundaries, in terms of the 'what is in my grasp'. As a story, I find this a remarkable example of an individual's frame of reference for what can and cannot be achieved. It tells me that what we see as unachievable is a matter of opinion, focus and competence.

Here is another example of 'you really have no excuse'. Shaquem Griffin, who in 2018 was drafted into the Seattle Seahawks in the NFL (National Football League). Shaquem is 22, he's an outstanding physical specimen, he's a linebacker in a sport that has its share of rough and tumble and no tolerance for anything other than excellence. When he attended what they call the 'Combine' which is, in essence, a test of various skills. He ran the quickest 40 yard dash for a linebacker since 2003, bench pressed 225lb x 20 times, which is 3 more than his identical twin. Oh, I should have said: "he's only got one hand". Yep, let that sink in a moment, one hand. He had his left hand amputated when he was four due to a condition that stopped it developing.

I think we can all look in the mirror and say, "I/we might need to get our shizzle together". It's a great story to tell yourself, your team and anyone else that's having a moment…. "listen this fella only had one hand and he's knocking it out the park….do you have all your limbs? Yes. Get unstuck, it's time to start Living Brave".

Living Brave is definitely about knowing what you are really able to achieve; however, at the same time it is also about the ability to envision a future, set out your path and by Facing Into your fear, with the force of your will, make it happen. It's also about a level of defiance that pushes back against the doubt of your own voice and the doubts of the many voices that may surround you.

I can only imagine what would happen if a young man of 5ft 3ins, walked into a careers officer and said that he wanted to be a basketball player in the NBA. Think about what you'd say if someone who was 5ft 3ins said, "I'm going to play in the NBA". You might be polite with an "oh great, well good luck", but I'm guessing most of us would stop there, as our minds would be going, "Yeah, good luck pal".

Or a one handed young man of any age, imagine if they said to you "I'm going to get drafted into the NFL". Many of us might be polite, but you'd have to say, most of us would doubt their chances. Even knowing that story I think, "really?"

Now in many respects, people like Roger Bannister, Elon Musk, 'Muggsy' Bogues and Shaquem Griffin are outliers, so let's not pretend they are the average, however, perhaps what they represent the most is the element of Living Brave that sits in all of us. I don't want to get all evangelical and whoop whoop, however….you have to admit, just about anything is doable.

Living Brave is about identifying realities and considering them carefully. But also about daring to envision, about working hard and about fostering a level of crafted, elegant defiance that pushes back against both your own doubts and those of others.

SOMETIMES YOU HAVE TO JUMP OFF THE LEDGE

Living Brave is both a mindset and a lens for re-framing the world in terms of how you approach life at all levels. But sometimes it's even more than that, it's about actually being brave and taking a risk, stepping into the line of fire, knowing you may fail and that it might hurt, that you might, or even know you will suffer.

On December 1, 1955, in Montgomery, Alabama, Rosa Louise McCauley Parks, age 42, refused to obey bus driver James Blake's order that she give up her seat to make room for a white passenger. Interestingly and not everyone knows this nine months before Parks refused to give up her seat, a 15-year-old Claudette Colvin refused to move from her seat on the same bus system, yes 15 years old…..think of her age, sex, the context in 1955 of her geography and the political and social context. It blows my mind.

All these examples are people that were stuck by their particular context and in their own way approached their 'stuckness' by working through the Stuckness Equation:

- Knowledge Gap (KG)
- Barrier to Action (BA)
- Uncertainty Factors (UF)
- Motivational Drivers (MD)

UNSTICKING A GREAT EXAMPLE WITH IAN RITCHIE

Ian Ritchie is a great example of Living Brave. I worked with Ian when he was the MD of the Rugby Football Union (RFU) and he's a fascinating character, a large man physically and intellectually, with a genuine humanity that's wrapped around a rod of iron. He manages to be both engaging and yet maintain an incredibly strong perspective and direction. He is approachable and, if you have your facts straight, he'll listen and even shift his position if your argument holds up. He is hugely respected.

During one of the sessions with the RFU senior team, I gave Ian some direct feedback which he baulked at and didn't agree with. It made him uncomfortable mainly because he hadn't experienced that kind of delivery before. It stung and it meant he was being asked to shift his behaviour. Ian challenged it directly, in the moment, in a very elegant manner. But he didn't get the response he was hoping for and I Faced Into it, holding my ground and reiterating counsel and observation.

He was in that moment stuck, not in a big way but just stuck in that one moment.

Now, this is the crux of it, the moment in time that defines Ian. He could leave, force change (particularly as he was paying for the session), he could seek a way to save face, to prove he was right. Or he could reflect and ultimately make the adjustments that might be uncomfortable, but which would add value to himself and those around him.

That's when Ian shone. During a break he reflected, then re-entered the room and agreed to try a new approach. Although he relinquished his position he can still be acknowledged as Living Brave. He didn't shut us down, like John in the example on page 45, he let it play out, trusted our experience, role-modelled and became the advocate. Ian was Living Brave in everything he did and that's why he has been, and remains, so impactful.

He reviewed the equation to unstick himself, just at that moment. Below I'm hypothesising his thoughts:

Knowledge Gap (KG)	"Could be I don't know something and could learn?"
Barrier to Action (BA)	"Ok is this my ego, even a little?"
Uncertainty Factors (UF)	"If I stop, I don't know how this might play out"
Motivational Drivers (MD)	"How much do I want to be a role model?"

Living Brave is about recognising the futility of being 'right' when the only reason you are fighting to be right is so you can be right. It's a frame of reference called 'Right Fighting' being a 'Right Fighter' doesn't mean your energy is going into a healthy conclusion for all involved but to the securing of a victory. It is motivated by, the need to win and of the illusion of control. It's understanding that true power sits within true vulnerability. When you openly acknowledge your weakness no one can hurt you with it, so instead it empowers you. When this is balanced with a true sense of personal and shared vision, the one drives the other.

UNSTICKING ELVIS PRESLEY

In 1968 the producer and director Steve Binder was asked by Elvis Presley: "Where do you think my career is at?" Binder replied: "I think it's in the toilet." He then walked Elvis outside to demonstrate that, without his entourage, no-one would have the faintest idea who Elvis was. It turned out they didn't. The pair walked along the road and without an entourage to draw attention to him there was no reaction from passersby. Elvis was famous but not 'relevant'. His star was waning and he recognised this. Think back to the Ian Ritchie example where he recognised that even if he wasn't going to accept everything, he should listen. Elvis listened, too. And Binder then directed the Elvis 1968 Comeback Special, the catalyst for Presley's rebirth.

Binder's story reminds us about the value of true counsel, which has nothing to do with friendship, although the two may co-exist. It's about Binder having a Living Brave mindset, one that says: "I'm going to be honest and tell you the truth. You may not like it, and it might mean we can't work together. However, it will be the truth." So, there's Elvis Presley with an entourage telling him how the world still loves him, that he's a megastar. And the Living Brave, Steve Binder goes: "No you aren't."

I really love this story as it resonates so strongly with the everyday reality of life in the workplace and particularly working with leaders. The variance of what people want to say and what they actually will say is often directly proportionate to their financial situation and place in the hierarchy. I've come to see 'habitual carefulness' as a mask for uncertainty and fear. You might be careful the first few times but, if that filter remains always in play and displayed in actions, it becomes a way of being. That then becomes your brand and, ultimately, the way you are experienced, it becomes what people expect of you. Ultimately, as individuals, teams or organisations, we must accept that we are what we habitually do.

These stories speak to me, and I hope to you too, about the realities that exist in life and how they only have as much credibility and power as we give them. When one of these 'realities' is challenged by a new mindset or behaviour and a new set of beliefs and behaviours are formed from them, the old ones not only disappear but we often find it hard to imagine we once held that belief in such high esteem.

Elvis reviewed the equation to unstick himself. Below I'm hypothesising his thoughts:

Knowledge Gap (KG)	"Could be I don't know something and could learn?"
Barrier to Action (BA)	"Ok is this my ego, even a little?"
Uncertainty Factors (UF)	"If I stop, I don't know how this might play out"
Motivational Drivers (MD)	"How much do I want to move forward?"

A PAINFUL MOMENT OF GETTING EVEN MORE STUCK

John, the MD at a well-known financial institution wanted to ready his middle managers for huge change ahead, in terms of process change, product adaption and cultural shift. He engaged me and my team to look at his leaders and create a development programme. We did and long story short, it was very well received by participants with great feedback and was having a trackable impact.

The work with John and his team, went brilliantly and we were all congratulating ourselves on a job well done at the end of the first workshop, with great commentary about the experience with one quote "we were a 3 maybe a 4 at this end of this session I think we are an 8". My colleague and I thought, 'great we are on track with some hard work ahead, but on track'. We got to a moment where John and his senior team had to move to the second part of the developmental process, which involved demonstrating personal change. In the morning of the second session, we had a break for tea and coffee, about 1030. This was when there was a halt and a screech of the proverbial brakes, my colleague and I went out the building to chat through next steps, on returning 10 minutes later it had all taken a turn. John didn't want to continue and best of all sent one of his team to tell us, didn't let us back in the building and wouldn't come down to see or talk to me. He'd come to the sudden realisation that being different as defined by his and his owns teams definitions would require actual change.

His fear was in the interruption in the business, it would take away from the breakneck speed that had been set as the pace required, any move to actual leadership, as opposed to command and control, would require a duality of focus that he couldn't maintain. He was stuck in his stuckness.

If we ask the question, "what is the antithesis of Living Brave?" it is "Living Fearful". What I often see is that the 'fear' is wrapped up in logic, it makes sense "we don't have the time" or "this would get in the way", however when it's the goal you set yourself, it is often an indication as to where the individual or the team is.

John's journey through the equation, I hypothesise looked like this:

Knowledge Gap (KG)	"I know all I need to know"
Barrier to Action (BA)	"There is nothing new for me to learn here"
Uncertainty Factors (UF)	"I don't want disturbance, I want continuity"
Motivational Drivers (MD)	"I am fearful of the reality of change"

You will notice in the above they are statements, not questions, which is indicative of a fixed frame confirmation bias as opposed to an open, learning, curiosity-based mindset.

John's journey through the equation might have looked like this:

Knowledge Gap (KG)	"Could be I don't know something and could learn?"
Barrier to Action (BA)	"Ok is this my ego, even a little?"
Uncertainty Factors (UF)	"If I stop, I don't know how this might play out
Motivational Drivers (MD)	"How much do I want to develop myself and the team?"

Things to reflect on:
1. Do you define yourself as Living Brave?
2. Do you believe that you require permission to be Living Brave?
3. Do you see Living Brave as requiring seniority?
4. Do you see your ability for Living Brave depending on the position you hold?

5. Do you believe you can be Living Brave if you have no power or direct control?

6. Do you think more than one person can be Living Brave in any one situation at the same time?

7. Do you think Living Brave is only for the workplace?

8. Do you believe Living Brave is as easy as just saying it?

9. Do you believe Living Brave is a craft?

10. Do you actively seek feedback?

11. Do you seek counsel from others that both reinforces and challenges?

CHAPTER

THREE

WHAT LIVING BRAVE
MEANS TO YOU

This is where we look at

Flicking the first domino | The Envisaged Self |
The inconvenience of inconvenience

What Living Brave Means to You

"The truth is, we all face hardships of some kind, and you never know the struggles a person is going through. Behind every smile, there's a story of a personal struggle."

- Adrienne C. Moore, actress

Living Brave in no small part requires a 'leadership of self' mindset. I call it 'having your own house in order'. For you to truly lead yourself, there has to be a sense of foundational strength in your own world because, when that's out of kilter, it will impact your ability to be authentic, transparent and present in the workspace.

IDENTITY

Living Brave starts with you. This is more than personal 'brand', which is how you show up in the world and though an output of identity it can feel a bit Machiavellian or forced when we use that word in isolation. It's a good word, needing meaning and context. This is about your personal identity. Who are you? What is the genuine experience of you? How do others experience you in interactions? Can you strip away what you have learned and adopted in order to get on and focus instead on how you would like to be? What makes sense to you? What makes you feel best about yourself?

Every journey begins with the first step and a series of steps add up to a journey. That is what you are about to do, create a path defined by you, in the context of your life. That's what high performing teams and organisations do: create a path that they have defined and engaged with, and head towards it.

Living Brave is about a journey of vision. It's about you as a Leader of Self, imagining a brightly-lit lighthouse on the horizon, one that pulls you towards it with such intensity that everything you do is aimed, targeted and geared towards reaching it. That lighthouse is your vision of yourself. You can see the words Umbrella Belief on the lighthouse in the drawing, this is introduced on page 126.

The ability to imagine the future in a way that motivates you is a key skill for the individual, the team and the organisation. It's true to say that everything you experience in the world that has been created, started off by being imagined. How else would anything ever have been invented?

If you are planning a birthday party, you imagine how it will look and what people will be doing at it; if you think of yourself getting fit, then you think of what it would look like to actually be fit; if you are an architect planning to build a house, you are going to be thinking about what that house is ultimately going to look like. I think it is pretty safe to say that everything a human being has planned to be or has actually done was pre-empted with imagination creating a strong representation of the final outcome.

Imagination and visualisation are two of the most powerful tools that are NOT used by most of us most of the time, yet they are inbuilt from birth.

When thinking about how you want to be Living Brave, it's important to recognise the power of a strong visualisation that serves not just as a target or goal, but which when invested with a huge amount of emotion, pulls you towards it. Something that, most importantly, catalyses, inspires and that, in itself, is its own motivational source.

A LITTLE DOMINO MOVES A BIG DOMINO

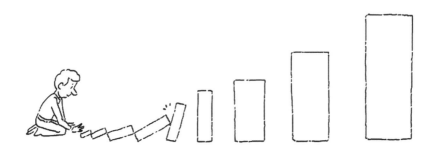

Everything starts somewhere, Lao Tzu said "the journey of a thousand miles begins with one step", makes sense, you can't always jump to the end. It is an inherent truth in leadership and team development that there is often a driver to get to the end as soon as possible or see the effort to get there as too difficult. How do you grow a plant? Well technically you don't, you set it up to succeed, the right soil, the right environment, the right sustenance, regular watering......get these factors right and you are on the way. The thing is you have to set the dominos up so that the little steps lead to the final goal.

The first real step in Living Brave is 'envisaging' if you have nothing to head for then, where do you think you are going? This quote from Alice in Wonderland sums it up nicely:

Alice: "Would you tell me please, which way I ought to go from here?"

Cat: "That depends a great deal on where you want to get to"

Alice: "I don't much care where"

Cat: "Then it doesn't much matter which way you go"

Alice: "So long as I get somewhere"

Cat: "Oh, you're sure to do that, if only you walk long enough"

Let's set the first domino....

ENVISAGE AN EMOTIONAL CONNECTION

"There is nothing noble in being superior to your fellow men.
True nobility lies in being superior to your former self."

- Ernest Hemingway

The first step towards Living Brave is the desire to be able to define yourself, your team, your department, your organisation as Living Brave. It's about choosing Living Brave as your frame of reference and as your lens through which you view the world.

This doesn't mean that you have to do away with all previous points of reference or that you can no longer align with company values. The idea here is that, with nothing else in your arsenal, Living Brave is a great point of focus. If there are other frames of reference then Living Brave can create a very powerful initial lens through which you can scrutinise other things such as values, mission statements and competences.

This step is key. Living Brave is just two words. However, it is highly symbolic, a metaphor. The words 'Living Brave' are aimed to reinforce the act of Living Brave. They're a challenge to you and those around you to re-calibrate and change behaviours that are found within and around us.

This starts with the question: "What is Living Brave to me/us?"

It means that, as you consider the reality of the world around you, you frame it through a Living Brave lens, which is:

1. How do I/we begin Living Brave?

2. How do I/we stay Living Brave in response to what is in front of us?

It also means that, as you consider your own actions, you frame them through the filter:

"How is what I am about to do, or am doing, Living Brave?"

This is a phase of visualisation and aspiration. It's the start of literally imagining the Living Brave version of yourself and asking yourself, the team and the organisation to imagine the Living Brave version of itself:

"What is the Living Brave version of me/us?"

When I was a young man it was imagining the me that could safeguard himself from the damage inflicted by my home environment. That required understanding what my Living Brave would look like. In later life, it meant defining what Living Brave would look like for me as a whole-life approach.

You can imagine a response to a particular need: "What does Living Brave mean in response to this situation?" However, it's far more powerful to do the deeper work by asking: "What does Living Brave mean to me/us?" Then, as individual situations arise, your response becomes more habitual, calibrated, refined and thus stronger, as the responses, you enact become increasingly yours and reinforce your own story as Living Brave.

The questions leadership teams are encouraged to ask are:

- What do we need to do?
- What are we going to do?
- How are we going to get there?
- What can stop us?

These are all perfectly good questions, but far more powerful is 'Why'?

INCONVENIENCE JUST ISN'T CONVENIENT

"Why?" is not a question that is complex or even new. Simon Sinek challenges people and organisations to not fixate on the 'What you are doing?' but on the 'Why are you/we doing it?'. The point here is that once you answer the 'why?' then you galvanise everyone to a common calling, a shared purpose. I happen to think Simon Sinek is right and his examples and perspectives are excellent.

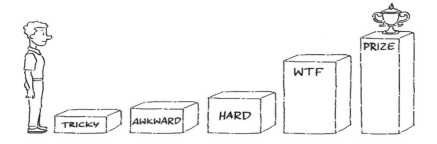

For me, there's something missing. It's not the 'call to arms' or the 'what shall we do?', it's the will to 'Face Into' the reality of the human condition.

What I see, time and time again is that people are 'up for it' until risk, inconvenience or hardship is perceived to outweigh convenience.

This is oddly strange. It's not that the inconvenience outweighs the reward. It's that it outweighs the convenience! Consider things you want to achieve, you'll often find that it's not that the reward has decreased, or that the hardships of getting there have increased. They are often the exact ones you knew had to be faced, it's just that the experiencing of them is not convenient.

That means that the desire, the habit, the instinct and the reality of you being someone who is Living Brave is, I believe, quite profound. As you develop and people recognise the impact it makes for you and those around you, it creates confidence and gives permission for others to follow suit.

IF IT WAS THAT EASY, WE'D ALL DO IT

Living Brave comes with risk attached. It means that you take up more space in the world due to your personal impact, curiosity and intent. This will be welcomed, valued and nurtured by many but feared and therefore attacked by others as your Living Brave may be perceived as an assault, on their domain be that intellectual, emotional or resource driven.

Neither will you get it right all the time, I know I don't, Living Brave does not mean, "I am right" and "I get to be a pain in everyone's behind by my response to any push back being "I'm Living Brave"". That will wear thin a bit quick in anyone's book, it will mean calibration, feedback, situational sensing and personal reflection to constantly tune your Living Brave engine.

The biggest mistake you can make is to believe that you are now 'awesome' and 'correct' because the moment you think you've cracked it that's when you stop paying attention.

Energy needs to be invested into the will to 'Face Into' to the endeavour, to staying the course and learning skills that drive you towards acting elegantly. You will hear me use that word a lot, 'elegant'. I particularly like the idea of craft, refinement, the skill of learning manifesting in high quality outputs.

The individual should consider:

- How do you want to be spoken about?
- What do you want your impact to be?
- What impact are you trying to make?
- What won't you do?
- What are you prepared to do?
- What are your lines in the sand?
- What is wrong now, if anything, that needs putting right?
- What counsel do you need that you are not seeking?
- What do you care about beyond your own needs?

The team should consider:

- What do we want our brand, story and legend to be?
- What is the impact we're trying to make?
- What are we about?
- Where won't we bend?
- Where do we add value to the world?
- Where do we draw the line on what's right and wrong?

The organisation needs to consider:

- What do we think about legacy, versus the now?
- What genuine value do we want to add to the world?
- How will we balance commerciality and humanity?
- What guidance should we give our people?
- What space should we make for individuals?
- Where should we step aside?

- How do we recognise our true blind spots?
- What is our value other than commercial success?

This is where you have to be very honest with yourself. Is it powerful? Does it fill you with a desire to strive? Will it push you to do the things that you don't want to do? You can, of course, create your own questions. Let these be a guide to the approach.

THE COMPLEXITY IS IN THE SIMPLICITY

Envisaging a future you is a very important life skill. It's not just about dreaming up a good picture but about creating something so powerful that it hijacks your everyday excuses and forces you to do something different.

When the image you have in your mind impacts and affects your emotional state, then you know you've nailed it. Your unconscious mind holds the history of your life and the innate chemistry of your unique DNA. There's much debate as to how 'pre-loaded' we are with behaviours at birth but, by the time you reach 18, you're sure to have 'felt the world' for good or bad.

When we envision a future self, it includes the best of what we are already plus the aspiration of a potential self.

It's interesting to note that one of the quirky things about our unconscious mind is that it can't seem to distinguish between fantasy and reality. It's your conscious mind that frames what's true and what isn't, which means that you are in control of both what is real and what is not. Meanwhile fear lies to you by insisting 'you aren't good enough' when what you should believe is 'you are, if you try'.

YOUR UNCONSCIOUS MIND NEEDS THE DISCIPLINE OF YOUR CONSCIOUS MIND

The unconscious mind is a very specific piece of you that can be incredibly childlike in its behaviour. It experiences the world without filters, whereas your conscious mind interprets. The conscious mind is like the desktop on your computer and can only hold so much at a time; the unconscious mind is your hard drive, your cloud storage and those old USBs in the drawer. It's everything you ever did or said, from day one.

The information that we put into our mind as an infant, adolescent and as an adult are often not always very reliable. However, it remains with us constantly. It's rather like a silent and invisible twin, one who sits on a spectrum which ranges from 'misguided and ill-informed' at one end to 'well-informed and insightful' at the other.

Neuroscience tells us that the brain is elastic and capable of forming new paths of memory and alignment all of your life. This means that you can teach an old dog new tricks and that you are able to learn new ways of approaching things. It will take effort and maybe inconvenient but, if you apply yourself, you can do it.

All this starts with an end game, a vision, something that pulls at you emotionally.

This part of the Living Brave process demands genuine effort and thought. It requires you to reinforce what you are doing well and start the process of redefining yourself as a stronger, perhaps even completely different, version of yourself. In doing that the domino pieces of your mind go forward with both what you already are and what you hope to become.

Once you have the envisaged version of yourself, you should visit it on a regular basis to check that you're still on target and ask yourself if the new you still adds value to both yourself and others.

ENVISAGED SELF

It is true that nothing ever got started that wasn't imagined first. It's also safe to say that nothing ever got finished unless it had emotion invested in it.

You have to care, you have to want it, you have to be prepared to suffer at some point in some way, to achieve the envisaged version of yourself. Perhaps even suffer a lot, if you're to move on through the blockages of your own emotional responses and those of others. That's what Living Brave is, it's the question in relation to the envisaged end game that you can ask yourself in those moments of preparation, frustration and suffering:

- "Am I/are we Living Brave in relation to (insert envisaged goal)?"
- "Is what I/we are doing Living Brave in order to achieve (insert envisaged goal)?"

It's the statement you make to energise and push forward, to navigate, to weather the storm, to attain the envisaged goal.

- "Right, this isn't Living Brave if I/we are going to (insert envisaged goal)"

- "This is not Living Brave if I/we are going to (insert envisaged goal)?"
- "Living Brave now, come on, let's go"
- "This is not who I/we are, this is not Living Brave, I'm adjusting, to Living Brave mode"

It doesn't have to be these exact questions or statements although they can be. But you should own this with your voice or that of the team. The point is that the envision piece needs to be accessed in order to engage your actions. An envisioned version of the Living Brave version of you, the team, the organisation, has to be the button, the switch, the slider, the volume control that, once you start turning it, flicking that switch and moving it along, is so strong in your mind and the collective mind of the team, that it engages an emotional state which will reinforce, galvanise and empower you not just to start but to continue.

At the most simplistic, primitive, human level this is about your motivation which is either moving towards something you want or moving away from something you don't want. It's basic, but it's just that simple.

You have to want it or even need it. It has to be important, not just a whim. If it's of little consequence, then it's probably just a target and targets, in this context, aren't enough.

Create time. Get a notebook. Draw, write, doodle, say things out loud, hear how they sound, discuss with others and mull it over. You're done when your gut says, "this is the envisaged path, this is something to believe in, I'm excited by this, it's something to fight for and which I will ensure happens".

Fig 3: Envisaged Goal

1
Can I say it simply?

6
How genuinely important
is this to me?

2
Am I clear on my purpose?

conscious choice
Envisaged
Goal

5
Do I know the repercussions
of not doing this?

3
Do I understand the why,
of why I want to do this?

© 2018 LivingBrave-Guy Bloom

4
Do I know what the benefit
will be?

DEFINING YOUR OWN DNA

You have to imagine a thing before you can make it true. It's a fact that human beings interpret things in different ways. Our personal values and the beliefs we hold to be true are all down to the lens we use to filter and frame the world.

Imagination and visualisation are two of the most powerful tools but are vastly under-utilised. There is a clear distinction between fantasy and visualization.

- envisaging with the intent to act is visualisation
- envisaging with no intent to act is fantasy

Things to reflect on:

- How connected am I to my Envisaged Self?
- How emotionally invested am I in my Envisaged Self?
- What daily efforts do I put into moving myself closer to it?
- What is my clarity on the outcomes this will achieve?

FOUR

CREATING THE LEGEND

This is where we look at

The power of Legend | The makeup of heroes | Calibration |
Putting on our Big Pants | Your Consuming Story |
Understanding Fear | Finding permission

CHAPTER FOUR

CREATING THE LEGEND

"If you want to be remembered as great, if you want to be a legend, you have to go out there every single day and do stuff."

- J. J. Watt, Athlete

Part of understanding ourselves is understanding the way people talk about us, the way in their paradigm they have experienced our actions. While people's experience of us should, in many ways, be in alignment with our behaviour, their impression of us will often be different from the one we believe we've generated. We're at the mercy of their interpretation.

STORY AND LEGEND

The 'story' then is what people tell of us when we're not present. It exists in their conversations about their experience of us. Individuals, teams and organisations all have their own story, the conversation that goes before us and after us, the stuff that gets talked about over dinner, the conversation that's heard in the margins when someone leaves a room.

Your 'Legend' however is what people talk about when you are done, when you've finished the job and moved on, when the project is completed. It's that future state that seems so far off, but which always, inevitably, comes. The craft is connecting to that future time and creating an outcome-driven vision for yourself that pushes you to adjust both brand and story to a higher level of output because the internal Connection to that future

Our Legend

Legend drives you. The immediacy of your 'story' feeds the 'Legend' of you, and the long-term experience of us as individuals or as team members.

Legend is an emotive statement, but it has been selected on purpose. It only works, of course, if you care about what your Legend is.

Your 'story' is more present tense. It's set in the moment and focuses on the now.

The thinking around 'story' is over-used and its impact has been reduced by its general usage. 'Legend' challenges you past the story of now to a future state that you might not even be around for. And it's deliberately more challenging. What are you willing to do for future good when daily pressures are ever-present?

Think about the question "What does this do to my/our Legend?" and how that can be applied to individual, team and culture need. In this thinking move past the now and focus on thinking that moves you to a longer point of reference.

Individual

- "What will this do to my Legend?"
- "What is this doing to my Legend?"
- "What did that do to my Legend?"

Team

- "What will this do to our Legend?"
- "What is this doing to our Legend?"
- "What did that do to our Legend?"

Culture

- "What will this do to the Legend?"
- "What is this doing to the Legend?"
- "What did that do to the Legend?"

Fig 4: Non-Reflective Model

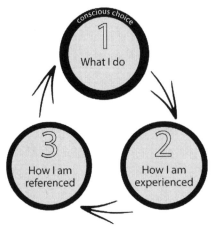

Story and Legend are inextricably linked. Stories are the jigsaw pieces of the Legend. The longer we live, the more we interact, and the more people who look to or at us, then the more stories there are to ultimately form our Legend.

Stories are important for anyone who is a leader, positional or not, as the smallest of actions can be magnified and reviewed. Something as simple as rolling one's eyes is open to huge interpretation... bored, thinking, something in your eye?

Put most simply, when we give our story and Legend no thought, we are operating in a 'non-reflective' state. In both of the following models, you can change the 'I' pronoun focus to 'we'.

On the other hand, when we through conscious choice, are being 'reflective'. Then we operate in a more calibrated and alert manner.

The story gives people the experience of you that forms the jigsaw pieces of your Legend. Your story is the way people talk about you in the moment, the frame of reference that they have for you in relation to all the things they experience about you personally and all the things that they hear about you, regardless of whether they're true.

You could imagine a pair of glasses that have your name down the side instead of a designer's name and whenever people talk about you, they all put on that pair of glasses. It's through the lens of those glasses that you are seen, and through these glasses that your actions are not just witnessed as a fact

Fig 5: Reflective Model

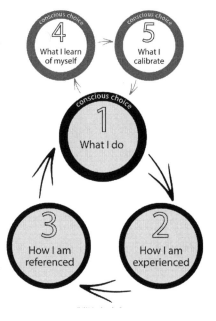

but translated. It's as if the lenses are coloured either for you or against you. It may well be that everyone shares the same colour of lens around the 'story' of you, but they may all have slightly different perspectives.

If the story is a poor one, then you have the opportunity to create Trust, to be Accountable in what you do, be Brave in your new behaviours and directly Connect to needs outside of your own need.

THE LEGEND EQUATION

As with everything offered, it could be simpler or more complex, so you will have to find your own way with the models presented in this process. The reason that I offer them is to make sense of the underlying factors that exist within the complexity (and often the ambiguity) of a topic.

As you look at the Legend Equation, do so with the intention of focusing on something greater than the imprint you want to leave or the immediate reaction someone might have of you. Go beyond that.

Fig 6: Legend Equation

$$\frac{\text{Brand}_{(now)} + \text{Story}_{(reflection)}}{\text{Interpretation (CONSCIOUS CHOICE)}} = \text{Legend}_{(Sum\ total)}$$

© 2018 LivingBrave-Guy Bloom

BRAND – THE IMPACT

Brand is the ideal of how you, the team or the organisation will be experienced and thus spoken about in the stories that people share. In time the stories will multiply and the Legend of the individual, team, department, product or service will be born. Brand within reason is easy to shift and manipulate. Stories and Legend once cemented, are much harder to change.

STORY – THE REFLECTION

How people talk about you, the team, the organisation in real time due to how they've experienced you in current and recent situations. Your story is the reality of people's experience. You cannot escape any alignment (or lack of alignment) between your intentions and the actual impact of the experience people have of you. Individuals, teams and organisations are all susceptible, especially in the digital age, to the way people experience and share their experiences. You can control your intent in the way you want to impact and, with feedback and calibration, you can influence the outcomes significantly. Personal calibration is a craft and perfecting it should be a lifelong quest.

When what you do or what you are responsible for is experienced (by a customer, internal or external) your story is out of your hands. In the main, the overwhelming reaction and the stories told will be a battle between the good and the bad. The way you win is to have an overwhelming number of good stories to drown out the bad.

LEGEND – THE SUM TOTAL

When you are gone, what will people say about you? Legend is where the brand (the impact of you) and the stories (the conversations around what happened) all come together and the strongest ones create a singular frame of reference for who you, the team and thus the organisation are.

A little thought experiment here, "are you who you think you are and are you experienced the way you think you are?"

A key way of thinking about this is to remember how we as children (now adults) think about our parents. We experienced the things they did in the moment, the way they faced out to us through their reactions to things (brand), we reflected on effects of particular occurrences and set the meaning and the points of reference according to the way we experienced them (story). As we matured those stories cemented and became a fixed frame of reference (Legend).

The question is:

• Do I/we care about how we are referenced after we are done here?

If the answer is 'yes' then you can mould your brand and your story into the creation of a Legend. For you, it's the energy source that drives and sustains and from this great things happen, people are engaged, teams are created, and organisations thrive.

Individuals grow and contribute, teams form around the desire to enable others and become part of something greater than the task.

Organisations navigate the complexity that is known and unknown as they increase spans of control, engender trust and reward the kind of contribution that enables rather than denies.

In this space, success is achieved because of people, because of the team dynamic, and because of an executive that enables, advocates and rewards the behaviours that drive this way of operating. In a 'yes' scenario the senior team is unlikely to market the success of the commercials as being down to themselves as they will recognise the component parts as something they cannot take credit for, even when they have enabled and nurtured the space and expectation to do so.

If the answer is 'no', work still gets done, some useful, some not. Large chunks of energy get focused on activity and, often, on internal politics and validation-seeking that distracts from looking out rather than in. Teams strive for survival and even compete with other teams to the detriment of overall commercial success. The organisation may increase in size but shrink in internal confidence, operate from a need of endemic safety as opposed to bravery and often fall at hurdles that cannot be overcome without the innovation and cumulative institutional wisdom caused by the momentum of market conditions.

In this space, if success is happening it is likely to be less sustainable and likely to be despite people working collectively, but due to a few high performers. Teams are more transactional, less likely to innovate or predict and more likely to react and respond to in-the-moment stimuli which often results in an adverse hero culture.

Organisations in this place require great product and a favourable market. It's where an organisation is having commercial success in spite of its culture, rather from the reality of the experience. The problem here is that executives often believe that the success experienced by the company is one that they can claim as their own: "I was there during that period, thus that success reflects on me". The truth is that this is sometimes correct and sometimes not at all.

These truths all culminate in a set of world, organisation and personal-truths that have to be understood as to your Legend, the team's Legend and the organisation's Legend. Each one of three factors are like polar points, armed with a huge magnet that can pull on the doubts and fears of the individual similar to something you see in the movies, where an evil spirit knows your true fears and sees past the social veneer and into your emotions, speaking deeply to those things you hold to be true.

One of the most exciting elements of a Living Brave journey is the decision to start building a Legend. Your Legend is your aspiration. It's the culmination of stories that together create legacy thoughts, memories and frames of reference. It is the way you want to be remembered when you are done whether that's personally, on the project or in the organisation.

THINKING BEYOND THE NOW

Dealing with 'now' is vitally important in the eyes of everyone around you. It's especially important if the news isn't constantly good. You need to be seen to address the issues in hand while also reminding people of the bigger context.

People are more willing to contribute their energy to enabling someone to achieve a goal if that goal resonates. The stronger your belief in your Envisioned Self, the more trust people will have in your actions. If I write this book and it's not that well done, you might see what I am getting at but still dismiss my efforts. However, if I tell you that I recognise that this is my first book, I recognise I have a lot to learn, I have sought counsel along the way and worked with an editor to make it work as best we can, that I am striving to learn the craft, that I am driven by the fact I have two children I want to feel proud of me, that I want to leave something that can enable them on their own journey, then you will, I hope, feel more engaged with the effort and understand it in its bigger context.

So, it's worth getting one thing straight: you, like me, like everyone, care about your story and your legend!

IT'S NOT MACHIAVELLIAN. IT'S YOUR LIFE'S WORK

What scares people is that the idea of a 'Legend' can appear, to some, as a contrived idea. Often, I hear people talk about not "wanting to be political" or "I don't want to be like that". Well, you live in society, you live in the world, and you aren't divorced from it. Having conscious control or an unconscious competence around your story and Legend doesn't mean you are a Machiavellian character. It just means that you are intelligent enough to understand that these things are a reality. They need to be managed, albeit not over-engineered. When you approach these things through a Living Brave lens, it's done with intelligence, elegance, integrity and good intention.

THERE ARE HEROES, THEN THERE ARE HEROES

Like the heroes that we grew up with, we can be more than just a set of actions and outputs, we can stand for something, we can demonstrate our belief in things greater than ourselves. It's not just something we could or should do, it's something that all of us involved in living in this world must do.

Isolde Motley[14] of Life Magazine (1997) is reported to have said 63% of Americans believe "There are fewer heroes than in the past". But that was 20+ years ago so, as is generally the case in these matters, things have probably got worse, and I think they have. What we consider heroic has also changed.

Think about the heroes of old who were mostly universally lauded: Robin Hood (brave), Neil Armstrong (brave), Martin Luther King (visionary/brave), Lassie (faithful), Winston Churchill (determined), Thomas Jefferson (inspiring), Batman (it's my book, I can have him in if I want: courageous), Amelia Earhart (brave), Maya Angelou (wise), Oprah Winfrey (savvy and emotionally intelligent).

Can we see a difference today? Yes. There are still modern-day heroes and heroines, however, their achievements are often more fleeting or with the social media phenomenon we are at some point exposed to a fault in their makeup, which takes the halo away and leaves them like the rest of us 'fallible and human'.

The majority of heroes of yesterday were heroes for their determination to excel, for their values and moral compass, whereas a disproportionate amount of today's heroes are admired for their wealth, beauty, money, even notoriety. True heroes do exist, but it takes focus and clarity to find them. Even when they have demonstrated determination and true grit in achieving something, this is overlooked, and it becomes about the fame, power and wealth. We live in an Instagram moment, where you can quite literally be famous for being famous, which in itself is fine, until it distorts the reality of actually functioning in the world.

It's something pervasive that has infected the organisational world, which was already seen as losing its unified conscience and moral compass. For many of us it feels like society, now primarily led by the social media tsunami, has taken a dive off the personal values platform and suddenly those that watch and report on this kind of thing are pointing out that we haven't got a safety net in place.

We definitely can't leave it to government, media or organisations to find a direction. The truth is it sits with all of us on an everyday level of behaviour to believe in a set of envisaged driving Legends that encourage our aspirations and that inspire us as we interact with each other in a manner that drives us forward.

I'm going to go so far as to say that the majority of 'heroes' in the public arena are not substantial enough or sufficiently fulfilling. They don't nourish the spirit. In essence, many 'heroes' aren't fit to be called such and many are both superficial and superfluous to the needs of the individual and the population.

Of course, there are heroes, many in the world of sport, where the mental discipline and coaching environment forces a singular focus. There are many admirable people such as Tiger Woods (golf) and Lewis Hamilton (Formula 1), who are admirable, inspiring even, and in the terms of sport, yes, heroic. Neither Woods nor Hamilton hit the clubs, do drugs or disrespect the sport that provides them with such opportunity. Hold on, apply the brakes…when I started writing this book this was true; we have since discovered that Tiger Woods had an affair and behaved very badly indeed.

We also have some people who without a doubt fall into the category of hero: Aung San Suu Kyi was placed under house arrest in Burma for a total of 15 years over a 21-year period. Amnesty International hailed her as a "symbol of hope, courage and the undying defence of human rights". Hold on, hold on, apply the handbrake again and let's do a 180…that was true when I started writing this book. Then on Monday 12th November 2018 at 19:59 Sky News[15] reports "Aung San Suu Kyi stripped of Amnesty award after 'shameful betrayal of values' over Rohingya".

Let's start again…Wang Weilin the 19-year-old student who stepped in front of a tank in Tiananmen Square; Sir Ranulph Fiennes, OBE the world's greatest living explorer and chopper-offer of his own frost-bitten fingers in his shed; Benazir Bhutto assassinated while seeking election in Pakistan; Malala Yousafzai, a young political activist shot in the face by the Taliban as she defied them by going to school. There are indeed still people who go above and beyond to such a degree that it is hard for many of us to truly identify how they do it.

There is a point I want to home in on. It is paramount that we accept that we often look for heroes in the wrong places. You have to be sure that you know what you are looking for and where to look for it. Many look to the media to show them heroes, rather than use the media to find them, which often means we are presented with someone who is media savvy, has a manager or, at the very least, is attractive to the audience, but not necessarily worthy.

We are often only left with those pre-selected for us to choose from, which is a flawed approach.

Famous people can be heroes, be they in the media, sport or wherever, but they are not the only ones we should be considering and that, of course, is where you come in.

LOOK IN THE MIRROR, IT'S YOU.....OR IT COULD BE

So where to start? I think the answer is very close to hand because I believe that when you look in the mirror you are looking at the face of a hero, maybe a hero who already has a true sense of who they are and also, perhaps, a hero who has only an inkling of what they are capable of becoming and who hasn't yet taken the steps to achieve all they are capable of.

I'm talking about looking within yourself and to others that are around you, about engaging with others who recognise the journey you are on and who are willing to accompany you or, at the very least, support you on that journey.

THE BEST HEROES ARE YOU AND I

Once you start to make this intellectual step it starts to become clear that you aren't dependent on the validation of others or the opinion of someone not operating from the same platform as yourself.

YOU AREN'T THE BOSS OF ME

The opinion of someone you don't see as valid need not figure in your personal validation process. You calibrate with the opinion of others. But you validate yourself.

Of course, others influence various parts of your life, perhaps parents or your boss, but they don't validate you, they calibrate you. When you use others to calibrate, they give you their opinion of their experience of you and how they would like you to continue or to change. The level to which you amend your actions is linked to the span of control they have over you, your willingness to listen, your desire to change and your respect for their opinion.

When you start Living Brave, others can't validate you. Only you can. Praise, displeasure, advice, counsel are all data points that you can review from a distance before deciding, in terms that are relevant to your context, how you deal with that information. You then own the choice.

The thing here is how you validate yourself. It is about how you define yourself in the current moment, not what you were or did, not what you will be or hope to become, but what you are, and what you are doing, now. The past is a data point for learning from, the future a projected data point of possibility, not fact. You are not what you were, nor are you what you will be. You are what you are doing now. Your focus must be on the now.

If the you of today is a mirror image of your past and, as you move into the future, your actions remain the same, then you will be that story and that will become your Legend.

However, your definition of yourself is open to review, reinforcement, calibration and fundamental change.

Being the hero of your own story while Living Brave means staying the course and reinforcing or moving towards the person you want to be.

You have to become the person you need to be because it is your story, no one else's. I am absolutely convinced that the very best heroes are us, that's you and me.

We are the people who do the incredible things. Being an action hero in Hollywood is not heroic, being a professional football/soccer player and scoring an amazing goal is not heroic.

Being the primary carer for your invalid mother at age 11 is heroic. Getting up at 5 am to get the kids ready for school, making it across town, working in an organisation where you might not be valued, getting back home and still loving and nurturing your family is heroic.

Swallowing the bitter pill of feedback from a peer, boss or family member that really is spot on but hurts and, instead of ignoring it, looking within and making changes, that's heroic and a symbol of you Living Brave.

I'd like to offer the idea of the 'everyday' being the bravery that exists in our lives:

- Integrity
- Accountability
- Courage
- Hard work
- Belief
- Understanding
- Love
- Affection
- Compassion
- Enduring
- Saying Yes or No
- Committing

'FACE INTO' THE CHALLENGE

Living Brave is in many ways about how you 'Face Into' the thing that gives you anxiety. The term 'Face Into' is indicative of the act of doing the uncomfortable. In the world of Living Brave, you must be ready to look to the storm and walk into it.

When you Face Into something, you are recognising what requires your attention as a Leader of Self, Leader of People or Leader of Organisation. You know when the weather changes you pull your clothes in tight around you and realise that you have no choice but to keep going, to weather the storm, to put your head down, grit your teeth and move forward. This is true of weather conditions and it is true of the emotional, social, cultural and business realities that we deal with. I can't sugar-coat it, some things are easy, a breeze, plain sailing if you will. Others are not. They are complex, painful and draining. That's when we Face Into it.

FACE INTO BEING THE LEGEND OF YOUR OWN STORY

Living Brave can operate in two places, in the moment and in a future state. In the moment is where you are faced with particular issues that are challenging you, whereas in the future it means that you don't know what that future is, but that you have prepared yourself mentally for the unknown, and that you have literally trained yourself to be ready for the complex situation.

These approaches have a root of wanting to be Living Brave and seeing the answer to the situation as coming from a Face Into it mindset and approach.

Think about the way in which you want to define yourself, the way in which you want your Legend to be heard, the conversations that you want to be had about you. These are all drivers for you to define yourself as Living Brave both in the moment and as a way of being in the right mindset.

There are moments where we have to engage with ourselves, not as things should be, might be, could be, but as they really are. And there is no better way of doing this than accepting the truth of your context in its glorious fabulousness and its glorious awfulness. It's time for the Big Pants.

BIG PANTS

Facing Into an issue is one thing, however, there are moments where there is often a need to put your individual or collective Big Pants on, to recognise levels of commitment, to be proud and remain motivated by the good things already achieved. To truly own and be Accountable, Brave and Connected (pages 156, 177, 188) for things to happen and to challenge those that have not.

WHY YOU PUT YOUR BIG PANTS ON

The desire to be alive, to not be less than you are, it is about wanting to be of value and relevant. Don't confuse that with being famous or popular. Living Brave means, you are 'alive' in the true sense of the word. You don't believe your place is to be submissive or subservient, you recognise there are hierarchies and people who deserve respect and you are willing to lead or follow in order to add value and to contribute.

This is something you can recognise should be true for a team and an organisation's culture, where there is a sense of energy and vibrancy that is couched in an environment that is performance focused but also has the ability to care, develop and nurture not just the chosen few, but everyone.

A true test of Living Brave is the balance that is struck between the time given to the human element of interactions, conversations around talent, focus on the individual taking responsibility for development and the organisation's drivers such as commercial outputs. These conversations manifest themselves in 'time' and 'expectation' of personal investment being a key factor in the strategic key performance indicators for the health, wellbeing, resilience, sustainability, story and legacy of both team and organisation.

All these things should factor into the brand value and even the commercial value of an organisation in terms of its investment and expected future commercial success.

It's not about 'caring' in the context of let's dance around the mulberry bush and give each other a hug. This is about the genuine belief that people, team and organisation have an experienced and perceived energy and soul that is felt both internally and externally, and which add to the desire for people to engage in a career or purchasing a product or service.

You put your Big Pants on, to Face Into the belief that there are things that are more important than the discomfort of your context.

ASK THE QUESTION OF YOURSELF AND OTHERS

"Am I/are we Living Brave?" a question to be asked whenever you recognise a need for Trust, Accountability, Bravery and Connection. You ask it to focus in on the catalyst emotion, the Umbrella Belief (chapter 7) that drives you to Face Into putting the Big Pants on.

It's asked when you and the person next to you are stuck, it is a call to arms, a catalyst and a reinforcement.

You can ask it of yourself when striving to own your space and hold strong against situations in which the identity you want for yourself is threatened. This idea of identity is key to developing your narrative and that of your team and organisation.

As an individual and team:

- What is my/our identity?
- What is my/our purpose?
- Who am I/are we in the world?
- How will I/we make a value difference?
- What will I/we stand for?
- What will I/we stand against?
- How will I/we learn?

- How will I/we calibrate?

As an organisation:

- What is the identity we want to create?
- What is our purpose beyond profit?
- What is this company in the world?
- How will we make a demonstrable difference?
- What will we stand for?
- What permissions will we give?
- How will we listen and truly hear?

THINK NOW AND THINK THEN

Living Brave is effective in two places, in the moment and in a future state. Consider the way in which you want to define yourself, the way in which you want your Legend to be heard, and the conversations that you want to be had about you. These are all drivers for you to define yourself as Living Brave both in the moment and as a way of being.

CONSUMING STORY

I would challenge you to start with the Envisioned Self, we have spoken about and turn it into a Consuming Story. You need that to drive you in a way that is linked not just to the intellectualisation of an outcome, which is connected deeply to your emotional state. You must want it. Passion is a powerful tool for action.

A Consuming Story has to compel and to connect deeply to an emotional state otherwise it is merely a target. Don't confuse this with being emotional, they aren't the same thing. You can be present in your emotions, without being emotional. You can be angered, without being angry. You can be upset, without demonstrating that response. This means you are committed enough to the Consuming Story that you are emotionally invested, I don't mean foolishly so, this is not cult membership, however, it should metaphorically be a fire inside of you.

The desire for a Consuming Story in the short-, mid-, long-term is something that you can manifest through the creation of Umbrella Beliefs (chapter 7) and the actions of the Living Brave Mindsets (chapter 8).

These components take the desire of a Consuming Story and move it from the ethereal to the actionable. I'd like you to reflect on yourself and the thinking about what a Consuming Story might look like.

Take some time to review and then invest some quality time in working through these thoughts, turning them from something in your mind to a written format:

These questions can be asked of yourself, the team or organisation:

- If I was/we were being written about, what would the stories be?
- Overall what would be my/our Legend?
- What would I/we be proud of?
- What would I/we not be proud of?
- Where do I/we hold my/our own?
- Where do I/we back away?
- Where do I/we add value?
- Where do I/we add less than I/we should?
- What worries me/us?
- What scares me/us?
- What excuses do I/we use (time, control, money, etc)?
- What makes me/us happy, that I/we could do more of?
- What adds no value to me/us, that I/we could do less of or stop completely?

The work to be done here is reflection and consultation. It does not have to be carved in stone, however, it must create a reaction and a reason for you/others to truly care.

THE FEAR OF FEAR ITSELF

In the film Batman, The Dark Knight, the Joker says: "People can handle anything if it's part of the plan." Tell people you are going to blow a bus up next Wednesday and though they are horrified, they can deal with it, as it's part of a plan. Just blow up a bus and people go completely bonkers (understandably), but the reaction is different, because it's a shock, it's off the radar, we didn't expect it, it wasn't in our game plan and we weren't able to prepare.

This analogy shows us that unfamiliarity can create emotional and actual chaos as people come across the unknown. It tells us that if we know the likelihood of something happening and prepare for it then that unfamiliarity becomes familiar.

It is how people who live in chaos create order, they practice and they assign probability to the reality of something happening. With further practice for the unknown by imagining a 'what's the worst that can happen?' scenario and using it to explore, practice and review, you can meet the challenge head on.

It relates to a story I heard of an American platoon that was under fire from the Viet Cong during the Vietnam War. The story goes that as the bullets were pinging off trees one soldier shouted, "Hey Sarge! Not as bad as basic training right?"

That's about the best thing I ever heard for the importance of training and entering into a Living Brave mindset prior to the need for it.

I have trained most of my life in the martial arts, trained in Hong Kong with Bruce Lee's teacher's sons (Ip Ching and Ip Chun), created a reality-based self defence, trained in tactical firearms, learned edged weapons and have been a 4 x martial arts Hall of Famer. But I have never been attacked once!

I know, I know… as I wrote this I realised I sounded almost disappointed. Of course, the level of effort I put into training was as much about the interest and the love of the craft as anything else. However, it was also about a mindset of preparation.

I don't believe I couldn't have had fights. I believe the preparation meant I sent out signals to the world that meant that I didn't have to. Being ready is powerful.

There is a great quote in Frank Herbert's 1984 film Dune[16]. Actor Kyle MacLachlan, playing Paul Atreides, at one point reflects:

"I must not fear. Fear is the mind killer. Fear is the little death that brings obliteration. I will face my fear. I will permit it to pass over me. And when it has gone past, I will turn the inner eye to see its path. Where the fear has gone there will be nothing. Only I will remain."

This is something I've also witnessed in the sports arena and heard in conversations I've had with military and emergency services: the pre-emptive thinking, the mental and actual rehearsals that set you up to experience the unknown space.

That's why we reflect on the who we want to be as individuals, as a team, and as an organisation; it is why we turn it into a Compelling Story: with the intent of moving forward as it drives and holds us to account.

YOU CAN BE THE HERO OF YOUR STORY

I have always liked the idea of people being the hero of their own story. The word 'hero' is a strong one and asking you to be a hero of your own story may excite you, it may worry you.

We spoke earlier about heroes, here we take aim on ourselves. Heroism has a volume control and can be a very personal thing that no one else is privy to. At other times it is an overt act that can earn the applause of and be rewarded by others. But for you, writing your story, when you commit to paper the desire to be Living Brave then, make no mistake, you will be a hero for doing so.

Creating stories with you as the hero is not a new thing. It's a tried, tested and a very powerful concept. Here it takes the form of having the book of your life put in front of you. You can read in it what you have done to date, the good and the not-so-good. You can also see blank pages ahead of you, each page representing a one-year period, and you then have the opportunity to write your own story, not in the minutiae of knowing the unknown, but in the context of who you want to be and how you want to be, what you will stand for, where you will flex, where you will not. This is again a great frame of reference for individuals, teams and organisations.

- What is the story I/we would like to write?
- What are the hurdles to this being real?
- What are the strengths that exist within me/us?
- Who can help on the journey?
- What needs to be learned?
- What are the limiting beliefs?

Henri Nouwen[17] writes that "real greatness is often hidden, humble, simple and unobtrusive". I like this way of thinking and encourage you to think along the same lines. The word 'real' in that quote becomes more powerful the more I consider the impact of the word, especially if you add the weight of your personal belief to it and say it with passion and honest belief.

ANYTHING CAN BE AN ART FORM IF YOU MAKE IT SO

I offer the idea of Living Brave as more than a set of actions or simple project. It is, in the frame of reference of this book, transformational for those who live within this frame of reference. Saying you are doing it is not going to cut it. Living it, putting in the effort, will.

Think of it as a craft. Like anything else that you want to get good at the intellectualisation is easy, it's the effort that follows that defines integrity and validity.

I mentioned earlier that I teach martial arts and so meet many people who want to become good. Some do improve, but there are a lot who don't. They like the idea of it more than the reality. They buy all the gear but, years later, still have no idea. The effort of constant learning and calibration has been replaced with stopping at the start line, attending a few lessons, coming infrequently and yet still identifying to themselves and their friends as a 'martial artist'. The worst thing I could imagine for Living Brave as a concept is that it was adopted by the professional voyeur who is keener to identify with the idea of Living Brave than with the reality of actually living it.

YOU ARE ONLY AVERAGE IF YOU LET YOURSELF BE

Superman might be able to fly, but so can Michael Jordan. Wonder Woman may have a lasso that makes people tell the truth (she does, take my word for it!), but Warren Buffet can sense the next market move. Inspector Gadget might have gizmos that save the day, but Alan Sugar can take a gizmo and turn it into a fortune. What I'm pushing at is some people are gifted. Some can look at a column of numbers and immediately see there's something wrong, others can hop on a horse and ride as if they were born in the saddle or listen to music and reproduce it as if they'd been practising for years. There are those within the human race who are blessed with knowing their gift, but many of us do not. We work hard, try even harder but recognise, at some point, that we are, I am afraid to say, normal.

It's not okay to be average, you might statistically be so at certain endeavours but not as a person, as a team or an organisation.

Average indicates 'not special' and having met literally thousands of people in an organisational context as well as socially, none of them has been average. Each of them has had something unique, at the very least a foible, at the most extreme specific behaviour traits. When I think about it, I really don't know any average people, and that's because I have learnt over time that whenever I think someone is average it's really because I don't know them well enough. No one is average. The fact you are this far into this book already defines you.

Unfortunately, many people allow themselves to behave average as they submit to the expectations set by others or which they heap upon themselves. We aren't born average; we make ourselves like that. No one is average, we can though habituate our thinking to being submissive to the fear we have of stepping into the role we want for ourselves. We fear our fear. Leaders recognise this and enable others to free themselves.

So Super Heroes are 'nice to have' but not aspirational in terms of the everyday world and I'm sorry to say the self-help mantra "you can be whatever you want to be" is, in essence, incorrect. The real mantra, the one that gives you the opportunity to succeed, is "you can be whatever you want to be, within the confines of whatever you're capable of achieving". The realisation is you are almost certainly more capable than you imagine, when you and others step off the threshold of fear.

This, I am afraid, is a fact. It's a non-debatable. You cannot achieve the impossible and, if you do, it never was impossible, even if it appeared to be outside your capability. If we cut through the hyperbole the impossible cannot be achieved. This, I am keen to point out, is why it is called 'impossible'.

Achievement in this parlance is recognising that life is not then achieving the impossible but sometimes achieving what didn't seem possible. It's in this context that I say it's not about being a Super Hero, but just a normal, everyday, run of the mill, it sits within all of us, yes, even you......hero.

A DROP BECOMES A DELUGE

In some ways this is a subtle and elegant thing, it is the whisper in the crowd, the sense of things being different, a moment in time where good people (that would be you if you were uncertain) stand straight and tall. Then it becomes the voice of many people, it moves from a feeling to an opinion, then from a consensus to a belief and, ultimately, a culture.

We all have the inalienable right to be Living Brave and, regardless of hierarchy, we are all Leaders of Self. No one requires permission to be the hero of their own life.

In the workplace, you may well be waiting to be given permission to be a leader of the organisation or a part of it. But you aren't waiting to be a leader within the organisation.

LEADERSHIP REQUIRES NO PERMISSION

Leader 'of' the organisation requires permission, leader 'in' the organisation does not. Leader 'of' the organisation requires positional power, resource and permission.

Being a leader 'in' the organisation is understanding that you are the leader of your own actions and, by Living Brave in your intent and actions, that becomes an expression of leadership.

Where people get it skewed is when they only see leadership as hierarchical and positional. Remember a role may have an expectation of leadership, but leadership itself does not require position.

Thus, management is hierarchical and power based while leadership is behavioural and comes from the personal choice of whether to lead or to follow.

Things to reflect on:

- What it would mean to factor in a Legend to your thinking?
- What fears would you have to Face Into?
- Do you believe you need permission to be a leader of self?
- Do you recognise yourself as the CEO of you?

FIVE

UNDERSTAND THE TIMELINE AND STEP INTO THE LEADER SPACE

This is where we look at

How we all got here | The reality of media overexposure |
Why I trusted James | Being a leader of self |
Questions to affirm ourselves as a leader

CHAPTER FIVE

UNDERSTAND THE TIMELINE AND STEP INTO THE LEADER SPACE

"'I am not an angel,' I asserted, 'and I will not be one till I die: I will be myself. Mr Rochester, you must neither expect nor exact anything celestial of me - for you will not get it, any more than I shall get it of you: which I do not at all anticipate.'"

- Charlotte Brontë, Jane Eyre

Leadership is a mindset, not a job, you lead because of your own decision to do so, it requires no position. We will get to that later in the chapter, however first I believe it's important to understand the timeline that got us all here. It's important because to really get Living Brave you have to see the ridiculousness of control and the pettiness of profit as a linear focus.

The history of us all can be summed up as frankly, you don't have very long on this world, so live a life where Living Brave adds value and don't get caught up in the distraction of social media telling you its narrative.

Living Brave is a mindset, a methodology, an approach. It's a way of navigating the complexity that we encounter in the world. The world is a beautiful place. It offers us things such as babies being born, puppies to fuss, friends who tell us silly jokes (and even rude ones that we can't repeat), and sunsets to admire. Recently I've been watching a cat that the owner has dressed up as a shark and placed on an electronic vacuum cleaner[18] going around a kitchen. It's got 12 million hits. I might be two million of them, and every time I watch it, it just reminds me that the world is a beautiful, crazy place.

So, the world is a complex place. It's a difficult place and a dark place in many ways. We have diseases, we have bullying, we have abuse, we have wars. And, as human beings, we're trying to find our path in the world. We're trying to navigate to who it is that we want to be and to whatever it is that we want to become. And if that's not enough, we have to do it while the world presents us with both beautiful and beastly things.

So how does the world feel right now? Well, statistically, the world has never been so good. We have a life expectancy longer than it's ever been before. We have fewer wars and less disease. But it still feels like there's more doubt, more anxiety, more fear. Where does that come from? I'm a firm believer that it's the digital age that is having that impact.

HOW WE GOT TO WHERE WE ARE

The mini-history scene set that follows acts as context, it is defining the landscape and it is doing so at a global level, recognising that we live in the world, we are not separate from it, even though sometimes it might feel that the world is too much to think about and that we are powerless in it. I want to offer another view that is directly linked to a new narrative that exists in the digital age, a narrative that we see play out in the political and social media space, as people realise that corporations and many institutional players have in many cases lost their way or struggle to keep on track with their responsibility to society.

BETTER THAN IT'S EVER BEEN?

I will start by saying; it has always been a bit tough, actually let's go a step further, as historically it has been really difficult staying alive.

- In the 18th century Sweden, every third child died, in 19th century Germany every second child died[19]
- Pre the 1900's it was a bit grim in the sense of the technology that was out there, you have to remember that it was not until 1928 that penicillin, the first true antibiotic, was discovered by Alexander Fleming[20], Professor of Bacteriology at St. Mary's Hospital in London

- In 1918 there was a deadly influenza epidemic that infected around 500 million people[21] globally, resulting in the deaths of some 50-100 million people (that's about 5% of the world's population) and there was, of course, World War II from 1939-1945, killing over 60 million people, which was about 3% of the 1940 world population[22].

The fact that you live in the 21st Century and probably in a 1st world country means that life has already dealt you a pretty strong hand, regardless of individual circumstances.

Looking at the above statistics, a lot of people had to fight to survive and even that probably didn't help a lot of people who make up these numbers. So in the context of history and thinking about things on a global platform, things aren't tough like they used to be, not by a long shot.

So yes we do live in interesting times and let us all be thankful that we live in 'that new iPhone is very interesting' as opposed to 'all the people I know are dead from disease or war' interesting. This is important as a huge amount of the messaging around you is often geared to 'it's awful, isn't it?'. The truth of the matter is that individual situations may well be awful, but cumulatively speaking it is actually getting better, a lot better in fact.

The facts are quite simply overwhelming:

STANDARDS OF LIVING, VIOLENCE AND DISEASE

Increased standards of living

- Infant mortality rates have fallen internationally by 60% over the last 50 years[19]
- People living in poverty has decreased from 75% in 1981 to 57% in 2005[23]
- Life expectancy worldwide is 30% higher than in the 1960's alone and has nearly doubled in the last 100 years[21]

Reduced violence

- In the US (as an indicator) between 1973 and 2009 crime has dropped from 48 to 16 per 1,000 people[24]
- People dying in armed conflict per million (total global population) has dropped from 235 in 1950 to 2.5 in 2007[25]

Decrease in disease

- In the US (as an indicator) cancer rates are on the decline and lower than they were in 1975[26]
- Access to proper sanitation has increased by 50%[27]

So the world is safer[28] and we will live longer; that's not a promise, just so we are clear.

THE TECHNOLOGY PROMISE

The internet is in your hand, which means that the sum of all human knowledge is in your hand; you can talk to anyone on the other side of the globe, something that if you'd have shown it to someone a mere 100 years ago would have probably been considered the stuff of wizardry.

We are also present in this world in a time of technological revolution and evolution, one that has in the scheme of things only just started.

Just to get a bit of a timeline going the pre-industrial age is seen as about 1930 onwards, so this means that before the 1900's we weren't that far away from wooden houses and candlelight. The steam engine was invented in 1765, in England, the first place outside London to have gas lighting was Preston, Lancashire and in 1816 it was already giving way to 'lighting' by 1880. In the US, the spacecraft Apollo 11 was in 1969, the IBM personal computer landed in 1981 (coining the term PC), the internet as we know it really landed about 1990, with Google coming into the public consciousness around 1997-8; mobile phones really became viable around 1990 and it may surprise you to know or remember that the ubiquitous iPhone only launched in 2007.

SOCIAL MEDIA AS A WONDERFUL CONNECTOR AND A MAGNIFIER OF SOCIAL IMMATURITY

Technology has always brought change, many years ago it was a great job to be a litter bearer (where you carried someone on a chair on your shoulders) for a person of wealth, then they invented the wheel and that job disappeared, it's always been like this. The well-used example is the Spinning Jenny: a key development in the Industrial Revolution. In the weaving industry, it destroyed the one person homestead, where one person could spin yarn at home, when in 1764, a man called James Hargreaves invented a device that would work eight spools, this over time growing to 120. He produced more and did it cheaper than everyone else; he also had to flee his hometown as people reacted so negatively, his house was broken into at one point and the Spinning Jenny destroyed, such was the hatred of it.

The theme continues today; however, often wrapped up in the myth of 'going to cheaper workers abroad', though in actuality and using the US as an example the US lost some 5.6 million jobs between 2000 and 2010, according to a study by the Center for Business and Economic Research [29], 85% of job losses in that period were attributable to technological change, largely automation, not by losing out to international trade.

We are also seeing a move to a greater social immaturity as new generations are framing reality through a lens of their relationship with social media and digital applications. The digital world often portrays itself as better than reality, with digital you can communicate immediately, research instantly, contribute without frontiers, and comment without repercussions. This often distorts people's relationship with both commercial and personal relationships, the promise of speed, sharing and transparency often isn't played out in real life.

WE ARE OVER-EXPOSED

Here's a statistic that blows my mind. Roger Bon[30], University of California, believes that people are every day inundated with the equivalent amount of 34 GB (gigabytes) of information and 100,000 words of information a day. Between 1980 and 2008, the number of bytes consumed by Americans increased by 350 per cent. 20GB is a good portion of the works of Beethoven so 34 GB is a lot…..every day. This is important, it's a deluge.

Imagine back to when the Vikings invaded, they would destroy a village, burn it to the ground, steal everything, but you only got to hear about the raid depending on your proximity to it. It may very well have been that it would have taken hours, days, weeks, months, even years depending on where you were geographically in relation to the act. Now if Vikings invaded, you'd see a live stream of it happening.

Of course, what happens is that events come straight through to your smartphone. This has been a remarkably quick development. In 2012 around 52% of respondents to a survey by Deloitte [31] had a smartphone or tablet, in 2017 it was 85% and, amongst 18 to 24-year-olds, it was somewhere close to 95%.

THERE ARE NO SAFE SPACES UNLESS YOU PROTECT THEM

There are now very few sacred spaces where you can be safe to regenerate. Not in your bed or before you go to sleep. Even when you're having a moment on the loo, there it is, straight through on your mobile phone.......of course you have to look.

It used to be that when work wanted to make contact with you, they had to wait for you to go back to work. But now, of course, you don't get that.

There used to be a cartoon called Earthworm Jim. You'll have to be a bit of an aficionado to know or care, but, in one scene a character said, "I shall take over the world, starting with the lactose-intolerant". Well, it made me laugh and when you look into it, it turns out 65% of the world is actually lactose intolerant[32]. Humans are the only mammals that drink milk past weaning and 65% of humans are intolerant experiencing abdominal pain, flatulence, nausea, even diarrhoea. As it did with the digital evolution, mankind created a market for milk that didn't exist naturally. We have had around 10,500 years since we domesticated[33] the cow and this remains true, the change in our brains required to take on board the amount of data, coupled with the social and emotional intelligence to process it is a blink of the eye in comparative terms.

My point is that we take time to acclimatise. We are organic, not electronic. We can't just reboot our system.

In terms of the digital age and the information age, we haven't even had the 10,000 years we've had to adapt to milk. We've had about 30 years.

Chamath Palihapitiya[34], ex VP of Facebook stated he "feels tremendous guilt" over his work on "tools that are ripping apart the social fabric of how society works". Ex-Facebook President Sean Parker has stated how the site was "deliberately designed to exploit human vulnerability". Just take a moment to think about that, let it sink in. You knew it, but they said it.

THE ABILITY TO DIGEST

This has had a huge influence in the way those who are supposed to be leading us now manifest behaviourally, politicians for example now speak to us in soundbites, because they don't believe that we can take the long-form message. We have corporate leaders who are forcing a set of actions and activities on the workforce, forcing it to move faster because of their own fear of innovation and of what the next challenge to their organisational model will be.

The media is feeding us a 24-hour stream of data that is predominantly negative. For example, when Paris was attacked by terrorists on 13th November, 2015 there were 130 victims[35], whereas 400 people die of cancer[36] in France every day. The mainstream media focus encourages a belief in the terror on every corner but statistically, you're more likely to contract cancer and die. Neither is a great option but the point exists. In fact, according to the US Consumer Product Safety Commission, the average American is statistically more likely to be crushed to death by a TV or piece of furniture than to be killed by a terrorist [37]. Yet I know which one you fear the most. It's not your flat screen TV.

This is affecting us as individual humans and as a society and the impact is obvious. 14 million workdays are lost to stress in the UK each year[38].

In the US 40% of the workforce[39] do not take their full holiday entitlement due to fear of what will happen if they're away from the workplace. In terms of fairness, we have 50% of household wealth sitting with 10% per cent of the population[40]. And, in terms of trust, the Edelman Trust Barometer[41] global survey says trust was at an all-time low globally against four major indicators, government, organisations, non-profits and the media?

So we don't even trust charities?!

What does that mean to us? Well, for me, the story of Living Brave is one that gives us a way of directly pushing back against the pressure of the world.

MY CATALYST FOR CHANGE

Living Brave came out of my personal need for change, one that felt very real at the time though I recognise that, on a spectrum of trauma, it would rate low for some and major for others. My father was married four times and my mother was married three times. My father's fourth wife was the mistress he had during his second marriage. So, you can see no trust issues or relationship issues for me in any way! I once came home to discover that out of three bedrooms, my bedroom had been moved from the end into the middle, my father was with his partner in one end room and my mother was in the other with her partner. Again, no damage done to me in any way at all because of that! I'm having a flashback now just thinking about it and getting slightly warm. One day I came home from school and found that my mother had tried to kill herself by taking an overdose. Another time, after I had damaged something belonging to my father, he took me into the garage and, with a rope, he whipped me.

Now, I share that knowing that it provided my catalyst for trying to find what Living Brave might mean to me. I know that other people could look at that and say, "Guy, you had it really easy". Other people might go "Gosh, that was horrific". Everybody's context, everybody's volume control is on a spectrum and it's all set differently for the challenges that we encounter.

STEPPING STONES

For me, I was simply trying to understand what was happening to me. I felt weak. I felt that I was a coward. I was challenging myself to say, "where is your bravery? Why aren't you being brave? Why aren't you living brave? What would that even look like?" So I discovered the vocabulary and mindset to be somebody who would be Living Brave in life, to extricate myself from an emotionally damaging situation. I was able to do that, but I still didn't have the parts of the mechanism that would enable me to help others, and it always stuck with me as something I wanted to achieve. I wanted to be able to give other people the opportunity to be Living Brave. Because, when we have that anxiety, that doubt, that fear, that frustration, when we feel under pressure or threatened in the world, to have a direct way of combating that can, I feel, be very powerful.

We maybe have friends who gossip or a boss who's a bully. Perhaps we have a sense of our own doubt about whether or not we're attractive or intelligent enough. Or maybe the world just feels a little bit heavy and we feel it in ourselves, too, or see it in others.

The component parts for me were what I was looking for. I would think about people like Claudette Colvin in Montgomery, Alabama in 1955, when the law said that if a white person wanted a bus seat, that it had to be given up. At just 15 years old she said "no". I wanted to know where that bravery came from. More recently I remember Malala Yousafzai who was shot in the head by the Taliban[42] in 2012 for wanting the education she was denied as a female. Again I wanted to understand, where did that bravery come from?

JAMES AND THE CIGARETTE

Then one day years into my adult life, I was in a car park and came across a gentleman who'd arrived at the same time. I was going to visit a client and, as I walked across the car park, this gentleman was beside me. There was a young man smoking a cigarette, back when you could, and he took his last puff and flicked it onto the floor. I remember to this day this man, James, saying "Excuse me, fella, would you mind picking that cigarette back up and popping it in the bin?" This young guy looked at James and I think he was making a judgment call as to how senior he was in the organisation and whether or not he should actually pick it up and put it in the bin, but he did. He picked it up, put it in the bin, and James went, "Thanks very much."

We went into reception where I signed the Visitor Book. I was expecting James to show his pass and be sent through because, obviously, he worked for the company. But he didn't. He signed the book as well. I was more than surprised. Here was someone who'd just taken issue with somebody in a car park in an organisation he had no span of control in. I was fascinated as to what drove that, the willingness to contribute outside of his own need, the bravery to do so, the sense of accountability required, the need he felt to trust himself to be the hero of his own story and the Umbrella Beliefs that drove him.

It suddenly came to me where my personal bravery was. My personal bravery was linked back to when I was a child and wishing I could extricate myself from a very personal situation. My bravery had been isolated to my personal need.

When I started to think about people like Claudette Colvin and Malala Yousafzai and James, I recognised that their Living Brave actually sat outside their own particular need.

I managed to take some time to have a conversation with James and he was able to explain how he saw the world. What became apparent in speaking to him, was he had a set of Umbrella Beliefs (page 126), something he believed in that was more important than whatever was in front of him. He had an absolutely vivid, strong representation of where he was trying to go and the person he wanted to be in the world. I recognised that I had inadvertently done the same thing in my own life. I knew what bad was because I was in bad. But what I wanted to do was move to a strong representation of something that was more nurturing to me and which wouldn't damage me emotionally so I, too, was refining my 'Umbrella Belief'.

I instinctively found that I trusted James, with little or no evidence of his trustworthiness, and in a very short space of time. Of course, time reinforces or challenges the data we have on someone but, right there, in that moment, I trusted him. His starting place was one of giving trust and that seemed to create a reciprocal reaction from me.

James also was accountable. That was absolutely clear in conversation with him. He put no responsibility on anyone else, even if the responsibility actually should have been with them. He recognised that he had to be the person who performed the actions. I was able to link that back to my own life and recognise that I'd also been accountable even though somebody else, because of the age I was, should have been responsible for me in many different ways. But I had taken to the responsibility for extracting myself from the situation. So, it's about having that Umbrella Belief. It's about being accountable to yourself in fulfilling that.

As we progressed in conversation it was clear that although James wouldn't place the mantle on himself, he was brave. Not fearless, but brave. He was willing to place himself in harm's way if he felt his Umbrella Belief(s) was at stake. He was willing to be unpopular, although this was never his intent.

I also could see that James was very connected to ideas beyond his own need. He was willing to contribute to others and his ideology required that he hold an Umbrella Belief in the greater good, calibrated with a personal need. He also didn't defer to a later time. He wasn't bewitched by an agenda of getting to a meeting. He recognised it was up to him to define himself as Living Brave when something happened in front of him, that he wanted to apply his thinking and perspective to. It had to be done in the moment. He was connected to the aspiration and the moment.

James was fully willing to be somebody who contributed, and that was absolutely key. He recognised that he was the catalyst. He was both the action and the power behind it, so he had to be willing to lead, to be a first follower, or to pitch in wherever needed. Again, I recognised within myself that I was exactly the same. Nobody would come and save me. There was no white knight to come and take me away. I had to be the contributing force to make the changes that I wanted to make.

So, for me, what I then had was a clear sense of what it might be for us as individuals, teams and work environments, to be able to ask, "do we want to operate with a mindset that is Living Brave?" If we are, then, when things are not going our way and we find tensions that we want to challenge ourselves against we want to be able to ask, "am I Living Brave?" and to always answer "yes". For that to happen we need to have clarity in our Umbrella Beliefs and to have an absolute commitment to being accountable, whilst being absolutely connected to the moment we find ourselves in. With this in play and the bravery to Face Into feedback and calibration, we have something very special.

If you can say 'yes' to these things, then even if you're not getting what you want, you are Living Brave. Because Living Brave isn't about things always going your way. Living Brave is simply about defining yourself as Living Brave. What happens to you, happens to you, literally 'c'est la vie'.

If you're looking to create trust, to be accountable, brave and genuinely connected then you need to make the adjustment towards it, to be able to define yourself as Living Brave. As a leader of others, it's about role-modelling in order to create a culture where you can expect it of others.

YOU ARE A LEADER OF SELF, THAT MAKES YOU A LEADER

What I want here is that you really start to see yourself in a timeline, one that you can recognise as being part of as a human being. That you have a sense that it has never been easy, that you are not owed anything, historically it has often been far worse and actually in the timeline of things, you are blessed with this starting point. From this jumping off point, you can now really start framing your particular need so that, as you read through this book, you can define what it is you're aiming for.

Looking at the questions below from the end of Chapter 2 and ask yourself if anything has changed since you thought about or captured your thoughts on the following.

1. Do you define yourself as a leader?
2. Do you believe that you require permission to lead?
3. Do you see leadership as requiring seniority?
4. Do you see leadership as being about the position you hold?
5. Do you believe you can lead even if you have no power or direct control?
6. Do you think there can be more than one leader at the same time?
7. Do you see leadership as being only at work?
8. Do you believe leaders should know the answer?
9. Do you believe leadership is straightforward?
10. Do you believe leaders can operate without feedback?
11. Do you seek counsel from others that both reinforces and challenges?

It may well be that what has happened is that you have had your thoughts confirmed, perhaps reinforced, challenged or perhaps this has given you permission and a license to consider yourself in a manner that you have never considered before.

1. Do you define yourself as a leader?

You are a leader, either by position or by life. You may have a position in an enterprise that requires not just management, but also leadership. You may hold no position of any jurisdictional consequence, however as discussed earlier you require no permission, no license to be a leader of yourself.

2. *Do you believe that you require permission to lead?*

No one has domain over your emotions, your mindset and your actions other than what you allow them to have. This means that you can think, feel and react as you see fit. You will need to calibrate to the outside world as you try to connect, engage and add value to it, however, this means you are learning the elegance of defining your strength within it. Not subjugating yourself through ongoing submission. A backwards strategic step is fine but continual acquiesce means you lose yourself.

3. *Do you see leadership as requiring seniority?*

Leadership has no seniority and that's a little tricky for some people to wrap their heads around. Management has seniority in the context of positional power and hierarchy. Management defines role responsibility and within that will require leadership. Leadership is 100% behavioural and when you consider what sits within the behaviours of a leader they are open to everyone.

4. *Do you see leadership as being about the position you hold?*

Feeding straight off Point 3, your position has no need for positional or resource control. You are a leader of self, in every part of your life, in which you may well be in a management role. That management role may well be a team leader, supervisor, manager, head of, director of, VP, executive, the title is whatever the title is, the seniority is whatever the role offers. Understand that 'leadership' behaviours are generic truths (curiosity, transparency, honesty, integrity....add more here), they are human truths for anyone living in the world. Leader of self means 'leader'.

5. *Do you believe you can lead even if you have no power or direct control?*

You may have no span of control, you may have no positional power and you may be outgunned however you can be Trusted, Accountable, Brave and Connected you can have an opinion and offer it, you can work hard to make things a success even when you don't believe in them. Note: Great piece of advice, if you want to prove someone wrong? Prove them right! This works because if you are wrong and you tried to genuinely enable the success of the thing you didn't agree with then you are trustworthy due to your intent and commitment, even enhancing the story of you as someone who even in disagreement pledges to make something work. This works because if you were right all along and this endeavour did not work, then it did not fail because of you, in fact, you were the advocate and a driving force.

This is Leadership of Self, not being a saboteur but an enabler. You expect to be heard, you expect to be listened to, respected and in return, you will work to make things work.

6. *Do you think there can be more than one leader at the same time?*

Generally, there only needs to be one person in ultimate control of a given situation however regardless of role or position there is no reason why leadership behaviours should not be on show from everyone in the room as they work in the context of the moment. When I say we are all Leaders of Self, I mean we are all turning up Trusted, Accountable, Brave and Connected. This means there are as many leaders in the room as there are people and they are all respecting the management hierarchy and responsibilities that are in place.

7. *Do you see leadership as being only at work?*

The act of fulfilling your role responsibility may well start and end at the door, however, that is the task, not the mindset. As a leader of self, you are a leader of your own actions, thoughts, opinions, and your own Trusted, Accountable, Brave and Connected engine. This is like being a friend to someone or a parent when you are away from the friend or the child you aren't directly doing an act of friendship or parenthood as you are engaged in other activities however you still define yourself as being a friend, a parent. The act of being a friend or a parent does not require you to be in situ, it is how you define yourself, and it is what you are. It doesn't require permission, it is a reality based on your own context. You may or may not be a (senior) manager at work but you are a leader of self, this means that you own your own identity and presence in the world and in that world you may or may not hold management positions. Wherever you are at work, home, on the bus, walking in the park you are a Leader of Self and you operate in that context regardless of the role or task you inhabit.

8. *Do you believe leaders should always know the answer?*

There are of course times when a role would indicate that you should have an answer, however in the increasingly complex and time-bound environments in which we live, it is ever more likely that a leader will not have 'the' answer. Decisions are increasingly complex and have fluid states, so the decision of today can be correct or wrong within short timelines. The role of a leader is not to 'always' have the answer, but to create an environment where contributors are up to date, in the right roles, are willing to give discretionary effort, have the success of the enterprise as their focus and are accountable in their actions pushing themselves to the fore when required or pulling back when it is beneficial.

9. *Is leadership straightforward?*

Leadership is not straightforward or simple. It should be seen as a craft, one that requires conscious competence and consistent effort. This is a difference in seeing leadership as a task and role-specific, as opposed to identity-driven and a craft. The seeking of data that informs your calibrations may be likened to sailing a boat, the best or the worst captains both have their hand on the tiller, the success over time comes from those that have seen it as a craft (the role not the boat), these are the ones that over time will learn, reflect and demonstrate curiosity in their own competence. Thus they will ultimately gain more skill, insight and trust from those around them. It is not just being willing to learn when learning presents itself, it is the drive to seek knowledge and insight.

10. *Should leaders operate without feedback?*

We all need feedback, that's a fact. It is near impossible to see the back of your own head, we need information that allows us to calibrate our thinking, approach and actions. It is said "all feedback is a gift", which might be true, but not all gifts are equal. People may give you truly insightful data on your actions and the impact they have both in the positive and the negative, information that can catapult you once you have become aware of it. However just like when someone gives you an article of clothing, that they think will look good on you, sometimes they have a bad eye for these things. It is the same with feedback, it can come at you sometimes with bad intent or with good intent but badly positioned. Leaders have to seek feedback from those they impact on directly and indirectly. Leaders need the truth, getting it requires elegance and a story of you that engenders trust.

11. *Do you seek counsel from others that both reinforces and challenges?*

This is different from feedback which is in essence data and is mostly up to you to navigate it. When you have others who you can discuss real-world scenarios with, who are operating as either mentor (as they have more experience than you), coach (as they can challenge your thinking and hold you to account) or peer review (people at your level who are experiencing similar situations and you enable each other). When you have this counsel you are able to bring your thoughts, emotions and ideas to a place that will reinforce, be curious, challenge and enable your mindset and actions. It is up to you, to not be dependent on the relationship and that you maintain a healthy engagement and at the same time separation. However, trusted counsel is a true sign that you see leadership as a craft.

The key to the thinking behind Living Brave is your self-context, if you believe that you require permission to lead then you have not understood the mindset. We are talking about permission, though it is a permission that is self-administered, is self-assessed and it requires no external validation.

Keep in mind that management is role specific, hierarchical and involves resource ownership, you might be aspiring, junior, middle tier or sitting on the top table as a senior executive, the reality is you are in essence a manager of people and resource, with targets to achieve.

Leadership might be required in the role, but it sits within the person, you can hold the position that impacting in a positive way as a leader is directly related to the experience of you, which is the story of you which is the way you interact with the world. Those interactions, whether you are seen as trustworthy, accountable, brave and connected are not position bound, they are not the domain of a manager at any level, they are the domain of the person/team who brings the behaviour to the role they happen to be in.

Senior managers can make the decision as to whether or not you are going to hold a certain position; however, really understand this: no one has dominion over the manner in which you wish to approach the world.

This is exactly the same for a team, you may well have output defined, resources administered and cultures to operate in that are very loose or incredibly prescriptive, even suffocating though the same thing applies. The team can harness the Living Brave approach and define itself as Trustworthy, Accountable, Brave and Connected and in the face of any reality that is being faced, the team can then Face Into that reality in the manner in which they have decided.

Things to reflect on:

- How are you feeling at this stage of the book?
- What's changed at this point?
- How are you planning to turn the idea of new actions into a reality?
- If someone asked you what Living Brave was about, how would you explain it?

SIX

CONTEXT IS KING

This is where we look at

Hitting a lamp post | If the tail is wagging the dog |
How to get shot properly | The humour elixir |
Understanding the resilience equation | Meeting the Truth Triangle |
The Agility Capability Triangle

CHAPTER SIX

CONTEXT IS KING

*"It's not as simple as understanding what leadership is,
it's about understanding the context
and applying leadership relevant to that moment."*

- Major General Paul Nanson, CBE

THE LAMP POST TEST

Imagine you are walking down the street on your way to an important meeting. You are distracted while looking at directions on your phone and don't notice the lamppost in front of you. BANG, you walk straight into it, so hard it knocks you over and your phone drops and shatters. At that moment you realise you will be late, there are lots of people (who you don't know) looking at you, perhaps sniggering, perhaps showing concern... What is your reaction?

Type 1
Blames the lamppost, blames the people who put it there. "Stupid lamppost". They mind people seeing they've just been daft. They need validation from observers, they externally validate.

Type 2
Laughs at themselves, understands straight away that it is all down to them and declare "I'm such a twit". They don't mind people seeing they've just been daft. They don't need validation from observers, they self-validate.

People, teams and organisations that are accountable are, by nature or by learning, able to laugh at themselves and learn at the same time.

HUMOUR

Businessman, Allen Klein said, "our attitude is like a box of crayons that colour your world. Constantly colour your picture grey, and your picture will always be bleak. Try adding some bright colours to the picture by including humour, and your picture begins to lighten up."

Accountability is the ability to find humour in the past, present and future. Humour is, I believe, the gift that keeps on giving. It is the most humane response to stress, uncertainty, doubt and fear.....it's a resilience building, well-being generator and a fantastic litmus test of individual, team and organisational health.

Anyone, any team, any organisation devoid of humour is damaged. Any organisation that considers itself to be professional should be professional enough to not just allow but to nurture humour. Here's a thought: how about creating a culture of humour? Don't get that confused with 'messing about', 'goofing off', 'pranks and Whoopi cushions'. I'm talking about socially mature humour. Let me explain.

One thing I have noticed as a martial arts instructor is that when people want their first combative experience in sparring, in a contest or when being pressure tested, it brings elements of uncertainty, stress, personal doubt, a threat to their ego and even fear. The healthy reaction of everyone involved in this process, especially those with the duty of care, is humour.

The person about to spar often laughs nervously as they're aware they're about to get challenged, might be outclassed, possibly get hurt a bit. Then when they get hit, you often hear a version of "Gawd that hurt (laugh)!" If they, in turn, get a lucky punch in, you hear "Whoa I got him (laughing, through genuine surprise)!" They laugh in their moments of greatest success and also their greatest mistake. This is typical. Laughter can be an expression of the awkwardness, doubt, fear, relief, release, success and celebration we experience.

The caveat for humour is that it must have 'good intent' at its core. Humour is about recognising the truth of a given situation, it is fabulously connective and cements relationships. In contrast, humour that is damaging to the other person is incredibly judgmental and shaming, which is why some people shy away from it, but that's fear and that has to be Faced Into.

Humour requires nurturing, calibrating and elegance. It is not a blunt instrument. It is a rapier blade.

HUMOUR THE ELIXIR OF COMPASSION

Humour provides the elasticity that allows the unpalatable to be endured. It's an amazingly powerful tool. I notice that one of the first signs of a healthy leadership mindset and culture is humour. Without it, the individual, team and the culture are in danger of being damaged as it loses a key resilience tool. I am quite serious when I say that you can feel the spirit in a person, in a team and in an organisation. We can all sense the anxiety of the individual and the team and feel it in the environment when the only Accountability is that of 'task completion' and when the only release is in private moments with trusted colleagues, manager approved social moments or contrived corporate scenarios. The elixir is not 'fun and happiness'. That's like saying to someone "make me laugh". Instead, operate from a place of Living Brave that values moments of humour as they occur.

Think about the emergency services or the military. They often step into a situation that has not been covered in training or which is directly stressful, even life-threatening. I have socialised and trained with firemen, law enforcement agents, even Special Forces operatives. They often talk with, and demonstrate a distinct comfort with humour at times that are technically far from funny.

An example of this is Mark 'Ted' O'Brien, who's spent a lifetime in the fire service. He has been Head of Incident Command, Head of Learning and Development, and Director of Product and Quality for the Fire Service College, he speaks about turning up at a scene which most of us would find extremely harrowing. As his crew assess and ready themselves humour often comes into play. Imagine arriving at a car crash, a horrible mess including some things you have dealt with before, others which you haven't, and which therefore have to be figured out in the moment. There are old hands and new recruits, the public, other emergency service agencies. There is a cacophony of voices, actions required and personalities. Some people are in charge, some learning, some in pain, some calm, some aggressive. It's all happening.

Ted: "Often you'll hear that voice that says, 'bliiiiiimey' or 'right let's go', perhaps you'll hear someone say 'any ideas?' or a 'hey (insert name) don't forget to turn the hose on this time!'."

You can see that it isn't that the situation is comical; it's the fact that they are sufficiently in control to remain human. It means they 'have it', it doesn't 'have them'. The dog is wagging the tail of the situation, not the other way around. It's a subtle thing, however, it's a huge thing. To me it's the key to the car, it might be small, but good luck without it.

HOW TO GET SHOT PROPERLY

Perspective is the key. Humour allows you to have a highly professional outlook, to be human while being professional and to enable others around you through your own actions. It's about creating permission, a rallying cry that it's ok to be professional, to succeed or fail. It's about learning to see the humour in the moment as it was, as it is, or as you can imagine.

I was in Allen, Texas many years ago and a Law Enforcement Officer I was training with told me a story that always stuck. He told me how when in the military, prior to his current role he was participating in various training courses and the instructor on one said, "right let's talk about how to get shot properly". Of course, he said, "we were all a bit 'shot properly'....what do you mean?" The instructor goes on to educate. It turns out that the right perspective, aligned with the right level of Accountability, administered with humour is the way to get shot properly.

He recounted how his instructor trained him in this experience: "So, let's say you get shot. It's feasible there are three ways to get shot. One of them will get you killed, one of them will help you and the final one will enable you......so someone shoot me with your finger."

One of the group puts up their hand with their forefinger out and the thumb up, in the universally accepted mode of shooting someone with a finger.....and says, "Bang".

The instructor goes, "Oh god I've been shot, oh Jesus.....oh Jesus....I'm shot....help me....help me......oh God......oh God.....please, someone, help me." There is a pause as everyone looks around, many thinking, "well honestly I might actually do that". "Right" says the instructor, "that'll get you killed. Heart rate increasing, adrenaline pumping, leads to irrational behaviour, poor decisions, panic and, generally, a bad outcome".

The instructor says, "Shoot me again". There's another shot from the finger gun. The instructor reacts with a stoic face, "right I have been shot, I need to stem the bleeding, control my breathing and get help. Ok, so breathe, apply pressure, use the radio or call out"

Everyone looks around. They realise he's right. It will take training, repetition, mindset and professionalism but yes, this is the way to go. Many are thinking, "Right I hope this is me". The instructor says, "This is exactly what you have to do if you're going to live. It requires having a methodology to follow, staying calm and having focused actions".

The instructor then said, "Right, whereas that last example is absolutely the right approach, this is the approach that makes you a legend.....shoot me". The finger shoots him, "BANG". The instructor looks down at the imaginary wound, takes a moment, smiles and says, "bloody hellfire, that's just goddam brilliant (starts laughing).....some son of a bitch has shot me....typical....right then". The instructor pauses.

Someone from the group asks "Then what?"

Instructor: "Well then you do the last approach, so you don't die!"

Now personally I think this is hilarious and very, very clever. There's a certain emotional, intellectual, insightfulness going on that just rings true. What it's telling me and, I hope you, is that there always has to be a process (version 2). However, the situation benefits from the humanity that is brought to the experience and training of getting shot (version 3). There's something about this that is worth reflecting on for us all as individuals, leaders of teams and organisation cultures.

RESILIENCE ALGORITHM

What's wrong with the second version of getting shot properly? Nothing, it's perfect in its approach. Would you want version 3 of getting shot properly without version 2? Nope, not unless you wanted to die a laughing idiot. You need process, that's for sure, however, we know that people operate better the less stress they are under, that's a clear fact. Less stress equates to greater clarity of thought and, ultimately, better health over the long term. This is true of the person, the team and the organisation. You better believe that a team and organisation overall have an eco-system, just like a person has an immune system. There is a collective health as much as there is individual health.

Living Brave has a definite humour and process element. However, let's not get evangelical to the point where it becomes its own problem. I truly believe that one of the greatest capacities for resilience is a strong drive to create a Legend to be proud of, aligned to goals, driven by will, enabled by humour and which encourages recalibration and rejuvenation.

Fig 7: Resilience Algorithm

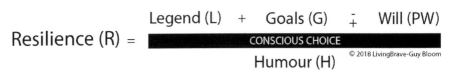

If we want Resilience (R), then the following has to be considered:

Legend: "Do I/we care about the cumulative story of my/our actions?"

Goals: "Is what we are striving for enough of a compelling story to excite?"

Will: "Is there an individual and shared will to achieve?"

Humour: "Is their room for compassion through humour"

HUMOUR AND COMPASSION

I do believe that humour is a version of compassion that manifests at a surface level and is a gateway to genuine and deep compassion and I did wonder why I haven't used the word 'compassion' itself.

I do realise that not everything has an element of humour, however the 'bloody hell, really' moment does seem to be a gateway to the human element of a situation. As if for many people, in particular in a social setting, it seems to be the pressure valve or the catalyst for if accepted, a stepping stone to dealing with the reality of the moment.

My current take on this is that humour in the context of compassion exists to allow compassion to be accessed, the phrase 'well….this is a bit painful' with a sense of the dark comedy in front of you is an extremely high level of adult communication. Humour in the darkest moments, when used with elegance and care, has the capacity to not fan the flames of a situation but to show that the moment is recognised and being shared.

I find this deeply human and deeply powerful.

OUR SUCCESS IS OUR LEARNING

We need to understand that the human animal is actually just that, an animal. Just like in any other animal reality, it's all about 'survival and hierarchy'. But we are also more than just a human 'animal'. We are also a human 'being' and that means we are so much more than just a set of instincts and reactions. But this is the key, we are all a consequence of 'instinct and reactions' living in conjunction with 'thought and intellect'.

The human condition is a balance of multiple dichotomies, the step-ping-stones of evolution have seen mankind emerge from being purely reactionary to having the capacity for thought and humanity. The human being is living within the reality of the human condition and it challenges us on a daily basis, to continue evolving.

Things to reflect on:

- How do I react to the lamp posts in my life?
- Where is your tail wagging you, instead of you wagging your tail?
- Where does humour exist in your life and where might it be used to greater effect?

TRUTH TRIANGLE

Living Brave looks through the lens of a triangle called the Truth Triangle. Your truth, be it as an individual, team or organisation, sits in the middle of this triangle and your particular frame of reference will determine which factors have a greater pull on you.

1.	Societal Truth	Bigger than all of us
2.	Organisation Truth	Cultural expectations, seen and unseen
3.	Own Truth	What you/we want for your/our self
4.	What you decide to be	How you contextualise and act on points 1, 2, 3

Fig 8: Truth Triangle

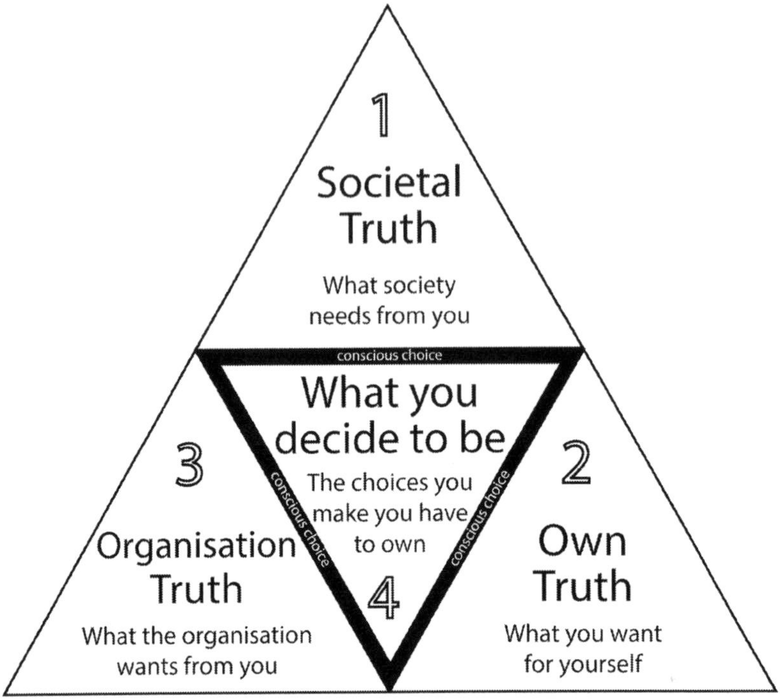

© 2018 LivingBrave-Guy Bloom

SOCIETAL TRUTH

It is key to understand what society expects of you, in the context of you being part of it. It's an easy thing to think that you are in the world, not a part of it, this is true for many organisations, in particular, the belief that we are in a battle to not just do well but win a battle of survival. This often creates an owner/shareholder narrative that starts and ends with 'they expect x and y'. What is really often meant is, 'for me to keep my value here x and y have to happen' and 'to get bonus x and y has to happen'.

When we look at society's expectations of business, we often find that there is a large gap between what is seen collectively as fair and equitable and what is really being experienced. Society doesn't want a great deal, it basically says, "do no harm, be kind, help others and try to leave things better than you found them". Yet as we have spoken about in earlier chapters, this seems to be a tall order for the many business leaders who are framing success as purely commercial and winning 'the battle'.

The truth is, this is true, business is a battle of sorts. However without meaning outside of the business or the task then the only way of defining a good outcome would be in commercial viability and anything that adds value to the bottom line and the sustainability of that enterprise. The internal dynamic of a business is not isolated to that business,

Society has a set of expectations, society says "don't hurt people", "don't kick puppies", "raise your children to be good people", "help others where you can"... Society also says things to the business world, "add value to the world where you can, at the very least don't do harm", "you have a duty of care to the people in your employ", "earn as much money as you want, however, consider how to make the parts of the world you touch better".

In the Living Brave frame of reference, this doesn't mean we all hold hands, wear hemp and start chanting, though it does recognise that society is affected and even infected deeply by the impact of the decisions that business makes both at a global and local level.

Large companies create a homogenisation of product; they can create, dictate or exasperate social trends and shift the social dynamic. This is not all done from a deeply Machiavellian position, it's done from the output of activity, activity that is often created from a good place. Mobile phones and the internet are an excellent case in point. They make sense and help us all; it means you are safer, more connected and more able to engage with the world. So for a family it means you can speak and see them from a different continent, you can look up basically anything and hold it in your hand. The only word for this is a big.....WOW.

The other side of this is that business can contact you at all times, emails bombard your inbox and if you are in a global context then as you go to rest others come online. The driving need in a global project, that all parts of the world are operating in unison, can drive a culture that lies deeply over the line of taking from people as they fear being out of the loop or seen to not be reactive enough. We see a cascading set of impatience from a CEO to those that are driving the need as they try to demonstrate up the line that they have control and can make things happen.

So there is often an Organisation Truth that says 'the world is like that, so you have to be on board' and a Societal Truth that we have around what 'is fair and right'. You know this from what just 'feels right' and from the conversations that you have with those around you. You know when expectations outweigh what is fair and equitable and with the advent of the same medium that feeds that anxiety, society kicks back by trying to hold those in positions of power to account.

Society needs individuals and organisations to care about society. The societal truth is that the world needs those in positions of influence and positional power to enable those around them to grow and become valuable in the world.

One of the most obvious ways of looking at this is to enable the Trust, Accountability, Bravery and Connection of individuals in a way that means as they operate in the world they are able to do so in a way that adds value to their family, friends and those that they interact with.

Another way of seeing this is the way a business frames its Corporate Social Responsibility (CSR). What do they do? Give some money, allow people to go and do something in the community once in while? All good stuff and long may it continue, but in many ways, that's a get out of jail free card, "we have given x% of our money" (tax write off), "we have let people out for a day to paint a school" etc…these are great things. However they are CSR, they are a tick to demonstrate "we are clear on that one". What would the impact be if it changed from Corporate Social Responsibility and was just Social Responsibility? What would it mean if we did the normal CSR stuff, because we should, but we framed the way we interact with our people to understand how we can help them be of value to the world? In the manner of who they can be in the world because of the learning and the environment we create for them.

So that's factor number one. What does society need from you as a human being and as a leader? Regardless of what any entity you work for needs or what you want, the question continues to be "What does society need you to be?".

Now you are going to react to this in a variety of different ways: on a spectrum of 'don't care', 'dunno' through to 'this really resonates'. To operate in a context of Living Brave you have to care; if you don't care about what society needs from you, then this isn't going to work for you. It's because the caring about what society needs is key to your ability to be Living Brave. There are some things that are bigger than you; they exist outside of your need, and by tapping into them you are reinforced by the understanding that some things are inherently true at a very deep level: don't bully people, help people learn and grow, enable others where you can, and don't be the cause of undue stress to others.

There are some things that are not institutional they are world truths, 2+2=4. Knowing this gives you strength, it's not what you think, it's true, the core societal truths can't be debatable, or they aren't truths. Now if you are thinking "everything is debatable", then that's your intellect arguing you out of what's real and that's a voice you need to turn the dial down on.

A societal truth empowers you because it's outside of your need, preference or want, you can hold yourself to task against a societal truth, and you can also bring curiosity and challenge to others against a societal truth. Think about it in your own life when perhaps you have instinctively replied or reacted with a "stop that" "no that's not right, it's not fair" or in the positive where you have reflexively felt your energy lend it to "let me help" "I'm going to do that", as you know it's the right thing to do. That's you knowing what's right and wrong at a societal level.

ORGANISATIONAL TRUTH

What does the organisation need? Here you have to factor in two questions:

- What is espoused?
- What is actually being performance-managed?

These two things might be in perfect alignment. The truth is that even in the most integrity-driven cultures, there is often a barometer of behavior, the hotter (the pressure that is being applied to managers in a business) it becomes, often the more autocratic and fearful the behaviour of the individual. As that is spread over a tier, project, team, the greater the experience of being micromanaged and feeling like a resource can be the experience of those that sit under or around that senior management team.

This organisation truth requires four factors to be understood:

Factor 1:   What the organisation markets to the world: vision, mission, purpose, values

Factor 2:   What is happening at a local level in your country, region, area, office, department, team

Factor 3:   What your line manager wants in relation to the above two factors

Factor 4:   The level of Trust, Accountability, Bravery and Connection you feel in relation to the first three factors

You know the things I am talking about here. The country manager doesn't agree with the steer from the centre, the MD of a business doesn't agree with the expectations of the group function, the department head plays up to the senior team but dictates differently, the team leader who recognises that as managers come and go as long as they get bottom-line results they are safe from repercussions. Or the team manager who recognises that as senior managers come and go and push different commercial buttons as long as they treat their team with respect they will experience minimal staff turnover in the face of the ever-changing focus coming down the line, thus maintain focus.

The dilemma for many organisations is: 'how do I/ we achieve what is right at a world/human/societal level whilst driving the commercials?'

OWN TRUTH

> "No one person can, for any considerable time, wear one
> face to themselves, and another to the multitude, without
> finally getting bewildered as to which is the true one."
>
> - *Nathaniel Hawthorne*

You have to have absolute clarity about 'your truth' in order to be able to calibrate how you behave.

- What do you want?
- What are your expectations?
- Who do you want to be?
- How do you wish to behave?

It is a key bit of understanding to grasp the difference between what might be selfish and what should be considered your right to expect or need. There are a few questions that generally hit the mark in gaining clarity:

Does what I want.......

- ...allow me to develop rather than stagnate?
- ...enable rather than harm others?
- ...satisfy a personal goal and vision?
- ...add rather than take from my energy and motivation?

If you are not clear what you are about and what you want, then what's the point of your existence? Remember it is one thing to be 'of' service to the world and the organisation, it's a very different thing to be 'in' service. Living Brave means that you are clear that your needs are relevant and though we all have navigated the realities of our context, we have to have clear boundaries around our own requirements that are subjugated due to the needs of others or our own fears.

To be clear on what you want, bear in mind that what you want:

- Can change as your context does
- Does not have to be fixed
- Does not require permission from anyone else to be of importance

It is very important to home in on things that add to your story, that enable and nourish you intellectually and/or emotionally and/or spiritually (in terms of personal need).

AGILITY CAPABILITY TRIANGLE

The Agility Capability Triangle layers neatly on top of each of the sections of the Truth Triangle. Imagine the Agility Capability Triangle as a model you can rotate and thus look at each section of the Truth

Triangle (page 114) through that lens. It provides an insight into the intelligence involved in each of those sections as well as working very effectively as an independent reference point that individuals, teams and organisations need to consider in terms of their Learning Capability.

Fig 9: Agility Capability Triangle

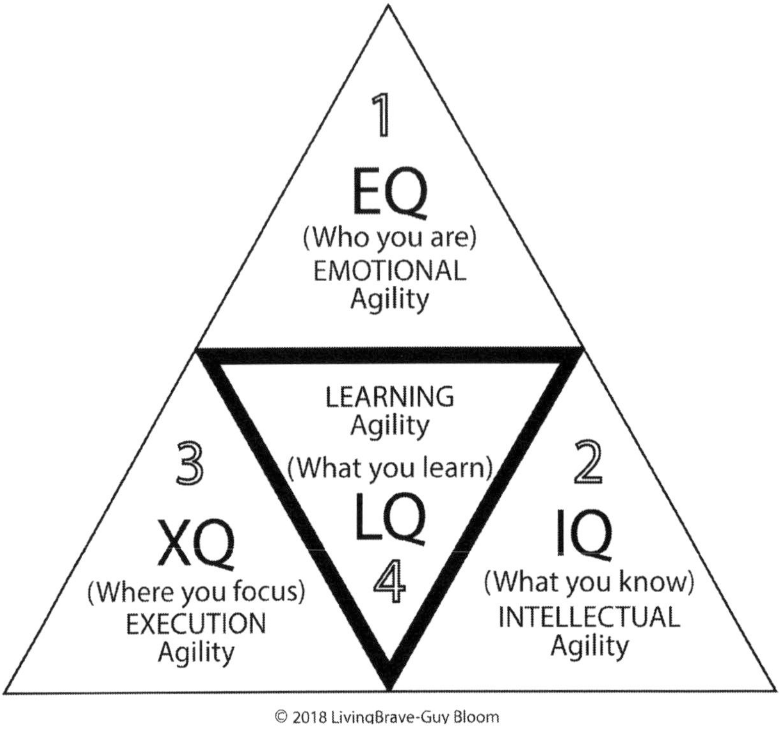

© 2018 LivingBrave-Guy Bloom

The Agility Capability Triangle is a model that helps to show the intelligence and agility required to truly understand Point 4 (What you decide to be) from the Truth Triangle.

There's a quote by F. Scott Fitzgerald which I love: "The test of a first-rate intelligence is the ability to hold two opposed ideas in mind at the same time and still retain the ability to function." It pretty well sums up the reality of one's life in any context.

The Agility Capability Triangle crucially addresses the complexities that are introduced when considering how the individual, team and organisation's capability to learn against the three intelligences of:

- **EQ (Emotional Intelligence)**

How insight at a social, organisation and individual level is gathered and understood

- **IQ (Intelligence Quotient)**

  How individuals, teams and the senior team manage multiple truths in complex, wicked times

- **XQ (eXecution Intelligence)**

  How adept the individual, team and the senior team are at moving to action, navigating hurdles, and reaching time-bound outputs

EQ, IQ and XQ all map to each part of Truth Triangle, as you need EQ in all these areas to have insight.

EQ (EMOTIONAL INTELLIGENCE)

Being alert to your own thoughts, behaviours, understanding and how they impact on you and those around us is a constant challenge. How is what you are doing on a day-to-day basis affecting or infecting your personal resilience and wellbeing? How is it impacting on those around you? Do you care enough to consider the way in which people leave the organisation feeling at the end of every day? Are they happy, growing and confident or unhappy, stagnant and submissive?

IQ (INTELLIGENCE QUOTIENT)

Do you know how to think, to learn, to gather inputs and to make sense of them? IQ is not a score, it is about how you gather in new learning, take on board the new information and how you look outside of your own horizon. What habits and methods exist within the individual and the business to onboard information that is needed to keep up with and even step ahead of change? This is also about the spread of information and the insight that is brought to it, which does require the application of analysis and the EQ to make sense of things. Information for a leader is people, process and profit. Think of the F. Scott Fitzgerald a few lines back, it's not as simple as what you know, it's the spectrum, the depth and the quality of what you know.

XQ (EXECUTION INTELLIGENCE)

What do you focus on? Where do you place your energy? Are you good at actually completing a task or project, not just in terms of the actions that overtly drive commercial outputs, but also in terms of the IQ & EQ of yourself, others and thus, ultimately, the organisation? As an individual does your focus ever move away from the organisation's need? Do you make space for the human elements and the development that goes along with this? Where is the organisation's XQ focus? If it's 100% task, there is something not right. If the human agenda is getting in the way of genuine output then something is not right.

Questions that drive EQ, IQ and XQ thinking:

- Are we capable of operating outside of the now and business as usual?
- Are we Trusted to see beyond the horizon to a place as yet unknown?
- Are we/am I, Accountable to the craft of learning?
- Are we Brave enough to admit what we don't know and seek insight and input from any level of our business and external entities?
- Are we Brave enough to understand that being in a state of 'not knowing' does not make us vulnerable, unless we treat time-served experienced as the only way of learning?
- Do we have the shared motivation to care beyond our own need to Contribute?
- Are we accountable to the business's learning ability by being the advocates and role models of developmental growth to prepare for the Tame (understood) and the Wicked (not understood) challenges that lie ahead?

When the factors within the Agility Capability Triangle are ignored or viewed simply as an intellectual exercise, then it's possible to self-sabotage as the factors tend to be transactional enterprises, but without the intimacy required to truly harness individual and cumulative capability.

The Legend that sits above both the story and brand is a driving force that should hold the focus of individuals, teams and organisational leaders because it is a culmination of IQ, EQ & XQ that people experience. There is no end of evidence in your business right now, start with your engagement survey and exit interviews, where people will evidence their experience of the over or underplaying of effort and competence in all three areas.

Things to reflect on:

- Consider the four elements in the Truth Triangle
- Consider the four elements in the Agility Capability Triangle
- Review, seek counsel, discuss, see if what you say resonates with others
- Explore where you are strong or weak

SEVEN

UMBRELLA BELIEFS

This is where we look at

Umbrella Beliefs being the hub of Living Brave |
Calibration and Validation | Which wolf you need to feed? |
Levers that drive action

CHAPTER SEVEN

UMBRELLA BELIEFS: THE HUB OF LIVING BRAVE

"Once you see the way broadly
you will see the way in all things."

– *Miyamoto Musashi, Go Rin No Sho*
(Book of Five Rings, 1645)

Umbrella Beliefs are what powers the Living Brave engine, have a quick look at the Living Brave Mindsets on page 147, you will see Umbrella Beliefs are at the centre.

An Umbrella is bigger than you, it covers you, in this sense, an Umbrella Belief is bigger than the thing that you are dealing with. The way to look at an Umbrella Belief is in the way it gives you a point of focus in the storm to say, "the belief I have in this is bigger than the stress the situation in front of me is creating". An Umbrella Belief holds you on track because you are compelled to move towards it. This is not the same as having a vision, purpose, strategy or plan. The word 'belief' means it's something deep-rooted enough to have an inherent pull on your emotional state and to create discomfort when you're not moving towards it.

An Umbrella Belief is not the same as a vision, purpose, strategy or plan.

Vision: Is the 'what?': the end game, what the result will look like. It is both grounded and stretching and thus exciting

Purpose: Is the 'why?': why care/why bother/why engage/why commit?

Strategy: Is the 'how?': the approach, the overall road map, the steps worked out so they can be understood and connected with

Plan: Is the 'when?': the plan, the tracking, the who and the deadline

There's a lot of existing material regarding vision, purpose, strategy and planning. In an organisational context, vision, purpose, strategy and planning are often devoid of a human element other than 'you can see what we want, so stay motivated'. There is often little Connection to personal drivers or emotional Connection to the individual who has to achieve the vision and the mission, who has to influence the strategy and work through the plan every day.

Umbrella Beliefs influence the way in which we succeed, fail, overcome or deal with the bad time, thus enabling the team to feel pride and empowerment.

Fig 10: Umbrella Beliefs

To create Umbrella Beliefs individuals, teams and an organisation's stakeholders need to think hard about the things that sit beyond the commercials, the things that act as a driver behind the goal or the output. Yes, you want commercial success. Yes, you want to succeed in your chosen career, however, those aspirations require an emotional driver that depends on pride, personal and shared value.

It is intrinsically linked to the concept of the Living Brave perspective on the 'manner of you' while you are doing what you are doing.

- You can have as many Umbrella Beliefs as you like
- They don't have to make sense to anyone else unless you're using them to engage others

The following is a simple, non-work example that has stuck with me for years. My next door neighbour, Margaret, was talking to her daughter, Eleanor. There was a heated argument going on between them and Eleanor uttered the immortal words: "I hate you!". Margaret replied, very calmly with no change in her tone of voice, "Eleanor, I love you". To which then Eleanor responded with words that came straight out of a Hollywood movie: "I don't want you to love me".

The question I have to ask is, what is it that Margaret believed in that enabled her to not shift her tone, her demeanour or her overall way of behaving? My observation was that she wasn't being hooked into the drama that her daughter was trying to create.

The answer, I hypothesise, would be the power that Margaret had in her own Umbrella Belief of: "I will love my daughter regardless of the context that we find ourselves in and I want the story of our relationship to be one where when Eleanor reflects back on conversations we've had, she will always have the image of her mother never attacking her or pulling away from her, but staying connected and fully present."

Having an Umbrella Belief meant Margaret could hold a position both intellectually and emotionally to a higher order than the situation in front of her. Often the situation in front of us may be something that triggers the emotional dynamics that are in play. Umbrella Beliefs are seen again and again in high performing individuals in any context in life and, this is key, the concept of an Umbrella Belief is that of the personal truth. Believing in something that's bigger than the situation you're in is a key differentiator for being able to hold yourself to be the person that you want to be. This also goes for teams. When a team has Umbrella Beliefs then it can hold itself to a personalised and therefore more connected way of behaving, 'this is who we are, this is what we do'. It may be, in part, aspiration, however, can become an inspiration as it moves closer and closer to reality.

This is why Margaret, in this context, is a leader. She is Living Brave through her unique set of personal Umbrella Beliefs which define her, positively validate her own story and lead to the Legend as spoken about by her daughter in years to come. She is a Leader of Self. She doesn't need permission to believe in what she wants to believe in.

When people are encouraged to have Umbrella Beliefs that align to and go beyond the task at hand, this is when people feel they are genuinely engaged as they are not being driven into a template of demonstrated actions to show their engagement.

VALIDATE INTERNALLY, CALIBRATE EXTERNALLY

I see too many people and teams who are trapped in a process where validation comes from outside. Falling into this trap is easily done and is often a continuation from a time when there was no data point to confirm their own capability or they have never established a clear set of Umbrella Beliefs about their identity and contracted that with the organisation.

Consider: recognition, calibration, validation.

- Recognition
  Where what you have done is acknowledged or valued
- Calibration
  Where you observe the reaction or are given feedback, and adjust accordingly
- Validation
  Where you define your self-worth

This is true for both organisations and individuals. It's valuable to gain feedback, observe reactions, consider the insights of others and combine them to review in the moment or reflect on. It's equally critical to not feel you need to react in real-time to the constant bombardment of others' reactions.

It's key to validate internally and to calibrate externally and not the other way around. If you're looking to external sources to validate, there lies a path to ruin.

INTERNAL BELIEFS OVERPOWER EXTERNAL MOTIVATORS

All the indications are that internal beliefs trump external motivators as long as they aren't stifled by fear. When external motivators, such as the desire to earn money, exist alongside the fear of not being able to afford a house, pay the bills and feed the family, then they will generally outweigh internal drivers.

This is why Living Brave is not always an easy path. It is, however:

- Hugely empowering to have Umbrella Beliefs that drive you to be a greater version of yourself.

- Hugely demotivating and even harmful not to follow through on your overarching beliefs because of fears, which are often catalysed by the behaviour of colleagues or more senior players in the organisation.

UMBRELLA BELIEFS ARE THE DNA OF BEHAVIOUR

People with strong Umbrella Beliefs have a way of holding themselves to account that often goes far beyond a set of values. Umbrella Beliefs are a motivational catalyst and provide something to aspire to. In my experience, it's absolutely true that individuals, teams and organisations that are mobilised by an agreed way of thinking and framing their context so they can Face Into the issues at hand have more resilience, wellbeing, engagement, innovation and sustainability.

The nearest thing I can see to a set of Umbrella Beliefs for an organisation is the Johnson & Johnson, Our Credo[43], crafted by Robert Wood Johnson in 1943, which drives the company to this day. It has aspiration and inspiration built into it and is a superb example of an organisation's Umbrella Belief.

Our Credo

We believe our first responsibility is to the patients, doctors
and nurses, to mothers and fathers and all others who use
our products and services. In meeting their needs everything
we do must be of high quality. We must constantly strive to
provide value, reduce our costs and maintain reasonable prices.
Customers' orders must be serviced promptly and accurately.
Our organisation partners must have an opportunity to make a
fair profit.

We are responsible to our employees who work with us
throughout the world. We must provide an inclusive work
environment where each person must be considered as an
individual. We must respect their diversity and dignity and
recognise their merit. They must have a sense of security, fulfilment and purpose in their jobs. Compensation must be fair and
adequate and working conditions clean, orderly and safe. We
must support the health and well-being of our employees and
help them fulfil their family and other personal responsibilities.
Employees must feel free to make suggestions and complaints.
There must be equal opportunity for employment, development and advancement for those qualified. We must provide
highly capable leaders and their actions must be just and ethical.

We are responsible to the communities in which we live and
work and to the world community as well. We must help
people be healthier by supporting better access and care in
more places around the world. We must be good citizens —
support good works and charities, better health and education,
and bear our fair share of taxes. We must maintain in good
order the property we are privileged to use, protecting the
environment and natural resources.

Our final responsibility is to our stockholders. Businesses must
make a sound profit. We must experiment with new ideas.
Research must be carried on, innovative programs developed,
investments made for the future and mistakes paid for. New
equipment must be purchased, new facilities provided, and new
products launched. Reserves must be created to provide for
adverse times. When we operate according to these principles,
the stockholders should realize a fair return.

There is something very powerful about this Credo, it sets a tone, it aspires, it challenges the EQ, IQ and XQ, it is a document made up of multiple Umbrella Beliefs and because of that it has endured and been the foundational strength of the organisation. This is a great example of how the individual's and team's Umbrella Beliefs can and feed into a general narrative that drives culture and resilience.

On a more individual basis consider this speech by Colonel Tim Collins [44] on the eve of battle to the 1st Battalion of the Royal Irish Regiment in Iraq in 2003. One key point is erasing your opinion as to the rights and wrongs of the war, and instead, consider the fear on the faces of his people and the need to bolster their confidence and to set the daunting boundaries of behaviour expected.

Colonel Tim Collins, eve of battle speech

We go to liberate, not to conquer.
We will not fly our flags in their country.
We are entering Iraq to free a people and
the only flag which will be flown in that ancient land is their own.
Show respect for them.
There are some who are alive at this moment
who will not be alive shortly.
Those who do not wish to go on that journey, we will not send.
As for the others, I expect you to rock their world.
Wipe them out if that is what they choose.
But if you are ferocious in battle remember
to be magnanimous in victory.
Iraq is steeped in history.
It is the site of the Garden of Eden,
of the Great Flood and the birthplace of Abraham.
Tread lightly there.
You will see things that no man could pay to see and you will have to
go a long way to find a more decent,
generous and upright people than the Iraqis.
You will be embarrassed by their hospitality
even though they have nothing.
Don't treat them as refugees for they are in their own country.
Their children will be poor, in years to come they will
know that the light of liberation in their lives was brought by you.
If there are casualties of war, then remember that when

they woke up and got dressed in the morning
they did not plan to die this day.
Allow them dignity in death.
Bury them properly and mark their graves.
It is my foremost intention to bring every single one of you out alive.
But there may be people among us who
will not see the end of this campaign.
We will put them in their sleeping bags and send them back.
There will be no time for sorrow.
The enemy should be in no doubt that we are his nemesis and
that we are bringing about his rightful destruction.
There are many regional commanders who have stains on their
souls and they are stoking the fires of hell for Saddam.
He and his forces will be destroyed by this coalition
for what they have done.
As they die, they will know their deeds have brought them to this place.
Show them no pity.
It is a big step to take another human life.
It is not to be done lightly.
I know of men who have taken life needlessly in other conflicts.
I can assure you they live with the mark of Cain upon them.
If someone surrenders to you then remember they have that right in
international law and ensure that one day they go home to their family.
The ones who wish to fight, well, we aim to please.
If you harm the regiment or its history
by over-enthusiasm in killing or in cowardice,
know it is your family who will suffer.
You will be shunned unless your conduct is of the highest, for your
deeds will follow you down through history.
We will bring shame on neither our uniform or our nation.
It is not a question of if, it's a question of when.
We know he has already devolved the decision to lower commanders,
and that means he has already taken the decision himself.
If we survive the first strike we will survive the attack.
As for ourselves, let's bring everyone home and leave Iraq
a better place for us having been there.
Our business now is North.

Consider the EQ, IQ and XQ that's present in this. He really was talking about the right thing, at the right moment, in the right place and at the right time.

UMBRELLA BELIEFS ARE A LINE IN THE SAND

Umbrella Beliefs are the front line, the unbendable truth about what you as an individual, team or organisation believe to be true. They are not carved in stone in the long term because, as someone who wants to be Living Brave, you always have to acknowledge that your position may require calibration. When you realise that's the case you can adjust. However, until the data creates that recognition, the Umbrella Belief holds you and others strong.

When an individual asks themselves not just what is the vision, purpose, strategy or plan, but what are the Umbrella Beliefs that preside over these process-driven needs, that's when you find the link to the emotion and to where your own and others' 'hearts and minds' sit.

We need to go beyond, "what do I/we care about here?" which in many ways can be answered with the output: "I/we care about the commercials, the project's success, my personal brand". These are not Umbrella Beliefs. They are the desire for the output. And that's not enough.

Umbrella Beliefs are more internally focused. They are linked to the individual's and the team's sense of self, the sense of what is right and the correct approach that will achieve the output.

CAN I HAVE MORE THAN ONE?

You can and already do have a lot of Umbrella Beliefs. They should have a clear sense of your perspective and a connected emotion. However, 'thought without action' is in effect 'ineffective intellectualisation' which is a grown-up term for fantasy, but without the dragons. Action has to be both believed in and performed. Without action to enable the intellectualisation it remains dormant or, at the worst, feeds sabotage.

Why sabotage? Because when people believe that things should be a certain way, especially if it's a general consensus, it breeds discontent and that never works out.

Umbrella Beliefs are fascinating to me and I hope they become so for you. The more you recognise them and the more you can connect yourself and others to them, then the greater the direct correlation to your own and others drive and commitment.

This is from a recent diagnostic with a board member:

Board Member:	"Getting this project to work is key. It's my consuming focus.
	This is my motivation and it's what I get up for."
Guy:	"What does success in this project get you?"
Board Member:	"Recognition, validation, bonus, promotion. And I keep my job"
Guy:	"What does it take from you?"
Board Member:	"Uuuumm... time with family, stress"
Guy:	"What's the motivator that sits under project completion?"
Board Member:	"Keeping my job, to pay bills, to provide for the family. I guess in reality, I fear failure and what that means"

What's interesting here is the root cause of this person's motivation. It's not 'to get the project done', or 'to be validated'. In truth, its output is to retain a job or perhaps get a better one, however, the key driver is to 'protect the family'. It's that last bit that we must recognise.

The commercial, socially acceptable conversation is about 'being motivated by the project' and this is true. It's just that there's also something deeper and Living Brave is about connecting to that in a way that taps into the raw energy of motivation. The true motivator is the Umbrella Belief around providing for the family. The craft is knowing what the real motivation is for yourself, ensuring that it drives good deeds, rather than fearful ones.

WHICH WOLF DO YOU FEED?

There is a legend in which a Cherokee elder is teaching a young family member about life. He says: "There is a constant battle between two wolves, one is evil, angry, envious, arrogant, resentful and ego-driven, and the other is good, it is happiness, humour, humility, contribution, truth. This fight goes on inside all of us".

The young child reflects and asks, "Which wolf will win?". The old man replies, "The one you feed." Umbrella Beliefs are your conscious decision to feed one of those wolves.

Understanding the beliefs of those you work closely with connects them to you. Within a team, there may be individual Umbrella Beliefs that work for different people but highlighting the ones everyone agrees on is healthy.

The key as an individual and a team is to not reject anything. If this connects to you, if you feel the intellectual and emotional pull to own this way of thinking and this is part of the Legend that you want to create for yourself, then it's valid. It doesn't require anyone's permission. As a team there may be individual Umbrella Beliefs that work for different people, some might be not only personal but private, the thing here is to share the ones that aren't private and to highlight the ones everyone agrees on, to add the weight of the entire group's motivation to this.

If the Umbrella Belief "I want to do this work in a way that doesn't infect my wellbeing and behaviour together with a healthy resilient version of myself both during and at the project's end" gets a rallying cry of "me too!" (and why wouldn't it?), that's powerful. Here are some Umbrella Beliefs you and the team may share:

Umbrella Belief	Explanation	What this looks like	Living Brave (considerations)
Clarity in uncertainty	• Even when there is a lack of direction from a senior team the role is to create clarity for those we lead	• When there's uncertainty or a lack of a coherent or engaging message, the goal is to ensure that people can make sense of things at their own level • This might mean offering a vision of how to behave at this moment so the team can agree its clarity and purpose	• Offering clarity into a space where you have the direct authority to do so • Being willing to step into the space where a senior team should be • Creating/taking permission to do this
Anti-Bullying	• Defend those who cannot defend themselves • Don't allow yourself to be bullied	• Not being a crusader and social justice warrior but recognising when someone is in distress or stress, or when you are • To offer observation, feedback, coaching and counsel and, if necessary, stand up to the instigator	• Offering observations on behaviour that may be considered bullish to bullying • Offering counsel or coaching • Taking a stance on behaviour that is damaging and raising it up the line
Dad/mum not just parent	• It's not just about providing • I am required to nurture	• Being present for my children in an engaging way. • Being sure to understand the	• Controlling work/life balance • Developing resilience so I can not feel fearful of not

		difference between performing tasks with them and becoming a positive part of their memories • Contributing not just to their success but to their emotional wellbeing • This may require a push-back on workload or taking charge over my own need to succeed, or over my fears about not being seen as ultra-valuable at work	being seen to be working • Reconnect with being present with the family • Negotiate working style with workplace • Seek permission from others or myself • Make the change and see if anyone notices or cares

The power of the Umbrella Belief lies in the personalisation. This is about you – or about the team if you are doing this with others. Umbrella Beliefs sit alongside the focus of actions in personal, social and commercial life. When we tap into things that we believe in, that are bigger than the issues, hurdles and barriers that present themselves, then we are in a position to Face Into these challenges because the Umbrella Belief has more power, and is, therefore, more empowering than what's in front of us.

Umbrella Beliefs do not need to make sense to anyone else, they just have to make sense to you. Although you can tell them to others, it's not about seeking approval. This isn't a strategy or a commercial plan. These are beliefs. An organisation can make demands about what you focus on and what actions they are seeking. However they don't have, and never should have, jurisdiction over what you believe. As an individual or team what you believe, though not needing to be a secret, is in essence, your own.

If you want people to buy into your Umbrella Beliefs, then yes, it makes sense to ensure they make sense to others and not just to yourself.

You can have as many Umbrella Beliefs as you choose and there can be more than one attached to each other. In fact the more Umbrella Beliefs you have around something, the more stability it has, as there's more than one thing supporting it.

Your Umbrella Beliefs are the lighthouse in the storm, the person at your shoulder whispering in your ear: "well done" "don't stray" "keep Living Brave" all with the intent that you don't lose touch with your own inner belief system.

Umbrella Beliefs feed and reinforce personal motivation, they engender Trust as people perceive your story as being integrity-driven. They drive your Accountability to behave in accordance with your Umbrella Beliefs. They challenge you to be Brave by staying Connected to something real to you and others.

Umbrella Beliefs create meaning that sits far deeper than the vision, the goal, the strategy, the action plan. They are something that is so personal and so important to you that the further you stray from them the less comfortable you become and the closer you remain to them, then the stronger and more empowered you are.

YOU WILL KNOW WHEN YOU KNOW

You'll know you have identified useful and bolstering Umbrella Beliefs if, when you feel under duress, uncertain, fearful, submissive or lacking in clarity, reminding yourself of them spurs you on with renewed confidence to improve the situation. You will also know if when you consider them, they energise and drive you forward. You should have a visceral reaction as they are both intellectual and emotional.

LEVERS THAT MOVE YOU

When you create an Umbrella Belief, that's only half the job done. You have to act in relation to it, otherwise, it remains an intellectualisation that serves no one.

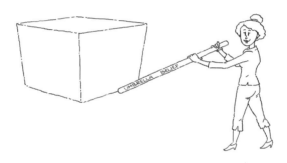

You need a Lever, something that can move things. Imagine a boulder as the thing you are trying to get movement on, it's the blocker, the hurdle, the barrier, the fear, the anxiety. It requires your concerted efforts. It needs you and a Lever, it is still you but it's you plus an energy drink.

The better a Lever is thought out, the more thinking that's gone into it, the more emotion has been connected to it then the stronger it is. The Lever is what we call on to apply the mindsets, that demonstrate our commitment to the Umbrella Belief and give us the ability to say we are Living Brave.

AM I WHAT I SAY I AM?

So, I have two sons, Milo and Hugo. I had different Levers before them, however, when they came along, they became the Lever of all Levers.

I talk to them about things that are sometimes 'what to do' though more often 'how to be'. As a coach/educator I try not to tell but rather to offer counsel, though of course telling also exists. I offer more 'things to consider'. Regardless of the conversations had, they watch me, they see how I really am in conversations and they have, and will continue to make judgements about the Connection between what I say and what I do and thus who I actually am.

My Umbrella Belief in this context is that I want to be a father that they're proud of and who's helped them on their own path.

I want my Legend with them to be "Dad wasn't perfect, but he knew what he thought was right, he had solid behaviours that he felt demonstrated his beliefs and (most importantly) that was clear in the way he spoke to people, acted with people, thought about things". I want them to see a clear link with the thoughts on a subject and the actions required to make them real. And I want them to see that sometimes the actions are easy and sometimes they aren't, especially when the environment and context are pushing for different behaviours.

With that in mind, I have a simple Lever that is uniquely powerful for me. When I face a situation that is challenging me as to whether or not I am Living Brave, I think "If there was a live video stream going on right now and my two boys were watching it with their friends, would they be proud of my behaviour and be saying 'That's our dad', or would they be embarrassed, even ashamed, and thus keep quiet?".

Even the writing of this makes the hairs stand up on the back of my neck. There's almost nothing I cannot achieve when I view a situation through that particular frame. It's a Lever that, once I think about it, I can pull on it and anything that's giving me doubt, uncertainty, stress, anxiety, fear had better be ready to receive a metaphorical 'ass-whooping' because, as in the words of Roddy Piper in the cult film 'They Live', that you probably have never heard of: "I have come here to kick ass and chew bubble gum... and I'm all out of bubble gum".

Those emotional Connections act like a shot of rocket fuel. If you can harness their positivity, you have something that empowers and holds you, and those connected to you, on target.

Things to reflect on:

Think about your Legend, Umbrella Beliefs, Levers and Facing Into issues as lenses which bring Living Brave into focus

- What are your key Umbrella Beliefs?
- What is/are your main Lever(s) that drive you to act on your Umbrella Beliefs?
- How committed are you to Face Into the behaviours that will drive action?

EIGHT

THE LIVING BRAVE MINDSETS

This is where we look at

Living Brave Mindsets | Trust | The Accountability Line
The Interview Question | Fear | Bravery | Connection |
Hummingbird Moments

CHAPTER EIGHT

THE LIVING BRAVE MINDSETS

"The true method of knowledge is experiment."

- William Blake, poet, painter, printmaker

We now have this whole way of framing the world, a set of 3 lenses (Umbrella Beliefs, Levers & Face Into's) that says you want to be Living Brave. We know that we don't need to get our Living Brave on if we run out of milk, we just go down the store. We get our Living Brave on when the situation is taking from us when it's making us less and when it is in some way destructive. Or with a frame of reference that allows us to approach the day in a positive mindset as you understand your own point of reference for the cut and thrust of life.

In the last chapter we looked at Umbrella Beliefs as the hub of the Living Brave Mindsets, they exist to hold us on course.

IT'S ABOUT TRUST

How we are experienced influences whether or not we are trusted. When people operate in a manner that means stakeholders, clients and direct reports don't trust them, it damages everything associated with them, so our ability to manage that is key. Remember being trusted, isn't the same as being liked. They are very different.

IT'S ABOUT ACCOUNTABILITY

Accountability is a crucial characteristic of Living Brave. The questions that many of us ask is "is this person a person of their word?", "Will they strive to be accountable, to own their thoughts, position and outcome in a manner that means, regardless of the outcome, I can believe in their intent to be accountable?"

IT'S ABOUT BRAVERY

The thing about being accountable is that you have to be brave in taking action. You may need to be brave enough to be the only person in the room who steps forward to be heard, to bring questions, to express an opinion.

IT'S ABOUT CONNECTION

You need to stay aware of the person/team/organisation you want to be, in order not to be pushed into a state of being that creates a submissive or aggressive response. Staying connected ensures that you maintain your focus on Accountability, on being Brave and on staying Connected to your true, aspirational and even inspirational self. It is about being Connected enough to contribute to the things outside of your own need.

The four Living Brave Mindsets represent the mindset and behaviour that when actioned drive us towards Living Brave, it is the supporting structure of Living Brave that determine mindset and behaviour.

Fig 11: Living Brave Mindsets

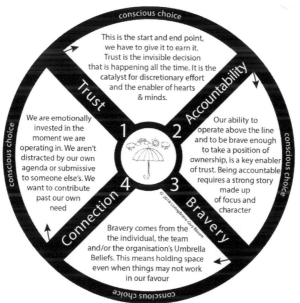

Each one of the mindsets works in isolation to enable great steps forward in mindset, methodology and motivation. However, when unified, the four form an incredibly robust frame of reference to one's own inner point of reference and dialogue and thus the way in which one faces the world.

MINDSET 1 – TRUST

I talk a lot about the role of Living Brave in generating Trust. Trust is a very important part of your currency in the world.

People gravitate towards, want to be friends with, engage with, place orders with, promote, give repeat business to, back up and help out those they trust.

It's the currency with the greatest value. It beats everything. It is the primary tenet of Living Brave.

- Do I trust him, her, them, myself?
- Am I trusted by her, him, them?

Jobs that are given out, deals that are made, relationships that are entered into are all about trust.

I am going to say No Trust = No Deal, in anything.

Trust is made up of many facets. They are, in many ways, pieces in the jigsaw puzzle that make up the complexity of your character, the character of a team or an organisation's culture.

- Am I trustworthy?
- Are they trustworthy?
- Do they think I am trustworthy?
- Are we trustworthy?

My intent is to give you a working model for how to frame Trust and at the same time how to maybe bring your own identity to it.

The component parts of Trust are what it means to be a leader, to reflect on your own personal trust, the team that you have and are in, and the business, the product, the service, and the interaction that you have with the customer.

I've got a couple of great quotes which I've picked up along the way around trust and unfortunately, I don't know who they've come from and I think this is more because they are generically true, rather than from one specific person.

The first one I have is "when you start to wonder whether you can trust someone or not, that is when you already know that you don't." It is worth reading that again, as it's a powerful truth.

I think that you can replace the word someone with team, business, product or service, so when you start to wonder whether you can trust that team or not, that is when you already know that you don't. When you start to wonder whether you can trust a product or not, that is when you already know that you don't.

I'm one of those people that instinctively give trust to people. I'm one of those people that says, "do you know what, I'm going to start from a position that says, I already trust you". Knowing of course that I can be let down, but I will do that. When it comes to a product or a service I flip that around. Other than for a few, I see it the other way, I'm generally pretty distrustful. I work under the assumption that the product or the service is trying to sell to me, to market to me, so I instinctively don't trust a product or a brand, in the same way, I do a person. Of course all of this has its degrees, but generally this is how it works for me and of course, there's every version in between for every one of us.

Trust is a pretty precarious thing to hold onto, we constantly do things that reinforce people's trust. At the same time, it really only takes one misstep, one breaking of the belief system that somebody has around what they think trust is in relation to you or the team or the organisation, and it's really hard to win that back.

In the social media age we live in, we know the ability for people to communicate at speed around their opinion of whether or not they trust the individual, the team, the organisation, the product, the service that's the stuff that stays on the internet after the fact.

You do something untrustworthy as a company it stays online forever, you do it as an individual or a team and that stays in the social memory banks for as long as there is someone to remember it.

There's a great saying 'a falsehood can get around the world before the truth has got its boots on'. And that's pretty well true. People will spread a rumour, their thoughts, their perceptions, their emotive reactions to an individual or to an experience that is negative far quicker than they will anything positive.

When people have good things to say, they tend to tell people close at hand. When people have negative things to say they tend to broadcast it.

Trust when it has gone, is a heck of a thing to try and get back.

When something hasn't gone quite right, we can bridge gaps, we can repair, we can put things back on track. Some people will be able to forgive and forget and let go of the past. But, on social media, slip-ups are held in a digital context and that means that when you put someone's name into a search engine, the good, the bad, and the ugly shows up.

Kintsugi by Myriam Greff

The Japanese have a beautiful art called Kintsugi[45], or Kintsukuroi which means 'golden repair'. It is the centuries-old Japanese art of fixing broken pottery with a special lacquer dusted and powdered gold, silver or platinum. Beautiful metallic seams glint in the cracks of ceramic ware, giving a unique appearance to the repaired piece. The images take my breath away, and, in the work I do with organisations, I use it as an example of how to remake a relationship. But relationship re-building, like Kintsugi, is a craft. And it takes real effort. My counsel is that it's far easier if you just avoid breaking trust in the first place!

In a commercial context Trust is a baton to be passed on, using Accountability as the delivery vehicle.

When we leave this place and space and we baton-pass to the next team and culture, we're not just handing over an organisation that has a good process and which is vigorous in the marketplace. We're actually handing over a legacy of stories and a Legend which the next person/ team will reinforce, grow or lose. Trust in a product or service is not simply in terms of its reliability, but also lies in how people interact and perceive the team and the organisation as a story. So, Trust is something that we're really passing through to those that come after us just like we are passing through any other product, service, process, strategy.

I'm going to offer you the idea of thinking about Trust with two main factors: 'story' and 'value'.

For me, when you think about Trust, you're thinking about the 'story' of a person and you're also then thinking about the value that they bring. You're thinking about their 'story' when you think about a team, a division, a department, a business, you're thinking about their 'story' you're thinking about the 'story' of them. You are also thinking about the 'value', the promise of what could be delivered. When I reflect on a business through its product, its service, the experience I have when I ring through and I talk to customer service people or somebody from that organisation comes into mind, there's the 'story' of them and then there's the 'value' that they bring.

Fig 12: Trust

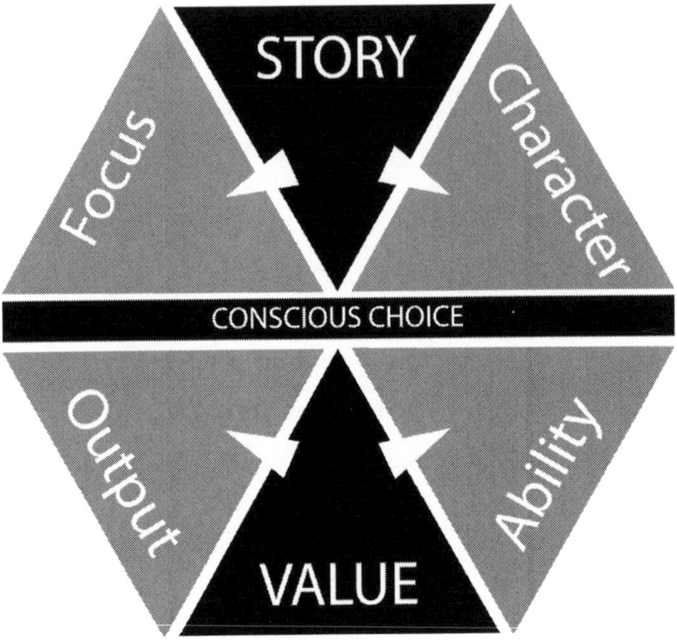

HOW STORY CREATES TRUST

When we are learning about the story of an individual, we look for clues as to their 'character' and their 'focus'.

Character

What's the game plan of the other person, short to long term? What are their Umbrella Beliefs? Who do they think they are? What is it that they want to contribute? How do they offer themselves to the outside world? What is the brand that they offer out? What is the story of them they are trying to get me to understand or buy into? How honest do they feel to me? How are others reacting to the experience of them? What is my innate reaction to them, that I might not have data for but is still a feeling I have to acknowledge?

Focus

I want to know if they act as the person they profess to be to me and others. I want to know if they are one person in all arenas or they consciously or unconsciously subvert their behaviour to fit in. Are they strong in their focus? Do they hold space, offering genuine curiosity? Are they willing to risk their brand in order to write their own story and hold to a positive and authentic Legend of their own imagining? What do they actually do in regards to what they said they would do? Are they actually playing an honest game as who they say they are matches what they actually do? Does the story of them match the brand they offer?

When trying to understand Trust in your context, think of the board team, a senior team, your team, your own behaviour and consider: "Does the 'focus' and 'character' add up to a 'story'?

HOW VALUE CREATES TRUST

When we are learning about the story of an individual, we look for clues as to their 'ability' and their 'output'.

Ability

When I think of a leader and the value they bring, it starts with 'ability', the possession of the means or skill to do something. It's about what they know through their experience, capability, skill set, commitment to learning, focus on personal growth, development and willingness to discover things about themselves and others in a truly transparent, curious way. In many ways, it is the relationship with knowledge. What do they know? What are they willing to find out? How focused are they on staying at the forefront or working to get there?

In my experience, a team's knowledge can get stuck, fail to grow and wear out if it isn't keeping ahead of or, at the very least aligned to, the changes that are going around them.

Professor Reg Revan[46] the Action Learning pioneer, had an equation around learning which says 'learning should be equal to or greater than the change that is going on around you'.

©Reg Revan

I absolutely buy into that. I think as an individual, as a team, as an organisation, we need to say one of the reasons that you can trust us and the value we bring to the table is that our knowledge has stayed in line with change.

Have you heard the anecdote about someone saying, "I'm an expert", to which another person responds "how long have you been an expert?" The answer is "nine years", which is followed by the somewhat tongue in cheek, yet possibly accurate remark, "does that mean you haven't learned anything for nine years?". We all know that the context of the individual, the team, the organisation is never fixed. It's always morphing, it's continually growing and it's always moving forward. This means our learning has to be at the least, relative to that.

Ability should never be fixed and our learning must never end.

Output

It's also about 'output'. What has been created? What has been done that is quantifiable? That what you have achieved is of high quality and of an output that matches the 'story' of you, and that it matches your ability through what others know to be your 'knowledge' base, is crucial. When you are offering yourself as somebody who is to be trusted, this is a key jigsaw piece of your brand. People want to know that when you make you a promise, you stick to it and you see it through to the end simply because that's what you do. The 'story' of you is that you have a 'focus' that you are the kind of 'character' that is willing to learn and to take feedback. So, your knowledge isn't fixed and if you have not done something to the level that it should be, you will learn, and consequently, you will improve your 'ability' to create a better 'output'.

You are striving for a reputation for doing the above as an individual. You can have a reputation for doing it as a team and you can have a reputation for doing it as an organisation. This can read "this is my/our story and this is the value that I/we bring to you, to the market, to the world".

So, we are clear that Trust has multiple segments and a lot of questions to be answered. It's not about likeability. It's about 'story' and 'value'.

WHEN GUY MET SIR STANLEY

As a very young man, I was a retail manager in a Curry's high street electrical goods store in the UK. I was quite new in the role and we were really doing a good job. The store looked good, the team was motivated, sales were on the up.

I had a call from my Regional Manager "Sir Stanley Kalms is coming to visit your store". I nearly threw up! Kalms was the founder, the MD, and a retail legend in the UK. When the big day arrived, he was flanked by an Area Manager, the Regional Manager and someone from Head Office. He said to the others "leave me and Guy to walk around", so we did, we went around the store, into the stockroom and I was answering questions with a heightened adrenaline level.

He paused: "I've looked at your figures, seen the customer comments, you run a tight ship, well done... you can calm down". I said "thank you" and said that I would calm down, but didn't. He then said, "let's go for a walk outside". We did so and about 20 paces from the storefront, he turned around, looking at the store and said, "you know sometimes you try so hard, and because you look so intensely at the details because you want to get it right, you miss the big things". I stared at him a little bit like some new monk in the monastery receiving wisdom without really knowing what it meant yet. He looked at me and said, "walk away for two minutes, then walk back as if looking at your store for the first time."

So I did that and came back, looking at the store thinking "right, so I am Stanley Kalms looking at my store for the first time... ahhhhh crap." There it was. I looked at him and said "I can't believe it, I checked and checked... I'm so sorry."

He laughed out loud and said "it's fine, none of my senior team saw it, either. Do what you need to do and then call my PA and let her know it's done." He handed me a card with a number on it.

After he left, I got the team together, said a massive 'thank you', told them the story and that fact I/we had only changed the display in one of the two windows of the store to the current promotion. The other still had the last season's promotion in it. They ran out to look.

I got a call a little later from the Area Manager saying, "well done". I realised then that Sir Stanley Kalms hadn't told them.

I called Mr Kalms' PA and told her I'd changed the window. She paused and said, "Mr Kalms says well done, thank your team and always remember to walk away from the problem, give yourself a break and then come back in with fresh eyes."

Of course, decades later I'm still telling that story. It was his Legend in my eyes and I want you to see that this is about Trust, his 'story', his 'focus' and his 'character'. I could talk about his 'value' to the organisation in the context of what he knew and could generate, however, important as that is, it's not the stuff of hearts and minds. It's not his 'focus' on educating and enabling, on nurturing instead of shaming or the 'character' of a man that didn't require to show others (Area & Regional Manager) that he was clever. It speaks volumes about the man and his not needing to be the centre of attention. That's the stuff of Legend.

MINDSET 2 – ACCOUNTABILITY

Accountability is both the experience of the person who is Living Brave, those who are experiencing them and those that are observing. As an individual when you are able to look at yourself and believe that you are being accountable then this is in many ways a form of empowerment in itself. When I can say "I am being accountable" then I am able to tap into my character, I am able to hold a position with myself and others that says even if I am proven to be wrong then one thing I and others will be able to say is whatever happened 'I/we was/were being accountable'.

This is so important because often we are paralysed by whether or not we are right or wrong and the truth of the matter is that you can't see into the future, you cannot mitigate all the risks and ultimately there are external factors that may very well regardless of your efforts prevent you from having success. Even if you are competent sometimes all the effort in the world does not mean that you achieve what you set out to. Often projects run for months and years with people touching them at various times, with their own agenda, competence and motivations and often you are only part of the team as a jigsaw piece in an overall puzzle.

Sometimes you have personal success sometimes the team has success in spite of your inputs, it's not straight forward. As global dependencies grow, as expertise is utilised ad hoc rather than full time, as people leave and the reason you started sometimes shifts, then success can become very subjective. Often even as a project succeeds, it fails to meet its original intended goal, projects shut down, they change direction and morph.

Very often it's understood by those involved, that the outcome doesn't always factor into whether you want people on the next project. Yes, competence is wanted but more than that 'Accountability' will be a massive deciding factor at both an empirical and emotional level.

NO SURPRISES AND OWNERSHIP

What people who have been alive for a while quickly realise, admire, and desire is someone that ensures there are 'no surprises' and thus 'ownership'. These are the two key outputs of Accountability that people truly value and wanting to be around people that are accountable is a huge driver for many people. It's something I see a great deal in organisations up and down the line, the one thing everyone wants is to work with and for people that are accountable. Don't you want to be around people that are accountable? People that are accountable for making sure your relationship be it friend, spouse, partner, peer, boss is healthy with no surprises, other than the odd party.

No one wants to be placed in a situation, personal or professional, where they should have known about something that was kept from them due to someone's doubts and fears, because they were not Living Brave. It's all about who you want standing next to you in the battle ahead, the person you want protecting your back in the metaphorical gun battle. As a metaphor, if you and a colleague were policemen and a gun battle broke out, the words you don't want to hear are "I'm scared of loud noises.....I just thought it wouldn't come up". No one wants to hear something that they should have already known about so they could have mitigated the risk.

Ian Ritchie, ex-CEO Wimbledon (All England Lawn Tennis Club) and the Rugby Football Union (RFU) said, "You can't plan for something you don't know about. I really demand of people the accountability to tell me the good, the bad the ugly. I need to trust people in knowing that I know the things that I should. This, of course, means I have to create and nurture an environment that develops the confidence and the bravery to speak out."

BE ELEGANT IN YOUR ACCOUNTABILITY

When I talk about 'no surprises' it's a mindset that means, be brave, say what needs to be said to whoever needs to hear it. Be elegant, yes. Pick the right moment, yes. But don't fudge it. Don't hide the truth or part-truths. Remember that your opinion is also a truth. The data is a fact. However, due to the subjective reality of the everyday need for an opinion, data isn't the truth, not really. It requires people's perspectives around the data to make it real for others. Stating your opinion is part of the Living Brave approach to 'no surprises'. Sometimes this will be easy. At other times you'll have to Face Into it by stepping forward to ensure that there are no surprises.

To be fully accountable requires both a 'no surprises' and an 'ownership' mindset. Consider this quote by French playwright Moliere[47],

"It is not only for what we do that we are held responsible,
but also for what we do not do."

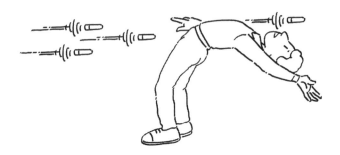

This quote nails it, when you think of Accountability, it is connected with Bravery. It is also connected with a willingness to do things that will, very often, put us in the firing line, or in a position that forces us to make an overt commitment to what it is that we stand for and represent. By that definition, whether or not we stand up to be counted, whether or not we have an opinion as a team, as an individual, as an organisation, will very much lend itself towards, not just the concept of Accountability, but to how brave are we in our Accountability. It's easy to set your Accountability too low as a justification for navigating the political climate, or simply because it's easier right now. Of course, those strategies are sometimes sensible. However, watch out, Accountability has a habit of putting you in harm's way to a greater or lesser degree. Because the moment you're accountable you're holding yourself to account and, of course, you're holding others to account as well.

It's very easy to espouse the idea of being accountable when things are going well when the money's flowing in and everybody's ideas are great and whatever we do seems to turn to gold. It's when things are not going so well that it becomes hard because people around us are looking for ways to dodge the bullet. They're looking to be blameless, and to be part of the winning team, not the losing one. They're looking to be the one that gets to say, "I did my bit, I was accountable in my space".

Accountability goes beyond your role responsibility and beyond your task list. It extends into whether or not you're prepared to operate within the enterprise, not just from a political perspective, but as someone who is actually trying to make a difference through your Connection, not just your outputs.

I think this is one of the true tests. It's one of the differentiators of whether or not people are leaders by position, by nature and/or by behaviour. A position can mean that you assume Accountability because you have the positional responsibility to do so. I've seen many organisations, where people take accountability for their area, for their span of control, for their resource, for their P&L but they're not interested in being account-able for anything that sits outside that. I see people take Accountability for the commercials, but not necessarily for the people. It can also go the other way around, where someone is so accountable for the people they're not taking care of the commercials. Everything requires balance.

YOUR NATURE VS. THE CRAFT

Being accountable without any sort of political, situational savvy can be quite career limiting. Bringing a zealot's level of Accountability into every conversation can mean that others are wary of showing or sharing their true selves. They fear that it will be spoken about in the moment, possibly while they're raw or while their boss is in the room or before they've got their words wrapped around what they really want to say.

When being accountable is working at its best it's a marvellous thing. But it can also be damaging, such as when you hear, "well, I'm just being accountable", "I'm just saying it the way it is". That can turn into a weapon and a weapon of choice because there can be for some people a kind of reinforcement, a pleasure, a benefit in being seen to be the one who is bringing Accountability into the room. This is often done by people who have an element of positional power and use it to be a leader who 'makes everyone accountable'.

Accountability has to have elegance in its delivery so it can be Trusted. I've often experienced situations where I am being accountable, and I'm also being sensible. I'm being careful about when it is that I bring my thinking into a space, my behaviour, which may have been a lot rawer when I was younger, a little bit blunter, if you like, required some crafting; it required some elegance. Someone once said to me, "it seems to me that you get paid now for saying the things that used to get you sacked". There's an element of humour there, though not wrong. The insights might be the same, however, the situational sensing and the craft of the delivery mechanism has got a lot better.

The reality is when I was younger, I used to be so 'intellectually curious' it came across as at best challenging and often disruptive. But now, older and wiser I can see that my curiosity though genuine was like a set of firecrackers going off, it had no direction or elegance. Now the insight, curiosity and counsel I create is managed and calibrated. I still hold myself and others to account, but with an increased delicacy, call it more of an elegance. The craft is balancing the personal fears of ourselves and others with the need of the room to hear something said and the sensibilities of the individuals involved.

Experience teaches that although it's easy to believe that you're owning your behaviours by taking action sometimes doing less, even doing nothing and simply waiting, is being accountable. This is why it's a craft.

ACCOUNTABILITY LINE

Let's have a look at a model for Accountability. It has a simple principle, that you are either 'above or below the line'. That's it. You, the team, the organisation are constantly being assessed and judged against this reality, the interpretation, the belief that feeds the conversations and feeds the culture of whether what is been asked, seen and felt is 'above or below' the line.

Fig 13: Accountability Line

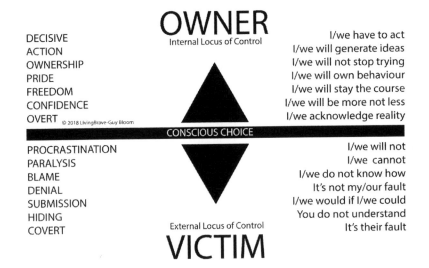

You know it in yourself when you drop below the line, that submissive, covert, blame place that sees you abandon the mindsets of Trust,

Accountability, Bravery and Connection and sees your behaviour drop below the line behaviourally, so you start to operate as a Sheep or Wolf (page 211-212).

You know when you do it, you see when others do. When you see it in a senior manager or peer it is deeply challenging to stay above the line and operate as a Sheepdog or Shepherd (page 208 & 210), this is when your Umbrella Beliefs (page 126) kick in, this is when you apply the Levers (page 141), this is when the passion you have for the Legend (page 64) you are enabling is brought to bear.

Above the line is a place that many fear, however it is what separates the herd, it is where you can hold a position that reinforces the journey you are on, reinforces your resilience and enables others. When you see it in others it is something that we recognise makes them stand out, which we can admire and in equal measure recognise that by them being Accountable they are in the game, one that they might lose. So often, we admire and fear accountability in equal measures. This is why it's a craft.

BRINGING THE ACCOUNTABILITY LINE TO LIFE

Many years ago, I was at a meeting of senior managers. Martin Long, the then owner of the UK company Churchill Insurance, was speaking to his top 100. They had just been purchased by a new owner, the voracious and commercially aggressive Royal Bank of Scotland. People who had given their all to the organisation were nervous. Martin had always promised, "I will never make anyone redundant. It happened to my father and was devastating to our family." Over the years, this promise had become not just his brand or his story, but his Legend. He spoke about the upcoming sale and integration and then opened the floor to questions. A hand went up and the question was asked, "You know how you have always said you would never make anyone redundant, well... (he pointed to the person sat next to him) you're making him redundant."

There was a pause. There was an expectation the Legend would do his thing. He replied, "Yes and that's still true, I'm not making him redundant, I'm making the job redundant." The response came back from the person who had asked the question, "Well he's still out of a job." Martin fired back: "Like I said, not the person the job."

His Legend went up in a cloud of smoke and his brand was irrevocably damaged, as he was no longer trusted in the same way. I'd never seen anything like it. It reminded me of a scene from a film called Misery[48] which stars James Caan as an author who has an accident and is 'rescued' by his greatest fan Kathy Bates. In the film she won't let him heal and leave, instead breaking his ankles with a sledgehammer. In the cinema, the whole audience went 'ahhh' and shifted in their seats. This was just like that. The news of Martins's shift travelled the length of the country within hours.

We could use this story as a vehicle to understand many of the models in this book. However, in this case, the focus is on Accountability. In that critical moment, he had the opportunity to operate above the line.

He could have replied, "You know, you're right. Things have changed and with that so has the context for my thinking. I've always meant what I said but in reality, perhaps I should have said 'I will try my best' rather than 'I never will'. However, over a decade of building this company, I have held to that. But things change. I am no longer directly in control and, even if I was, I would have to make new decisions. So 'yes'... Excuse me, what's your name? Fred? Fred yes, the organisation is making you redundant, I only hope that we ensure that it is done the right way. And your name? Simon? So, Simon that was a great question, a hard one for me to be honest, but that's my honest response."

A response like that would have been 'above the line' and have reinforced the brand, the story and Legend, it would have also given direction to the team as to how to answer that question.

Whereas Martin's actual response was 'below the line', it shook the room, took away the belief in the man, the manager, the leader and infected the business moving forward. In the moment he had an opportunity to like Colonel Tim Collins (page 133), set the tone however he took the energy out of the room and set a hare running that took huge amounts of discretionary effort from the organisation.

I sense that what happened was that he had never been in a situation where he needed to make people redundant on this scale or even at all and so hadn't revisited his Umbrella Beliefs in this new context. This wasn't a bad person doing bad things. It was a good man who let it get away from him by not redefining his position and refining his thinking accordingly.

Remember Reg Revan's 'learning must be equal to or greater than the change that's happening around you'? There's the example.

BELOW THE LINE

When you are a Victim, you are likely to procrastinate, to deny understanding or ownership, to blame others or the situation as opposed to acknowledging the reality.

Being in Victim mode does not mean that you are 'victimised'. It means that you are playing the victim due to a lack of Accountability for your reaction to a situation. The metaphor for this is the idea of an accident, where a car goes off the road and flips over. The driver gets out and says, "OMG I nearly died". The passenger gets out and says, "OMG I'm alive!"

You see, it's not about what happens to you it's about your relationship to events. Accountability sits firmly in whether you self-validate or externally-validate.

When we are 'below the line' we see procrastination and paralysis. There's denial about responsibility: "I didn't know", "I didn't understand", "It wasn't clear", "It didn't make sense to me". Often there's concealing information, and not sharing with absolute clarity what is happening or has happened. This can lead to submissiveness that manifests as a facade of smiling, committing to being part of the plan and saying "Yes, of course, I'm 100% behind this", when actually, there is no such intention due to fears, doubts and a lack of Accountability.

When people/teams or organisations don't take responsibility it often leads to a covert set of behaviours. One person being accountable can change everything. Equally, one person not being accountable can infect everyone else. It's like bananas. In the same way, you have to keep them separate from other fruit, or they rot them. People can infect others when not being accountable. Don't be the banana. Don't infect others.

THE INTERVIEW QUESTION

Many years ago I delivered a leadership transformation project into a construction company called VINCI Construction. 500 leaders who had experienced little to no leadership development in a 20 year period, good people with few of them having no reference points other than those internal to their ecosystem. When done it won a national training award in the UK, in the category Best Leadership Programme, so well done everyone.

However there was a session at the start of the programme that involved briefing the senior leaders, not the Executive Team, but in essence their direct reports, the Senior Leadership Team. There were about 25 people that turned up to a very cramped room and straight away you could feel the tension, magnified by people being nearly on top of each other. In the introductions, one of the attendees said, "well I don't even know why I am here", he paused and then said, "does anyone else?".

It was one of those days where you earn your money, though I digress.

The mumblings started, straight away there was a group of people that demonstrated below the line commentary:

- "I only got an email telling me to be here"
- "Well I asked and no one seemed to know the purpose of this session"
- "This is so typical, being kept in the dark"

At the time, I recall my head tilting to one side and then saying, "so if this was a job interview and you were offered a scenario that was 'if you had emails inviting you to a session that you knew nothing about what would you do?'. How would you answer that?"

At that moment, one of the room went above the line and offered the insight, "well I guess we wouldn't say 'I would get the hump, moan about it to others, turn up to the session and then throw my toys out of the pram, with the intent to disrupt the session whilst trying to get the rest of the room to agree with me' I am thinking I wouldn't actually say that".

There was a pause…..then someone else said, "so we look a right bunch of muppets really don't we?!". At this point, I said, "well……..let's perhaps start with introducing you to something called the Accountability Line".

The Interview Question is a tremendous technique for lifting yourself or others out of the moment, transporting yourself to a 3rd person position and bringing the clarity of what you know to be true to the moment and getting back 'above the line'.

GOOD PEOPLE SOMETIMES NEED TO RECALIBRATE

For me the worst scenario is when you have good people who want to be accountable, however, because of their fear of potential repercussions, or simply owing to the way the organisation is run, they start to develop a loose relationship with Accountability which is characterised by an unwillingness to be curious and transparent, to challenge and to bring innovation into the room.

The biggest issue with operating below the line is how long you spend there. The longer you stay there the more likely you will become habituated to it. It's a place that changes you and drives disconnection, disenchantment and disagreement.

People operating below the line try to sign you up to the 'it's rubbish, isn't it?' club, where the username could be 'disenfranchised' and the password 'discontent'. People operating below the line will drain your energy and put you in a place where, if you're not clear on your Legend and Umbrella Beliefs, you may experience a sense of needing to agree in order to fit in and avoid alienating yourself.

It's fair to say that we all drop below the line from time to time, it's human to do so and dangerous to pretend that we do not. There is nothing wrong in dropping below the line as a reaction to a complex or threatening situation, however you know you are Living Brave when like a bungee jump, you jump off the metaphorical bridge, enter free fall, fully in the moment of embracing the experience, the bungee tightens,

UMBRELLA BELIEFS

you, the team, the organisation recognise that you've had your moment and that the bungees which are tied to your Umbrella Beliefs snap you back into place.

Living Brave doesn't mean you should never go below the line. It means:

- Recognising when you are likely to go below the line and pulling yourself back
- Recognising you are already below the line and getting back above it

ABOVE THE LINE

When you are above the line, you, the team and the organisation demonstrate overt acts of ownership, increased confidence in the direction you're heading in, freedom from the negative inner voice, pride in actions and beliefs, action rather than procrastination and the decisiveness that comes from the certainty behind your brand, story and Legend.

Operating above the line doesn't guarantee success. But it does secure Trust and that, in turn, engenders faith in your actions so that people at all levels are more likely to rally to your support. This is powerful as it's a key driver for ultimate success.

Above the line behaviour is easy to rationalise however it can be harder to do in reality as the doubts, fears and uncertainties that we all possess are a natural barrier to operating in this space.

Operating above the line does require owning space, which you can read more when you get to Connection. However when it comes to the idea about what keeps you above the line? Well, it's your Umbrella Beliefs and Levers that can really drive you here.

Earlier I shared the Johnson & Johnson, Credo. Below is the one I created for Living Brave, it really resonates with me and is a cumulative narrative on what I believe Living Brave to be, it's a powerful Lever to get back above the line or to stay there.

Living Brave Credo

Don't hide.
You are intrinsically valuable.
There is no permission required for you to have an opinion.
Curiosity is not challenge it's okay to ask a genuine question.
Offering your observations and counsel is not opinionated.
Ask yourself "who am I doing this for?" The answer will guide you.
Holding a position is not aggression.
Learning is the route to your future self.
Learning is knowledge and experience.
It's ok to be scared, we all are about something.
Help others, don't create a dependency for you or them.
Say yes if you want to.
Say no if you want to.
Say maybe if you want to.
Being an elegant version of yourself is the goal.
Hurting others because you are being yourself is bullying,
don't be that person.
Not everything is a battle but recognise when you are in one.
The more you put yourself out there, the more successes
and the more failures,
it's not a paradox, it's supposed to be that way.
You have more impact than you think.
There is no 'being neutral'.
When all is said and done, stand for something, make some ripples,
leave a positive imprint in people's lives.

The whole idea of being 'above or below' the line is designed to be an easy intellectualisation, it's easy to remember and apply to yourself or others and one of the greatest gifts to give to others. However do not fall into the trap of simply saying "get above the line", as a catch-all frame of reference or you are in danger of being the Sports Coach who just shouts, "Run Faster", it doesn't give insight or help.

Reflect on:

- The thinking that keeps you above the line?
- Situations or people that nudge you below the line?

- The Umbrella Beliefs and Levers that you can use to stay or get back?
- How a team or organisation can operate above or below the line?
- How things such as emails and internal comms can be seen as above or below the line?
- What the impact to yourself, the team or the organisation is when you operate above or below the line?

ORGANISATIONAL ACCOUNTABILITY

Consider your own organisation and many of the larger organisations that we read about in the news. These are typical questions that we can ask on a larger platform of enquiry:

- "How are taxes paid?"
- "Are our people on a fair wage/salary?"
- "When we outsource our manufacturing to other countries, do we insist that there's a level of behaviour for people even though they are not directly employed by us? Would we do that even if it meant less profit for us?"
- "We talk about wellbeing, however, is that seen in the reality of the day to day expectations on output?"

If being accountable is going to have a systemic impact we have to constantly ask: "Are we accountable, not just for output, but in a way that supports our story?"

Most recently there was a fantastic example of a CEO and Accountability, I will let you decide whether he was above or below the line:

April 10th, 2019 the US Congress, Financial Services Committee brought in some of the country's biggest banks to answer questions. Representative Katherine Porter, law professor, attorney and representative for California's 45th congressional district interviewed the CEO of JP Morgan, Jamie Dimon. It went like this:

Porter: You're an expert on financial statements and you run a $2.6 trillion dollar bank. I know you are good at numbers and you've shared lots of opinions recently about how the US should budget its resources, and how families should budget their resources.

So I'd like to ask your help with a problem. I went to Monster.com and I found a job in my hometown of Irvine. At JP Morgan Chase. It pays $16.50 an hour. And I wondered if you'd indulge me…. (Porter at this point holds up a whiteboard and picks up a marker pen, she then writes up as she speaks)…..would you do the math on this and you do the $16.50 at 40 hours a week, for 52 weeks a year.

It comes out to an income of $35, 070. Now, this bank teller, her name is let's say Patricia, she has one child who's 6 years old. She claims for the one dependent, after tax, she has $29,100, we divide that by 12 it equals $2,425 per month. She rents a 1 bedroom apartment. She and her daughter sleep together in the same room in Irvine, California.

That average 1-bedroom apartment is gonna be $1,600. She spends $100 on utilities, that's $1,700. Take away the $1,700 and she has net $725. She's like me, she drives a 2008 minivan and it's $250 for a car, $150 gas (petrol), that's net $325.

The department of Agriculture says a low-cost food budget that is ramen noodles, a low food budget is $400. Her net worth is now -$77. She has a Cricket cell phone, the cheapest cell phone she can get for $40, she is now in the red with a net worth of -$117 a month.

She has after-school childcare, $450 a month because the bank is open during normal business hours, that takes her down to -$567 per month.

My question for you Mr Dimon is, how should she manage this budget shortfall while she is working full-time at your bank?

Dimon: I don't know. I have to think about that.

Porter: Would you recommend that she take out a JP Morgan Chase credit card and run a deficit?

Dimon: I don't know. I have to think about that.

Porter:	Would you recommend that she have an overdraft at your bank and be charged overdraft fees?
Dimon:	I don't know. I have to think about that. I would love to call up and have a conversation about her financial affairs and see if we can be helpful.
Porter:	See if you can find a way for her to live on less than the minimum I have described?
Dimon:	Just be helpful
Porter:	I appreciate your desire to be helpful, but what I'd like you to do is provide a way for families to make ends meet, so the little kids who are 6 years old, living in a 1 bedroom apartment with their mother aren't hungry at night because their $567 short from feeding themselves, clothing etc.... We allowed no money for clothing, we allowed no money for school lunches, we allowed no money for field trips, no money for medical, no money for prescription drugs, nothing. She's short $567 already.

Mr Dimon, you know how to spend $31 million a year in salary and you can't figure out how to make up a $567 a month shortfall.

This is a budget problem you cannot solve?

Now let me pause there for a moment and suggest you watch the video that goes with this, it can be found on YouTube, I think the video is very impactful.

There's a lot going on here and without turning this into a dissertation on the financial markets and their relation to society and culture, what I would like to highlight is the relationship of the organisation and society, the part it has to play in the reality of our everyday lives.

Leadership has to be more than profit, it doesn't have to become about the redistribution of wealth however it does have to factor in a level of 'above the line Accountability' that demonstrates that when we consider our place as Living Brave in the world we are able to see that the organisation is not just focused on Corporate Social Responsibility but just Social Responsibility.

Think back to the Truth Triangle (page 114), I imagine myself as a potential or current employer of JP Morgan, as I factor in my own truth it is very difficult to believe in the companies mission, vision and espoused values. When Mr Dimon says on the JP Morgan web site, "People are our most important asset" that feels very disconnected from the reality that people perceive.

This is where the break comes in Trust when especially in this information and the social connectivity-rich world we live in, people can consolidate their views and share their thoughts at pace. It's no longer good enough to have a great web site, with some strong words on, there's no belief in that.

What I'd have loved to have seen Mr Dimon do is say the following:

Dimon: Ok…can we pause for a moment? Thank you. I have never had this presented to me in this way and something is not right. Either your figures are off or we as an organisation need to ensure our people can live in relative comfort. I want to answer you, but I recognise I'm on the back foot here, I do want to do a brief investigation. Let me commit to looking at this over say 12 weeks, then coming back to you with my thoughts….as frankly, this makes me feel uncomfortable. Are we ok to do that?

Can you imagine the impact of that on the audience, I believe it would have been hugely effective. I believe it would have made him look very believable, it would have spoken to a much more positive story of himself and that of the organisation he represents. The bravery to have held space whilst acknowledging the vulnerability of the people involved and his own uncertainty, his willingness to not just be 'present' at the hearing but 'connected' to a greater need than his own.

We need our leaders to be willing to own Accountability not just in their P&L (Profit & Loss) but in their overarching actions.

IT'S ALL A CONSCIOUS CHOICE

The line that separates the 'victim' from the 'owner' is a 'conscious choice'. That means making a conscious choice to be the individual, the team or the organisation that we want to be. If it holds that we are responsible for our own actions, then it follows that whatever we do is our decision. What happens to us is not always something of our own making but the way we react to it is. We are the 'owners' or the 'victims' of our own thoughts and actions. The greater the power of our Umbrella Beliefs and the greater the power of the Levers that we use to activate those Umbrella Beliefs, then the greater our Connection to operating above the line and being fully Accountable.

The Accountability Line is a massively powerful tool for checking in on yourself and calibrating how to remain above it or get back to operating above the line. Sharing the concept of the Accountability Line before, during and after a conversation is a hugely powerful way of discerning where the other party believes you are operating from.

The key here is that individuals and teams that are Living Brave are not managing relationships in any part of their lives through data alone. They are intent on a human connection that does not necessarily equate to friendship or approval, but which supports the brand, story and eventual Legend. Let's be under no illusions, this will depend on the experience people have of you, which will be predicated on Trust which, in turn, will be partly forged from their perception of your Accountability, not just from the outcome of your actions.

It's also extremely helpful to be able to start shifting and reframing others' perspective. This can happen when the other party acknowledges that even if they're not happy with you, they agree you are being accountable. That's a powerful stake in the ground for you to reference later on or for them to acknowledge in retrospection.

Key questions to ask are:

- "What isn't working for me/us and am I/are we above or below the line?"
- "Am I/are we being a victim?"
- "Am I/are we owning it?"
- "What takes me/us below the line?"
- "What keeps me/us above it?"
- "What Umbrella Beliefs can I/we use to stay or get back above the line?"
- "What are the Levers that will catalyse action?"

BRAND, STORY AND LEGEND ALL SIT ABOVE THE LINE

Let's look at what ownership means in terms of Accountability. When you are in a place where you're saying "do you know what? I own my

Accountability", you make decisions, you take action, you take ownership, you have pride in what you do and have a sense of freedom about talking with absolute clarity without fear of repercussions. When people come across somebody that's being accountable, they trust that person's story, they trust your 'focus', they trust your 'character'. They understand that the person is operating from a place of high Accountability, therefore, they're not playing political games or safeguarding themselves.

Also, when you own your Accountability, with that freedom comes confidence. It's an overt thing. When you are around individuals, teams and organisations who are operating from a place of ownership in terms of high Accountability, they have confidence, they have pride, they are elegant and they have a way about them that says, 'whatever it is that needs to be done to get us to that place, we will do it with an elegance and a subtlety that ensures people come with us'.

If there are things to be said in terms of individual performance or quality of service or product, the conversations will take place in a manner that indicates you are not just taking Accountability for the conversation, you're taking Accountability for having the conversation the right way.

Telling somebody something that hurts and damages them is not accountable. It's about talking to people in a manner that leaves them better for or at the least safeguarded by that conversation, even when it's not news they want to hear. The experience that a person has should not be a 'tick the box' exercise. It has to be completely transparent and performed with integrity. That means that though someone didn't get what they wanted, they still have a sense of Accountability within the experience. That means they also have a sense of Trust around the experience and, as the experience is retold, it enhances brand, story and Legend. When you think about the story you want told and the Legend you are trying to create then you can really ask "who am I doing this for?"

Accountability means owning the mindset, the actions and the outcome. You don't control how people act or react. You only control your story. Remember this is not the 'getting what you want model'. It is the 'I was/am accountable' model.

You are defined by your actions, not by your thoughts. Think hard about that.

FEAR IS THE MIND KILLER

What fear do you have as an individual, as a team or as an organisation? What stops you from operating above that line? To cross that line and become an Owner, someone who has pride and curiosity, who is transparent with genuine integrity in their actions?

While someone is behaving like a victim they often believe they're fully accountable, when actually they're only being accountable for a certain subset of their actions. Often this is a 'hamster wheel' mindset in which the thinking is "let's work as hard as we can to create outputs and put ourselves into a commercially viable and strong place. Everything else can be done later".

The truth is that this thinking comes from a place of fear. What we end up with is people who are negating true Accountability and focusing instead on 'Accountability for action'. In other words, they are focusing on accountability for output, and not being accountable for the organisation's long term good and sustainability.

When Accountability is only defined in the workplace as being about task completion you know you've got a damaged organisation. The answer lies in looking at the accountable things that sit around that task completion. Are people being nurtured and developed? Are people in the loop as to what's going on? Are people being communicated with?

When Accountability comes from a victim space, when you see individuals and teams and organisations operating from a place of not taking Accountability, it is fear.

Usually, it's a collective fear generated by a set of behaviours from the senior team/manager who measure performance in a very specific way and give out punishments or withhold rewards. If there's a likelihood of being punished or not rewarded and you know that, by focusing on certain criteria with very narrow levels of Accountability, task output being the primary one, then everything else will be put to one side, because 'look at the commercials', 'look at the output', 'look at what we're achieving here'. If these are the rules, it becomes a get out of jail free card for Accountability around any other factors that don't feed into the short-term focus.

That's when we have a damaged organisation. That's when we have people who aren't going to give their discretionary effort, who aren't contributing to the story, but more to their own survival and their own well-being.

WE DON'T LIKE THE WORD FEAR, BUT THAT'S WHAT IT IS

When we look at what the fear is, it is usually around loss: loss of position, loss of credibility, loss of money, loss of reward. It's also the fear of overt or covert punishment or being held to account for things that are really just focused on the outputs. It's the fear of losing one's positional power, of losing the ear of the senior team because 'you're not on the bus' or whatever vocabulary might be being used. It's the fear that absolutely strikes into the behaviours of individuals and teams that I see all the time.

It's also the fear, rational, if justified and irrational, if not of being found out. The idea of Impostor Syndrome is alive and well in many senior managers, it has nothing to do with age, seniority or salary. Over two decades I have seen CEO's as much as a high potential at the start of their career sharing the anxiety of failure. The Peter Principle[49] is the idea that someone can be promoted to their own level of incompetence, it is both true and a figment of the imagination.

People are human and unless for example, the CEO of JP Morgan, Jamie Dimon is one of the 1-3% of the world who are sociopaths, he holds the same fears we all do. On $31 million per annum, it's not money he is probably worried about but credibility, legacy, social standing, personal brand, professional standing, ego, personal drivers all factor into a place where a person drops below the line.

Going below the line isn't generally about 'bad people doing bad things', it's about good people who have lost Connection with their Umbrella

Beliefs and have stopped using the Levers that drive them.

Conscious Choice is asking you "What is the fear?"

WHAT IS OUR COLLECTIVE ACCOUNTABILITY?

How does the organisation manage Accountability? In what ways do we take Accountability for having the tough conversations? Where do we take Accountability for allowing people to be curious and to challenge a strategy? If, for example, a senior team's behaviour is creating feedback or observations of doubt or disbelief from others, is there room and space to listen to those people? What are our accountabilities? As an individual, in order to define ourselves as being accountable, we must be somebody who owns our story, our personal brand, our position, our willingness to be curious, to be challenging, to be challenged, to be transparent, to take ownership, to have pride, to want freedom. So, if the organisation wants that, it has to allow it, to nurture it and to role-model it.

An organisation needs to enable people to answer:

- What permissions do we need to seek or grant ourselves?
- What license to operate are we looking to acquire?
- What permissions do we need to have for a license to operate?

Accountability is a thing of bravery. It's a thing of beauty. It defines an individual, it defines a team, it defines an organisation and, ultimately, it defines society.

TAKING IT FORWARD

The Accountability Line is a key way of thinking about how you are accountable and how you can help others to be the same. What I see in regard to 'being above or below the line' in this model is a simple way of self-calibrating and recognising where you are and what you need to do to get and/or stay above the line.

The most valuable use of this tool is having it as a constant frame of reference before, during and after events:

Before: How am I/are we approaching the Accountability Line?

During: Am I/are we above or below the line?

After: Where was I/were we on the Accountability Line?

MINDSET 3 – BRAVERY

Society is constantly evolving and, with an ever-increasing population, social networks and etiquette are changing fast, we have seen a huge shift in the conversation about what is and is not acceptable in conversation, marketing, points of humour, political agenda and social norms.

The internet has given voice to the voiceless and they can be heard within the media platforms who extoll 'Twitter Erupts' when we don't really know how many people that quantifies out of those interested in the conversation.

It's complex thinking in wicked times. Points of reference are shifting, "oh we can't say that now?" is something we may all have encountered.

I recently had someone point out to me, "you know whenever you create an example of a senior person, you always reference them as 'he'…just thought I'd point that out". You know that took me a moment and they were right, but I had to shift my thinking back to conscious competence to adjust and make changes in real time, took me a while but I think I am there now.

Not too long after that, I had someone else say "I'm a (stated a religion) and when you say 'holy moly' it makes me feel uncomfortable with the use of the word 'holy'". That one took me a moment as well, how should I react? Should I adjust? Should I not? Do I run the risk of becoming to vanilla and generic in my conversation or delivery?

The point is that bravery is often geared around the thing in front of us, it's not often about the heroic act, it's often about the doubt or uncertainty we feel and whether we go 'below the line' Accountability or 'Push or Pull' of Connection against it, recognising that whatever we do impacts on our brand, story and Legend.

HARRY SHOWS ME BRAVERY

I had a border collie, Harry. One day, while we were walking, a Great Dane came around the corner. In a world championship of who's the biggest Great Dane, this blinking thing would win. I've been around dogs all my life and know when one is in a good mood or not. And this one wasn't. It had that slightly 'I'm lost, agitated, scared and ever so slightly out of control/frantic' rolling eyes look about it. To put not too fine a point on it and at the risk of losing any street credibility that I may have had, I realised that in a metaphor of a boxing match, this was Mike

Tyson against Sugar Ray and I was the lightweight in this contest.

It growled, its mouth opened, and it lunged. I, I'm ashamed to say, didn't move an inch. I was welded to the spot. Then all of a sudden, there was a blur as Harry shot out of the bushes on the right-hand side, slamming into the side of the Great Dane. The Dane turned, bit him once, and that was the end of that contest because if I was a lightweight, poor old Harry wasn't even going to register on the scales.

But it gave me enough time to wake up. I suddenly became the one who leapt into action, grabbing a very large branch. I wanted to protect my furry saviour. Looking as if my underwear was on fire and I needed psychiatric help I was screaming and swinging the branch. The Great Dane looked at me as if to say "I'm off" and so it left (I like to think it ran away, but it probably just sauntered). Harry, made a full recovery, though he didn't move from under the kitchen table for nearly a week. The vet said it was shock and then said, "Brave dog you have there, a real hero!"

"A real hero!" Now that's a thought.

So, Harry saved my life or at the very least a visit to the hospital. He acted selflessly, without thought for his own wellbeing. I had seen Harry around bigger dogs prior to our rumble in the jungle and his reaction was to submit in a typical dog way, wag his tail and rollover. But on this day, when it really counted, he stepped up to the plate and went for it. As much as I love him for doing that, I'm also aware that he didn't think about it. He didn't weigh up the pros and cons, saying to himself, "Big dog that! But the boss is in trouble and there'll probably be a chewy stick in it for me at the end of the day."

Some people are the same. When something is wrong they instinctively take a stand and say that something is wrong. But many of us have ventured onto a corporate playing field that sees us indoctrinated, even slightly neutered. We're almost cloned into a corporate being, concerned with hierarchy, earning our stripes, playing the game, delivering the numbers, keeping our eye on the big picture and so on.

Harry didn't understand any of that. He's a dog, but he knew something was wrong and he spoke up in his own way.

Here's the rub: you have to accept that Living Brave is about the creation of a conscious competence to react to danger and threat to yours and other's intellectual and emotional wellbeing and to hold a position even though that might leave you a little damaged and bruised. Remember, it's always easier to play small and to be less. Keeping your head down means you are ok in the moment. However, in the long term, it affects both your integrity and how the world sees you.

IT'S EASY IF I JOIN THE CULT

Another factor I am very aware of is how there is a deeply safe and comforting feeling in looking to someone else to have the answers. It is one thing to believe in a person's Story, to believe in their character and focus, and thus feel good about investing your discretionary effort in the cause. It's another to abdicate all accountability to the will of the other person, the peer group or senior team.

It's also hugely dangerous as a senior manager to not recognise when the people have lost their bravery and you are being obeyed rather than followed. It's important to keep your eye on whether people are 'in' rather than being 'of' service to you or the role you inhabit. It might only be a pronoun shift but it all hinges on this.

THIS IS NOT THE CULT OF HEROISM

On a daily basis, I say 'Face Into it' as I reference a mindset of 'it's not going to be. My experience is that change, in no particular order, is a constant push sometimes a slow jog, a marathon and frequent sprints.

The idea of Bravery is sometimes shunned as being linked to 'heroic leadership', which is the idea that the managers within an organisation sometimes fall in the trap of enjoying the feeling of being the 'hero' and fall in love with that element of saving the day and being the one that sorts it out. Some, strangely, even getting a dark satisfaction with the failure of the business around them as they are the only ones that can step into the breach and go where others dare not.

Unfortunately, as they dominate the space, they do not create the time to develop people as they are too busy being the hero; the business capability gets worse, so they have to be more heroic.....and so the circle continues.

Though it's true, we aren't talking about that.

This is about the bravery that each person often has to find within themselves to move forward on their own journey. It's about a team facing the truths of their own doubts and finding a unified way to approach Living Brave and 'Face Into' a collective bravery.

It's how a business creates a culture that acknowledges its strengths, weaknesses and blind spots and then publicly Faces Into their collective cultural and individual bravery.

This creates permission and license for others to do the same and finally for the organisation creating a brand, story and Legend that attracts both talent and customers as the appeal of an organisation that is culturally brave and Faces Into their challenges, grows.

Through a Living Brave lens, the reality of bravery is that it is the antidote to fear at an individual, team and organisational level. No one likes to admit their fears and the more senior people become, so often the increased difficulty in the acknowledgement of fear as it signifies weakness.

To say "I am scared about this" is watered down to, things to consider, uncertainties, as yet undefined, lacking clarity on. The reason that flawed reframe works so well for people is that that language makes a lot of sense and sounds measured.

In truth as strong as we are, as many things as we may have under control, there's always something or someone that we are fearful of. I don't mean 'hiding in a cupboard scared' though I do mean that climb from doubt to anxiety to fear exists for most of us at some time, in some form.

There's something about seeing through the façade of fear that we create for ourselves as individuals, teams and cultures and at the same time being willing to take an intellectual position that is then demonstrated through an actual behaviour that is the essence of Living Brave.

I have come to think of this as:

- the scene from the Wizard of Oz, when Dorothy looks behind the curtain at the 'terrible' wizard to discover that in reality, he is an old man pulling levers and using a megaphone to sound loud.
- or the idea of our own fear as a shadow that turns out to be a lamp-post or a tree.

The truth of the matter is that we all have the doubt, anxiety and fear, normally it is quite easily alleviated by reflection, seeking counsel, sharing the load of the thinking.

The problem comes in organisations that have a stereotypical alpha approach, a workload culture that validates commitment in a distorted manner with a 'solve it or you are the failure', with a constant ramping up of ever-increasing timeline pressures, reducing resources, where only the people fulfiling the caricature of 'commitment' are recognised and rewarded.

These cultures can exist in totality across a business or in clearly defined areas where they have been allowed to thrive, they usually are hidden under a brand of high professionalism, high output and a core cult like centre that face out to the rest of the business, giving the impression that 'everything is awesome'. Though on closer inspection it is clear that 80% of the success is being achieved by 20% of the top players with the many reduced to being in service, often with reducing motivation and increased fear around being of value so they become more servile in order to keep their managers happy.

Sound harsh? You may only think so if you are senior enough to not realise that the world you are presented with by those that report into you might not be as it seems. If you suspect this is true, now might be a good time to realise you probably aren't as funny as you'd like to think.......disappointing I know.

FEAR HAS A VOLUME CONTROL

Fear isn't as straight forward as it sounds, it's easy to dismiss it for your-self and others, no one wants to admit they aren't in control, certain and being brave and it's a hard pill to swallow to acknowledge we have doubt, fear or panic.

It's easy to say you are in control or aren't doubtful when you are playing it safe.

Fig 14: Fear Volume

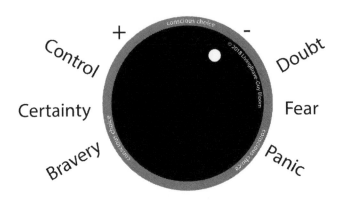

When we lose focus on our Umbrella Beliefs, don't have or apply the Levers and stop caring about our Legend, it's often a sign of fear around:

- losing our jobs
- been seen as inept
- not having control
- not being good enough to be there
- losing the favour of the boss
- losing credibility in the senior circles
- not keeping up with peers
- losing confidence with hierarchy
- looking for a new job and not getting one
- validating ourselves independently of the employer and its brand

There's something quite reassuring in knowing and accepting that everyone, at some point in their life, wrestles with anxiety, from simple nagging doubts through to outright panic.

LIVING FEARFULLY

When we are not Living Brave it means we are Living Fearfully. In the very worst cases, this leads to stress, depression, post-traumatic stress and deeply dangerous physical and emotional damage. In many other cases, it's far less obvious but just as insidious. I liken it to when you sometimes know you are not well however, as you are strong enough to fight it off, you are not ill enough to be 'ill'. Nevertheless, if you take a moment, you know you are not right. Yet you continue to function and while those around you know you are not right, it's not enough to comment on.

These are the moments of truth as individuals and teams we ask, "who will I/we be?" and "how will I/we exist in the world?"

FEAR CREATES STRESS

It creeps up on us and 'normalises' itself, becoming 'what we do' and 'the way it is around here'. The insight here is to know that just because something is standard, doesn't mean it's right.

It isn't unusual for someone to say to me, "when I left it was like a weight being lifted", "I felt emotional, I didn't realise the weight I'd been carrying".

Fear exists and its greatest trick is telling you, that you are the only one in the room experiencing it.

Reflect on these questions:

- How often do you hold back questions?
- When do you reduce the strength of your inputs aware of possible negative responses?
- When do you work harder than required as you fear not been seen as valuable?
- What circumstances have you experienced where you felt attacked but didn't feel empowered to hold space?

Think about your responses and to a greater or lesser degree you are surrounded by people responding from the same spectrum of response; if you think of 10 people the chances are they are distributed across it to lesser or greater reactions.

A great question is: "What am I/are we really fearful of here?"

IS THE 'JUICE WORTH THE SQUEEZE'?

Of course, no one wants to live in doubt or fear, so for some, it's easier to be submissive, to be 'in' service and to rationalise it as being politically savvy, or something you need to do to survive. Usually, that behaviour is coupled with a slightly deluded "it won't be forever", which is below the line on Accountability, 'waiting and hoping'.

Even if things are complex and difficult to remember, life isn't about easy, it's about challenge and learning. In the cauldron of life, experience is earned through hard work, determination and putting up with some form of inconvenience to your everyday routine.

It's sometimes difficult to see the back of your own head in terms of how you are really acting and rationalising, for the team to see its own reality and for the organisation to get far enough away from itself to look back and see with clarity and insight.

So, 'Is the juice worth the squeeze?'

Think of something real for you and/or the team right now and answer these questions:

1. "Am I/are we growing and developing in this situation?"
2. "Is this situation enabling me/us and those around me/us?"
3. "Do I/we feel better for being in this situation?"
4. "Do I/we have momentum in working towards a defined goal?"

If the answers are "yes" then the situation is adding value, if "no" then "what's the fear that's stopping new behaviours?"

BRAVERY ALGORITHM

Bravery is a word often under or overused. Some people won't accept being called brave as they are embarrassed by the praise, sometimes they accept the mantel of being brave when they did little to contribute. However, for me, it's quite an easy thing to understand.

A question that helps

Did you or those around you feel doubt, uncertainty, anxiety, fear and still move forward? If so then there's a level of bravery in those actions to a greater or lesser degree.

A metaphor to think about

If a person is not scared of spiders and picks one up, it is not brave. If they are scared and do, then it is.

When we are Living Brave one of the indicators that we need to Face Into the situation is when we recognise in ourselves or others, doubt, anxiety and fear. These are the tell-tale signs that tell us to apply a Living Brave approach by checking in with a question:

- Is this taking from me?
- Is it damaging me?
- Is it making me less?

The first Living Brave Mindset asks us to work towards being Trusted, the second Living Brave Mindset to work above the line and to take Accountability for our actions. If we are applying the thinking of Living Brave then there is a good chance there's a level of uncertainty so Mindset 3 brings the challenge to 'Face Into' being Brave and in Mindset 4 will look at the Area of Connection you are operating in to achieve this.

Trying to place this into a workable algorithm it looks like this:

Fig 15: Bravery Quotient

$$\frac{[Fear\ (3) + Accountability\ (B) + Connection\ (1)]}{\underset{Legend\ (3)}{\text{CONSCIOUS CHOICE}}} \times \frac{Committed}{Action\ (3)} = \frac{Bravery}{Quotient}\ (1)$$

© 2018 LivingBrave-Guy Bloom

The first part of the algorithm (Fear + Accountability + Connection) tells you what the benchmark is. It allows us to ask whether or not we need to move to action. These are the indicators, the factors that tell you where you and those around you are in terms of comfort, stretch or panic.

F (Fear): 0-10 (0-3 = Uncertain, 4-6 = Doubt, 7-8, Anxiety, 9-10 Fear)

A (Accountability): A or B ('A'bove or 'B'elow the line

C (Connection): C (Connected) or NC (Not Connected)

You can see how the scores self-assessed, in a partnership or done in group work give rise to the recognition of whether effort needs to go into reinforcement or remediation. That's a call to action to increase/decrease the ratings for Fear (F), Accountability (A) and Connection (C).

This is underpinned by Legend:

L (Legend):   0-10 (0-3 = Irrelevant 4-6 = Relevant, 7-8 = Important, 9-10 = Prime Focus)

If having a Legend is irrelevant to you, the team and the organisation, then addressing Fear, Accountability and Connection will never be a key focus. You have to want a legacy for the work you are focusing on.

The score has to be 7+ to even stand a chance of making a change, and 9+ to drive long term sustainable change. If the score is low, there is a need to manage the brand, to create the right stories and to have a Legend that enables pride in those involved.

Finally, the outcome of the individual, team's, organisation's fear, Accountability, Connection and Legend has to viewed against Committed Action.

CA (Committed Action):   0-10 (0-3 = Little, 4-6 = Some, 7-8 = Sizeable, 9-10 = All in)

Committed Action means a plan. One that is viewable and open to all. Without a plan of 'committed action' then nothing is going to change. You know it, I know it, everyone knows it.

This is where you often see a veneer of 'buy-in' without the actions that go with it. This is where you run the risk of paying lip service or receiving it. It's where you also need to understand that little will change if the score is not 9 or 10. This is because, as the struggles of daily life reach out to challenge our Bravery, then only 'Committed Action' will move us forward.

Decades of experience have taught me that 'no plan' means 'no completion'. The plan is the glue that holds everything together. The power of writing things down, putting a time against them, completing them, celebrating that completion, holding oneself or others to account, and consistently moving forward to stepped successes is about as powerful as it gets.

It's fair to say that, when you meet an individual, a team or organisation who are succeeding or failing, it often becomes self-evident when you say, "Can I see your plan?"

It may or may not surprise you to know that from an individual, to a team to an organisation often 'intent' is offered as a plan or strategy. Make a plan, review the plan, change the plan, add to the plan, adapt the plan, scrap the plan and do another one, seek counsel on the plan, lament the state of the plan, celebrate the success within the plan... do whatever you need to do but have a (goddamn) plan.

People who are below the line, not brave enough to hold space and not connected to a need above their own don't fear a plan, they fear the reality of it being checked on, being given feedback and coached around it. They fear reports, peers and managers who are Living Brave in relation to the components of Trust. When a person's 'story' is that they have the 'character' to 'focus' on the real questions, that the 'value' they bring is in the craft of the management 'ability' via feedback and coaching to focus and drive 'output' through the deliverables that people have committed to.......well that's when you see people paying attention.

When people perform well and see they are recognised that's key, however, what surpasses that is seeing underperformers managed; otherwise why give discretionary effort if the ramifications are little to non-existent?

BQ (Bravery Quotient): 0-4

Selecting the Bravery Quotient is subjective and that's ok. As an individual, as a team, as an organisation, the Bravery Quotient catalyses a conversation that reaffirms the known, brings the need for data and reflection to the areas that are not clear, and brings a challenge to the bits that we don't want to look at or deal with. It demands that we Face Into the matter at hand.

Level	Description	Action
0	Not relevant and not interested	Reboot needed
1	Fearful and without hope	Strong catalyst and guidance required
2	Fearful with hope	Permission needed from self or other
3	Believes, but still uncertain	Motivation and focused action essential
4	Living Brave	Reinforce, enable, get out the way

Putting the scores in the Bravery Quotient algorithm might very well look like this.

$$\frac{[\text{Fear (3)} + \text{Accountability (B)} + \text{Connection (1)}]}{\text{CONSCIOUS CHOICE}} \times \frac{\text{Committed}}{\text{Action (3)}} = \frac{\text{Bravery}}{\text{Quotient}} \ (1)$$

Legend (3)

© 2018 LivingBrave-Guy Bloom

Take a moment to think about something that you, your team or your organisation are not achieving, something that you know requires change. Then fill out the algorithm. Be honest and let your instinct guide you.

Let's be clear. When you fill out the Bravery Quotient Algorithm it requires absolute honesty from yourself as an individual and from the team or the room. It's a powerful team, meeting and conference process to create a benchmark reference on what the real state of play is.

This is really about saying, "Where am I/are we in terms of our strengths and weaknesses?", in order to discover where the energy and the focus need to go. The algorithm acts as both a visual metaphor and a benchmark for future activity. We get to ask "What score do I/we want?" Yes, of course, this is subjective. However, it's a start point for self-reflection and conversation. It requires Trust in each other's agenda, Accountability to do the work honestly, Bravery to Face Into the conversations and Connection to stay connected to the work at hand in order to make it work.

Especially in team discussions, it will become very clear, very quickly where people feel the real issues are. Of course, this will require people to be Accountable in the clarity and transparency of their own feelings, and also about how they feel regarding the behaviour of those around them.

MINDSET 4 – CONNECTION

There is something powerful about the experience of being around someone and them being fully connected. Someone who is:

- willing to contribute outside of their own need and agenda
- willing to be connected to the moment, to the person in front of them and to understand the power this has to engage, enable and engender Trust
- asking, "Is the me in my head the same as the me that people experience?"

Have you ever been speaking to someone and had the feeling that they are thinking about other things rather than the conversation they are having with you? You know how that feels, it's frustrating, awkward, it feels as if you are boring them, that you might not be important enough to them to give you their attention. From a customer service representative to a peer, stakeholder or boss. That feeling of them not being connected to the moment in hand is damaging in so many ways, it impacts on brand and the Trust that should exist.

Ask yourself the question, "do I ever do that to others?" Now you might be somewhere from a serial to an occasional offender and in your heart, you will know, if you think you never do you might want to think a little harder. When you think about Living Brave, it's about being connected, it's about parking your own reactions to individual personas and the situation and being present in the moment.

Without doubt, if you made one change right now and that was to pledge to always be connected to what is going on in front of you, you would find a huge difference in the experience of your life and in the lives of those around you. In a work situation, the more senior you are, then the more the impact of your connection is magnified by the very fact that you are senior. It is remarkably empowering and enabling for those junior to you to feel they are being listened to, rather than simply experiencing you pushing your agenda.

When we look at the idea of Connection we are looking at the idea that as an individual, as a team, as an organisation we are clear on how we are contributing past our own need. Are we 'talking the talk' or are we 'walking the walk'. This is critical to the individual's, the team's and the organisation's mental health, resilience and wellbeing.

When I ask a senior team, "what do you do that shows each other that you are contributing to needs outside of your own?". You might not be surprised to know often there is a pause that turns in a genuine tumble-weed moment, often exacerbated by examples that are actually transactional and role specific.

What I find time and again is the greater the Connection to the Umbrella Beliefs that we hold to be true, not just intellectually but in terms of Accountability and Bravery then the more energy, motivation, 'bounce-backability', grit and sheer will is accessible to those that are connected to what they hold to be true. The greater the Connection then the more

Sheepdog and Shepherd (chapter 9) behaviours become apparent, the lesser the Connection then the great the Sheep and Wolf (chapter 9) connections.

When we are Living Brave there is a Connection to both our Umbrella Beliefs and to the people that we encounter. People see, experience and hear the real us, through a lens of Trust: your Story (Character & Focus) and Value (Ability & Output). They see what we do in terms of behaviour. They understand what we believe. They experience what we are working towards. They get an insight into the real us, experiencing our Connection to these things. The more everything matches in terms of words and actions, the greater their Connection to us and the greater their Trust.

"You are not who you think you are. You are how people experience you". Take some time to consider that.

You are your willingness to be connected to the people in front of you and the only way to do that authentically is through a lens of willingness to be connected to something more important than your own need.

Look around your colleagues and ask yourself:

- Am I/are we connected to the other person when communicating?
- Am I/are we willingly connected to enable others outside of our own need?

A MODEL OF CONNECTION

Some years ago I was at a well-known global organisation the then HR Director was walking me around the executive floor introducing me to the senior team. One of the executives walked out of the board room, raised his hand, palm facing outwards and strode past, eyes fixed on his destination, never looking at his colleague or me, "No time," he declared and then disappeared into his office.

This behaviour demonstrated both Push and Pull. It was Pull, as he retreated from the minimum of social protocols and it was Push as he controlled the interaction by asserting his power to stop communication. This 'Push and Pull' utilised his positional power, a belief there would be no repercussions, a disregard of the other parties' needs, and no care for the impact this might have on Trust and relationship.

In terms of his intent, what was he trying to achieve from that chosen behaviour?

When he walked past us and said "no time" the action was clearly dismissive and the impact was hurtful. However, what is less clear was his 'intent'. Was it a habit, lack of thought or care, or action born from being overwhelmed by workload?

Each of the three areas in the model, Push, Connection, Pull consist of two parts:

- Action
- Intent

Action is the 'what you see', it's the 'what' people do from the behaviour of the person, the team or the organisation, and this is the experience you have of them.

Intent is the 'thinking that sits behind the action', it's the 'why of what' you/they are doing, be it on purpose or by habit. You may see intent through actions but at the same time, it may stay hidden from you.

Fig 16: Connection Model

THE LIVING BRAVE MINDSETS / 191

There is a difference between 'intent' and 'impact' and we're often at our most vulnerable here because it is our blind spot. It's the hairdresser with bad hair, it's being on stage not realising you left your zipper undone, or it's being fully aware that your intent is not good but not caring about the impact of that.

PERSON EXPERIENCES LOUD NOISE AND REACTS?

As I go through how the Connection Model works, I'd like you to see it through the example of a person who hears a loud noise in an adjacent room, which is disturbing them. They could react in three possible ways.

Reaction 1	Bangs on door, shouts at the person that answers it	PUSH
Reaction 2	Knocks on the door to see what might be done about it	CONNECTED
Reaction 3	Doesn't engage with the neighbour in future	PULL

PUSH

This action is seen as pushing against things with an intent to control and dominate. The intent may be from the need to assert control, or it may be a defensive reaction as the other person Pushes or Pulls.

Have you ever been in an interaction where you found yourself feeling threatened, uncertain, anxious or fearful and, because of that, your energy was focused on protecting yourself? You reacted by increasing the volume of your behaviour by fighting back, posturing, standing that bit more forward, raising your voice so you're not spoken over. This is Push.

Ever done this? Ever seen it? Ever experienced it?

I once observed an executive member as we walked to a meeting room for her quarterly financial meeting with the parent company. "This is going to be biblical," she predicted. And she was right. They challenged her figures aggressively and she replied in a similar fashion. As we left that meeting she turned to me and said, "Over 25% of my team's energy goes into preparing for these quarterly meetings."

That is a lot of energy going on defensiveness and safeguarding instead of being invested in positive action to move things forward.

Another classic example from a diagnostic my colleague was doing was a woman who said, "The thing about us is that we don't talk to each other... we reload." This is one of the best-ever descriptions of what it is like to be in a conversation with someone who is in Push. They are not 'in' the conversation with you. They are like a coiled spring waiting for the moment in which the other person stops talking so they can take over. They are reloading their gun. The gun is their voice and the ammunition is the data they intend to fire back.

You will easily recognise this in yourself at those times when you are impatient for someone to stop talking. You metaphorically reload your gun with facts, perspective, insights and rationale to fire back the moment they next stop talking. It takes willpower not to speak and, when you've said your piece, you know what it feels like. You know when you do it. Stop it!

The intention in such situations is to win, to be heard, to protect a perspective, to have a seat at the table, to be seen as strong.

YOU HAVE EXPERIENCED PUSH BEFORE

Someone asks a question of you that they could have asked prior to a meeting, but appear to have waited until then. When a person shakes your hand they are too close, perhaps holding your hand too hard or even too long. When in conversation someone plays resources Top Trumps, trying to control available funding with the fact they have more resources than you. Perhaps they utilise the name of a senior person to leverage their need by saying well it's not me but X said they needed it.

YOU'VE DONE PUSH BEFORE

When you have felt the need to fight back to protect yourself in a way that was combative. You have over prepared as you believe correctly or otherwise that you will be challenged in a way that could hurt you. Perhaps you have put your agenda ahead of others believing that as long as you do well then you are safe? You have publicly spoken against someone without the real effort to engage with them directly.

WHAT'S THE MOTIVATION OF PUSH

The intent is to protect oneself by direct control, by dominating and exerting pressure onto the person or situation that is in front of you. The method is to go onto the intellectual, physical or emotional offensive.

The questions that you need to ask yourself here are:

- What sends me/us to Push?
- What keeps me/us there?
- What is the impact on others?
- What gets me/us out of Push?

PULL

When in Pull we see the action of pulling away from interaction and engagement. You experience this in the way that some people don't engage with you when you try to make contact, or when someone is due to deliver on a commitment but become unavailable. You notice it when you realise that the person that you are talking to is presenting a fixed set of behaviours but has, in reality, checked out. They might still be in the meeting but have pushed back from the desk, closed their notebook, and are no longer engaged in the conversation offering ideas, challenge or support. They have metaphorically taken their ball home so the game can't continue.

An example of a senior manager being in Pull was given to me by an executive in the automotive parts trade. He said, "The IT director just doesn't want to hear things that will generate more work. He's put in place a Service Level Agreement with built-in complexity and online forms that, if not filled out properly, are rejected, even if the need is understood and important. Oh, there's no contact@theitdepartment.com, you have to know the actual name of the person you need to contact."

In this regard, the IT Director was in Pull. They had not just disengaged by pulling away, they had cemented their position by building a fortress of disengagement and arming the battlements with the arrows of process.

YOU HAVE EXPERIENCED PULL BEFORE

Not having responses to email or call. You suddenly feel a conversation is harder than it should be as the other person withdraws from being curious, support or even challenging. When it was much easier to purchase from a company than it is to get the same level of interaction from customer service. When it is clear that someone is saying one thing in a meeting but saying contrary points outside of that. You suddenly recognise that you are not inside the decision making process.

YOU'VE DONE PULL BEFORE

When you look for ways not to engage with a person, a project. When during a conversation you stop giving your thoughts and opinions and consciously or not make the decision to ride it through to the end. You have given in arguing as it's exhausting. You stop holding space on ideas and opinions as you feel negated.

WHAT'S THE MOTIVATION OF PULL

The intent is to protect oneself by indirect control, by submitting or escaping the person or situation that is in front of you. The method is to go into intellectual, physical or emotional withdrawal.

WHY NOT STAY CONNECTED?

The point of moving to 'Push or Pull' is control or self-defence.

- Push is saying: "If I/we force the point, enforce the position and come in harder or tougher then I/we am/are more likely to overcome perceived barriers"

- Pull is saying 'If I/we give in, keep my/our head(s) down and wait, the chances are this issue will go away'.

When you Push or Pull, then your belief is that you will succeed in a way that being Connected will not get you. This is not correct, it's just that you haven't developed the craft or you fear the reality of operating in this way.

Often, Pull is couched in being neutral, "I'm not being destructive. I'm neutral". However, you cannot be neutral when it comes to contributing to the success of an endeavour. If you're neutral, then you are not contributing, you're opting out and watching from the sidelines. And, if you're doing that then you're happy for something to fail. You can't claim you want something to succeed unless you're actively in the game. Being neutral is sabotage. Dress it up as you like, but that's what it is.

Both positions are below the line of Accountability, both demonstrate a lack of Bravery and most importantly both damage Trust as they sabotage the story of your character and focus.

The questions here:

- What sends me/us to Pull?
- What keeps me/us there?
- What is the impact on others?
- How do I/we get out of Pull?

CONNECTION

When you think of all the great moments you've shared with a person, a team, as a customer, client or stakeholder, I can almost guarantee it was in no small part down to the connection you experienced.

Connection engenders Trust. It speaks to the part of us that's looking to see if the other person is friend or foe. If there is Connection, we are far more likely to trust whatever they're about and to be more forgiving of anything we don't like.

Being connected doesn't mean you have to be in total agreement. It can work when you say "I may or may not agree, however, I am connected. I am here in the conversation. I am not distracted, I am present. You have my full attention. I have parked my need to win, to reload, to hide and am listening with the intention of reaching a great outcome." Not allowing the pressure of your own agenda or fears to overwhelm you takes practice.

It is easy to be connected to someone or to a topic you like, there is no craft in that and no Living Brave. The craft of Connection is in the experience people have of you in the situations where you don't like them, aren't interested in the topic, are focused on something else or fearful yourself.

NOT
PRESENT

PRESENT

Connecting to something larger than yourself is key and you need to be able to hold the two truths: your need and the needs of others. Remember the F. Scott Fitzgerald quote: "The test of a first-rate intelligence is the ability to hold two opposed ideas in mind at the same time and still retain the ability to function."

In some situations, you may need to hold more than two truths as you consider your connection to:

- your own need (individual)
- the needs of others (team)
- a larger need (organisation)
- a greater need (society)

The real effort comes in fully connecting to a person you don't particularly like or trust, or a situation that is not of interest, or not working in your favour. If you are seeking control and are operating below the line on the Accountability Line model, you may use Push and Pull as a way of gaining control. This strategy can damage your brand, especially if you believe you need to leverage your positional power to assert yourself and get your way.

Operating through Connection means that you are operating in a truly adult space, with the reality of what is happening in front of you, and having conversations about the truth of the situation as you see it, with the intention of understanding your own blind spots. This includes having the intent to:

- Reinforce your position
- Calibrate your position
- Change your position

Connected is a place of stability and curiosity. Push and Pull are places of rigidity and isolation.

HUMMINGBIRD MOMENTS

With Connection, you create what I call Hummingbird Moments. They are a moment of calm, where trust and engagement can be created.

A hummingbirds' rapidly moving wings are symbolic of being busy. They act as a metaphor for having a large to-do list that is ever present.

Yet, as busy as a hummingbird is, it remains still. It is not distracted. When it is in front of the flower collecting nectar, the effort being exerted is obvious but the bird still looks balanced and very much in the moment. It's in control, the exertion is masked by its skill, its craft. There is a ballet of movement from flower (meeting, task, conversations) to flower.

This is the beauty of operating from a place of Connection.

Our Umbrella Beliefs and Levers give us the will and motivation to have Connection to others. But while people acknowledge that we are busy, that we work hard and are active, the aim is to create Hummingbird Moments where we are neither Pushing or Pulling. We won't feel the need to push people aggressively and we won't punish by pulling away. We focus on the craft, elegance and story of ourselves at the moment at hand.

DO NOT BECOME A CARICATURE

It is very easy at this point to fall into a self-righteous position of 'being connected' in a kind of overworked caricature of almost yogic levels of mindfulness and presence.

Being overly still, holding the gaze of others as you 'look into them' (note, not 'at' but 'in'….in that knowing way), slowing your breathing down with a large mesmeric smile, as you are the one who's 'fully connected'. Let's be clear, we are not trying to transcend to a higher plane of consciousness, though feel free to do so and there's something quite unpleasant when someone attempts to overly connect and thus overplays the "I am fully present, please experience my karmic excellence".

A long time ago I worked for Churchill Insurance (UK based Insurance), which was purchased by Royal Bank of Scotland (RBS) who created RBS Insurance. This was back when Fred 'The Shred' Goodwin was MD of RBS so, as you can imagine from his nickname and knowledge of what happened in the financial markets, they were tough times. When Martin Long, the owner of Churchill, moved on after being bought out, John O'Roarke became MD of Churchill and Chief Operating Officer of RBS Insurance.

I moved from Churchill to being Head of Leadership and Learning at RBS Insurance, then the largest integration in the insurance sector. Heady times! I had a meeting with John O'Roarke at Coutts Bank, a part of RBS, to give him an overview of the training plans for full integration on system, process and culture.

Coutts has a prestigious setting and, as I arrived and was looking at a potted plant in the corner, I couldn't help but observe that it probably cost the equivalent of my annual salary just to keep the plants looking the part. This feeling was magnified because the carpet was so thick it was quite tricky to walk on. I walked towards the glass-fronted office, John looked up, stood and opened the door, shook my hand, asked if I wanted a drink and where I'd like to sit.

"Guy, how long do we have?" he asked. "What do we need to achieve? Is there anything you need before we get going?" The conversation then proceeded at pace. I was trying to over-validate both my efforts and those of the team, which he clearly realised, saying, "I can see what's been done. I can see the focus and the thinking that's gone into this. Please share that with the team."

He'd looked at his watch towards the end, but with no frustration, just for his information, and as we came to a close, he thanked me for my time, asked if I needed help collecting my papers, walked me to the office door, opened it, shook my hand and bade me well. I walked down the hall, got to the elevator, looked back down the hall to see that he had returned to his desk, looked up, smiled and raised his hand.

I have been telling that story for the last 20 + years because if I thought I was busy, my schedule was nothing compared to the scope and scale of what John was dealing with. Yet he created the perfect Hummingbird Moment. His agenda was calling him, his workload increasing by the moment, yet in the time I was with him he displayed complete Connection, totally there, no caricature. I trusted him and I add to the Legend as I retell the story.

The best way of seeing Connection is as a vehicle for the delivery of your message and the way it is experienced and received.

Decades of employee surveys, coaching sessions, forums, team diagnostics, exit interviews and conversations have consistently shown me that people don't expect to get what they want all the time. The point at which they become disenfranchised is when they believe they are not being heard. It's easy to listen, but to give a person, a team, an organisation the experience of being heard confirms the ability of individuals and teams to operate from Connection, even when the pressure is on.

You will often see in the military or the emergency services the ability to operate in Connection, in the middle of extreme situations that would drive most people straight to Push or Pull. However, they have been mentored, trained, coached and counselled to have conversations whilst the heat is on that stay in Connection.

When I spoke with Major General Paul Nanson, CBE, Commandant of the Royal Military Academy Sandhurst, this is what he told me: "Being connected to the moment in all its realities is paramount. You are holding the strategy, the process, the data streaming in, individual behaviours and unknown quantities. To operate in the military requires you to hold your place intellectually and emotionally and to converse with people in a manner that isn't about how long you've got with them, but about whether you've genuinely heard them, not just the words, but also the intent, the meaning and the expectation."

When real or metaphorical bullets fly, and the adrenalin flows, time often feels shorter and more anxiety laden. The capacity to offer a Hummingbird Moment and to be the one who maintains Connection is massively powerful. It is where a large part of the essence of Living Brave lies.

The key reflections for Connection are:

- What do you believe can only be achieved in Push or Pull? (Note that everything you think might need Push or Pull to succeed can be achieved in Connection)
- Which Umbrella Beliefs can keep you in a position of Connection?
- Which of your Levers will keep you in Connection or motivate you to get back there from Push or Pull?

NINE

SHEEPDOG, SHEPHERD, SHEEP & WOLF

This is where we look at

Living Brave Behaviours | Sheepdog Behaviours
Shepherd Behaviours | Sheep Behaviours
Wolf Behaviours | Conscious Choice

CHAPTER NINE

SHEEPDOG, SHEPHERD, SHEEP & WOLF

"I am not bound to win, but I am bound to be true. I am
not bound to succeed, but I am bound to live by the light
that I have. I must stand with anybody that stands right,
and stand with them while they are right, and part with
them when they go wrong."

- Abraham Lincoln

In writing this book I wanted to consolidate decades of insight, reflection and perspective and to make my conclusions accessible to those who don't think about these things as much as I do. Also, I've been wondering, after you've read this book, what conversations and metaphors might you offer to help make sense of the thinking to others.

I liken this to me and cars. I am not interested in cars. I just need to know how to drive one. I am not excited by a conversation about the internal combustion engine. Part of the challenge of applying the Living Brave mindset will be the way in which you can bring others to think about the approach (drive the car) even if they are not as inherently interested as you (the mechanic) may be.

I also wanted to be able to catch myself at points when I was Living Brave and points when I was not, in a way that was more emotional than intellectual. The Accountability Line and the Connection Model gave me real intellectual clarity on the thinking needed to answer these headline questions:

- What would you do if you were Living Brave?
- In terms of Trust, Accountability, Bravery and Connection where should you most focus?
- What are the Umbrella Beliefs that will hold you true?
- What are the Levers that will create action?
- What do you need to Face Into?

The ultimate question: "What would you do if you were Living Brave?" still remains. It's powerful and emotive. But what could be added to it? The answer and transferability is in metaphor found in the power of the characters associated with the terms Sheepdog, Shepherd, Sheep and Wolf.

Think back to the story on page 137, 'Which wolf do you feed?'. The power is in the understanding of what these four components represent.

In my experience people who are Living Brave, encouraging others to do so, and holding people to account for these key behaviours, get great value from seeing not only their own behaviours, but the behaviour of those around them through a lens that highlights the reality of what happened, is happening and should happen, in a fast and accessible manner. In the context of Living Brave, it really helps to frame your own and others' behaviours through a point of reference that everyone can learn quickly and use immediately.

I've always tried to find a way of identifying the types of behaviour that I've experienced in myself and others that's easy to grasp, even if it's not rooted in the sort of psychological language that would give it greater kudos.

OBSERVE THE BEHAVIOUR, DON'T DEFINE THE PERSON

I would strongly counsel that you don't say:

- "I am a sheepdog, a shepherd, a sheep, a wolf"
- "You are a sheepdog, a shepherd, a sheep, a wolf"

I can tell you now that that never worked for anyone. It doesn't help to define yourself or anyone else by the judgement of being a 'something'. I know I react badly to it myself and I know others do as well.

Fig 17: living Brave Behaviours

One thing I want you to note in terms of the way I am phrasing this is I am referring to behaviours, not to people. The reason is that behaviours are not fixed, though a person, team and culture may have habituated themselves as a way of operating in the world, they are often very fluid depending on the context in relation to the situation. This means that it's incorrect to say, "she, he, they, we" are x,y,z (sheep etc..). The truth is the behaviours that are being experienced and demonstrated are indicating that behaviour. In truth what we witness is a person behaving through the frame of reference of a sheepdog, shepherd, wolf, sheep, all moving in relation to the level of power, control, fear and the confidence they may be experiencing and their reaction to it.

The trick here is to not pigeon hole people with a descriptor that creates a frame of reference that then sets the manner of your interactions with them. Calling someone a Sheepdog doesn't help. They are not a Sheepdog, they are a person, what you can say is "I'm experiencing Sheepdog behaviours". You don't want to be pigeon holed and nor does anyone else. That will never help you or them. It's always what you are seeing right now in relation to the thing that is happening. What you are trying to do with any external frame of reference is use it as a tool, not a weapon. Any psychometric or preference tool is capable of taking away the persons ability to change if we define them by the language in the tool. So remember it's the behaviour, not the person.

It's really important that when talking to yourself and offering the thinking to others it's offered in the following format:

SELF

"The way I was/am behaving is sheepdog, shepherd, sheep, wolf. This is what I am seeing (example), hearing (example), feeling (example)".

OTHERS

"What I am observing is sheepdog, shepherd, sheep, wolf. This is what I am seeing (example), hearing (example), feeling (example)".

IT'S A LAYERED CAKE

Let us go a little deeper into the defining characteristics of a person and consider Trait and Type theory[50]. *Traits* are the underpinning, consistently present characteristics of a person that produce an effect on behaviour, *Types* are collections of traits that occur together in some individuals, in some contexts.

The way I would offer this thinking is that when you tell someone that's 'what they are', you are telling them their Trait. When you offer the observation of how you have experienced their behaviour', then you are discussing their Type.

The Big Five Personality Traits[51] are used in psychological profiling to give an essence of 'who you are'. The layered cake element for me comes from the fact that, in psychometric terms, there is no consensus as to exactly which traits are developable. It's easy to get drawn into the semantics of 'well even if you can modify your behaviour, it's only a veneer on top of who you already are'.

Of course, this may suit some people as they are able to excuse their behaviour as being 'just who I am'. Sometimes they may also resort to using badly interpreted psychometrics as a defence: "it's because my profile says I am an x,y,z".

I don't believe we should venture down that road. It's the intellectual equivalent of saying, "well it's because I'm a Sagittarius". Using that way of framing the world, supersedes all authority to the paradigm of the psychometric test and that's not Living Brave. Within Living Brave, we are Accountable and Brave, we can acknowledge a preference, we can acknowledge a conscious or unconscious bias or habituation. What we can't do is say, "this behaviour is pre-ordained by my psychological disposition, so it's not really me is it?"

Bearing all that in mind, I still firmly believe that you cannot control everything that happens to you, around you or to those connected to you. Life is life and it can be messy. We only really control one thing, the way we behave and the way we approach and react to things and the stronger our Umbrella Beliefs, the abler we are to develop the elegance and the craft around the impact we make in the world.

So, are you a sheepdog, sheep, shepherd or wolf? What's your answer? Which one are you? And is your answer definitive or contextual?

Let me supply the answer, you are not a sheepdog, sheep, shepherd or wolf. Go back to the beginning of the paragraph 'Observe the behaviour, don't define the person' and keep reading it until your answer is as below:

Q: So, are you a sheepdog, sheep, shepherd or a wolf?

A: I am none of those things, though my behaviour at different times is identifiable by those descriptions.

Right, you are now prepared to read the following descriptions and not disappear into your own navel with an approach that judges and shames yourself or others, but rather one that helps identify the experience for you to calibrate.

LIVING BRAVE BEHAVIORAL TYPES: SHEEPDOG, SHEPHERD, SHEEP, WOLF

The following is an overview of the cumulative behaviours belonging to each category: sheepdog, shepherd, sheep, wolf.

SHEEPDOG BEHAVIOUR

The Sheepdog defining behaviours are the desire to be of use, to have a purpose. It's not about being in control. It's about having a focus point that adds value. Sheepdog behaviours include energy, curiosity and drive.

Sheepdog mindsets flourish in environments where there is a clear vision, little ambiguity, and the permission to be curious, to offer and receive praise and to challenge when necessary. Other important factors are clear lines of power, knowing where responsibilities lie and not having to deal with politics that get in the way of honest conversations and actions.

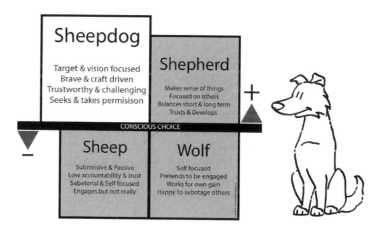

Sheepdog behaviour shows up in teams when members are both skilled at their work and striving to do their best. Sheepdog behaviour also means being happy to work alone when that's required.

Sheepdog mindsets thrive when they have clear targets, communication and an identified leader. However, they are happy to take the helm if a leader is not present. A Sheepdog has its eye on the prize and, should things start to fall apart, the Sheepdog will step forward to fill the gap.

Living Brave Mindset	Description	Rating
Mindset 1	Trust	High Trust
Mindset 2	Accountability	Above the line
Mindset 3	Bravery	3-4 Bravery Quotient
Mindset 4	Connection	Connected

I remember watching a UK programme called 'One man and his dog', it started in 1976, so today we would probably, rightly call it The Sheepdog Show. It was a Sunday show that had Shepherds with their Sheepdogs herding the sheep into a pen, it was better than it sounds.

One show I watched as a young boy, the sheep had to be herded behind a hill and out of the line of sight of the shepherd. On this one occasion, some of the sheep bolted, possibly shouting 'freeeeeeeedom'....I digress, the shepherd didn't know this and kept whistling for the sheepdog to move the sheep forward. The sheepdog saw the prison break attempt and hesitated as he clearly heard the command. Then he left the main flock and shot after the strays bringing them back to the flock and then continuing. The Shepherd didn't know this was happening.

As a metaphor this works brilliantly, the sheepdog mindset is high performance, the need is clear goals (sheep in pen), clear guidance (whistle commands), however, the freedom to also be in control of the delivery is key. The sheepdog frame of reference is to be 'OF' service not 'IN' service.

In the US military and Law Enforcement, there is a common turn of phrase which is "we are the sheepdogs". It's very powerful, these are people who give their all, are highly professional, they place themselves in harm's way, they obey orders and yet at the same time they are ready not to. They understand the boundaries they must operate in and will express themselves freely within it, whilst respecting hierarchy, but they are not submissive to it.

The "we are the Sheepdogs" is a very powerful frame of reference.

SHEPHERD BEHAVIOUR

Shepherds behaviours are motivated by the desire to enable, to protect and to ensure that things are fair. Shepherd behaviours stem from working from Connection. Contributing to the greater good, they manifest in a desire for sustainability and value creation. Shepherds accept that, while things might have to be done with a short term focus, this is always balanced with the long term and the need to ensure things are set up so the next Shepherds and Sheepdogs can succeed.

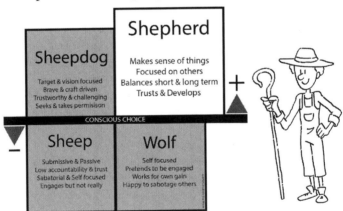

Shepherd traits include curiosity and a willingness to challenge the value of certain actions if they are perceived as damaging. They also balance the defence of the weak with a resolute approach when hard decisions are needed that affect the cultural (flock) whole. Shepherds nurture, protect and make hard decisions, even if others find their decisions difficult.

Shepherds focus on paying attention to both individuals and the wider population. They are able to handle short-, mid- and long-term timelines for actions, strategies and visions.

Living Brave Mindset	Description	Rating	Page Reference
Mindset 1	Trust	Trust	High Trust
Mindset 2	Accountability	Accountability	Above the line
Mindset 3	Bravery	Bravery	3-4 Bravery Quotient
Mindset 4	Connection	Connection	Connected

Who are the ultimate Shepherds? Parents. It's a role that sums up the difference between being in charge of some direct reports (children) and having a much deeper Connection. Think how the best parents run the gamut of nurturer, disciplinarian, coach, counsel, motivator, observer, trusted confidante, authority figure, leader, manager, protector.

It's an encompassing role, directing, standing back, holding to account, praising but overall it's about knowing the intended outcomes that you want for the family unit (team, organisation); whilst recognising you can't do it all by yourself and others will at different times lead and challenge.

The shepherd and the parent know from experience that the plan will never fully turn out in the originally expected outcome.

SHEEP BEHAVIOUR

Sheep behaviours are often expressed by the desire to join anonymity and perceived safety of the crowd (flock). Behaviours are, on the surface, very useful to managers who like to be surrounded by people willing to get on with it, often code for doing as told. Sheep behaviours include turning up and keeping below the radar, being submissive and not standing out.

Sheep tend to agree upwards about everything and then bleat about levels of dissatisfaction afterwards. Sheep characteristics can be destructive if they mask the truth of how the individual or team really feel.

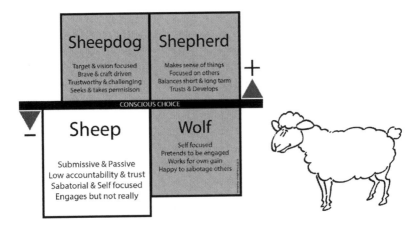

Sheepdog

Target & vision focused
Brave & craft driven
Trustworthy & challenging
Seeks & takes permisison

Shepherd

Makes sense of things
Focused on others
Balances short & long term
Trusts & Develops

CONSCIOUS CHOICE

Sheep

Submissive & Passive
Low accountability & trust
Sabatorial & Self focused
Engages but not really

Wolf

Self focused
Pretends to be engaged
Works for own gain
Happy to sabotage others

Sheep behaviour also creates an environment of mistrust in which real thoughts, actions and feelings are muted, covert and guarded.

Living Brave Mindset	Description	Rating
Mindset 1	Trust	Low Trust
Mindset 2	Accountability	Below the line
Mindset 3	Bravery	0-2 Bravery Quotient
Mindset 4	Connection	Push or Pull

There are so many examples of Sheep behaviour I barely know where to start. Think of how many news stories we have seen in recent years where people have 'kept quiet'. There's often a good reason from the perspective of the person involved, self-preservation or personal gain being the primary drivers. Think of the following scandals, UK politician expenses, Volkswagon emissions, Harvey Weinstein, Enron accounting…the list goes on and on. The common denominator is that a lot of people knew about 'Wolf' behaviours that they were witnessing but stayed in the safety of the flock. They decided 'safety first' and were Sheep. You won't probably have to think too hard about examples in your own context where you or others keep quite with ideas and challenge because its safer.

WOLF BEHAVIOUR

Wolf behaviour is selfish and driven by the desire for personal success or survival. When in conflict or fearing perceived threat the Wolf behaviour is fueled by the need to emerge as unscathed as possible. Sometimes these behaviours are overt and easy to identify, other times they are covert and often couched in social and organisation niceties. It makes the Wolf behaviour often the hardest behaviour to pin down, as cunning and deceit can be masked with benevolence and engagement. The reason this can often be the most complex of behaviours is that this behaviour can create a belief that this is political astuteness and good intellect…but it is not. It's self-absorbed, Machiavellian and destructive.

It rests on a simple premise, the Wolf's own survival and achievement are paramount.

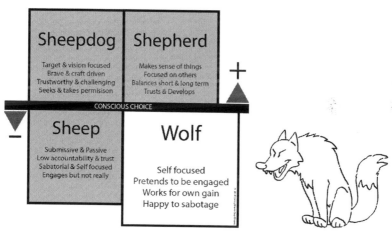

Wolf behaviour can be seen in a host of guises. Wolves may dress as a Sheep, Shepherd or Sheepdog. They rarely show their true motivation as that would reveal their true self and bring attention to their activities. Wolf behaviour is seen not in what is said but in the contradiction with what is actually done.

Wolf behaviour is truly damaging. A wolf is happy to see others fail and will often capitalise on that failure by stepping into the breach or utilising the shift of focus to their own advantage.

Living Brave Mindset	Description	Rating
Mindset 1	Trust	Low Trust
Mindset 2	Accountability	Below the line
Mindset 3	Bravery	0-2 Bravery Quotient
Mindset 4	Connection	Push or Pull

They make films about Wolf behaviour both in its overt and covert form. The Wolf of Wall Street is a great example of overt Wolf behaviours, through the real-life story of former US Stockbroker, Jordan Ross Belfort[52], seeing the film makes you think they must have embellished, though many say they didn't need to make anything up. Whereas Jordan Belfort is the zenith of 'it is all about me' with possible levels of sociopathy, he is representative of someone who's focus at its worst is anti-social at best disengaged. In terms of covert Wolf behaviours think of programmes like the House of Cards and films like The Talented Mr Ripley, where the anti heroes, with a very well crafted, almost forensic level of focus and craft have deeply Machiavellian intentions and act with great guile and skill in the world they operate in. This doesn't mean 'suspect everyone', it's similar to learning self-defence, you don't need to be on constant high alert with a 'who can you trust' mentality, that's exhausting.

I am absolutely convinced with Wolf behaviour that you know when the words and the actions don't quite match. You have data streaming in and your mind will filter it into a reaction, trust that, calibrate it.

IT'S A CONSCIOUS CHOICE TO ACT ABOVE THE LINE

Living Brave behaviours are Sheepdog and Shepherd. Both demonstrate a willingness to step up and hold space. They also help those who are demonstrating Sheep and Wolf behaviours to develop their confidence, personal insight and to increase their contribution with the possible outcome of them operating as Sheepdogs and Shepherds.

These questions really help focus the mind on being above the line behaviourally as a Sheepdog and/or Shepherd.

IN THE END, IT'S QUITE SIMPLE

Sheep can feel a lot easier than managing Sheepdogs and Shepherds because obedience is very appealing, it is also easy to fool yourself that you are a great manager when actually you have submission, not engagement. Many managers fear that by enabling people's true capabilities and dealing with their true feelings, they will increase the power of the other person and that they will increasingly push for what they see as right and push against what they see as wrong. It feels quicker to just have people do as they are told.

It also feels safer for many people to operate below the lone of Accountability and in the Sheep and Wolf paradigm. Sheep feels safe, 'if

I just do as I am told I will be ok' and Wolf can give the sense of control you don't feel you have 'I might not be in control of the situation, but I am able to damage or not really support, so I can control that'.

However, Sheep don't innovate or add value and the Wolf is always ready to move on or utilise stresses to their advantage. If you don't allow a Shepherd or a Sheepdog to be who they are, you breed resentment and end up getting Sheep or Wolf behaviours instead. For many managers it's easier to just have the veneer of engagement, to be a benevolent autocrat and to maintain control in a manner that feels like a heck of a lot less work.

It's by far the easier route and one that may well feel safest. It isn't. It just requires a Living Brave mentality to apply the Living Brave Mindsets, to Face Into and have honest conversations.

CONSCIOUS CHOICE MAKER

Every one of the core models in Living Brave have a shared factor, Conscious Choice, I interpret this as 'the action was considered and selected' or 'it was done on purpose'. Look at each model, just in case you didn't spot this:

Fig. No	Model	Page	Fig. No	Model	Page
Fig.1	Real You/Fake You	15	Fig.2	Stuckness Equation	34
Fig.3	Envisaged Goal	60	Fig.4	Non-Reflective Model	66
Fig.5	Reflective Model	66	Fig.6	Legend Equation	67
Fig.7	Resilience Algorithm	112	Fig.8	Truth Triangle	114
Fig.9	Agility Capability Triangle	120	Fig.10	Umbrella Beliefs	128
Fig.11	Living Brave Mindsets	147	Fig.12	Trust	152
Fig.13	Accountability Line	160	Fig.14	Fear Volume	182
Fig.15	Bravery Quotient	185	Fig.16	Connection Model	191
Fig.17	Living Brave Behaviours	206	Fig.21	If, Should, Can't, Do	261

By being a Conscious Choice maker, you can demonstrate your brand, enable your stories and create your Legend. You help to shape future evolutions of yourself and to draw others to you. Making Conscious Choices, and holding to them, in a public domain defines the nature of the person, the team and the organisation. There is nothing more accountable, nothing more Living Brave than saying "I/we did this on purpose". That's how the Sheepdogs and the Shepherds operate.

The way to consider Conscious Choice is to see it as a continuum of thinking and then decision making.

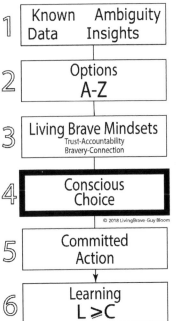

Fig 18: Conscious Choice Maker

1. *Inputs*

    Look first at the data, the known and unknown, the ambiguous, the insights and opinions you have from others. "What is and is not known?"

2. *Options*

    Reflect, thinktank, brainstorm and ponder the options that present themselves. "What could be done?"

3. *Living Brave Mindset Thinking*

    Apply thinking of Trust, Accountability, Bravery, Connection. "Where do Umbrella Beliefs & Levers need to be called upon?"

4. *Conscious Choice*

    Commit to action in order to apply what has been decided: "Where do you need to Face Into it?"

5. *Committed Action*

    There is no neutral, there is no "I'll see if it works out". You are in, or you are out. When you commence, it is with the precision of mind, emotion and action. "Where will Big Pants be needed?"

6. *Learning*

Learn as you go, as you implement the Committed Actions of the Conscious Choice, born from the application of the four Living Brave Mindsets. Discover the truth by seeking it out and by people feeling they can offer it without fear of reprisal. Remember your learning needs to be equal to, or greater than, the change being experienced. More effort, more change, more learning.

The difference between success and failure is seen in those that take an idea, fan its flames until a level of emotional engagement is achieved, and then apply a process that holds them tightly to account.

Things to reflect on:

- When am I the Sheepdog, Shepherd, Sheep or Wolf?
- What reinforces my/our behaviour as Sheepdog, Shepherd?
- What reinforces my/our behaviour as Sheep, Wolf?
- What behaviours am I/are we demonstrating?
- How am I/are we experienced by others?
- Do my/our behaviours enable me, the team and the culture, or do they damage?
- What is the brand, story and Legend because of this?
- Am I/are we enhanced or damaged by our Sheepdog, Shepherd, Sheep or Wolf behaviours?

TEN

PROCESS & APPLICATION

This is where we look at

The Living Brave Actions process | Context & Why |
Lay of the land | Capturing ideas & Sieving for Nuggets |
Risk Mitigation | Committed Actions | Calibrate to Conclusion

CHAPTER TEN

PROCESS & APPLICATION

"Kung Fu? Anything can be done with Kung Fu.
It refers to any study, learning, or practise that requires
patience, energy, and time to complete."

- Guy Bloom, 4 x Martial Arts Hall of Fame

Let's pick up the Conscious Choice idea and drive it forward into a definitive set of actions, utilising the thinking from within this work. If we don't, we're at risk of claiming "I'm Living Brave" but it not being true. We don't want to be the equivalent of someone who wears a sports watch, but never exercises. No, we don't want that.

At this point in the book, I hope you have the insight into the Living Brave mindset to give the same answers as me to the questions below:

Do you define yourself as a leader?	Yes
Do you believe that you require permission to lead?	No
Do you see leadership as requiring seniority?	No
Do you see leadership as being about the position you hold?	No
Do you believe you can lead even if you have no power or direct control?	Yes
Do you think there can be more than one leader at the same time?	Yes
Do you see leadership as being only at work?	No

Do you believe leaders should always know the answer?	No
Do you believe leadership is a craft?	Yes
Do you actively seek feedback?	Yes
Do you seek counsel from others that both reinforces and challenges?	Yes

Thinking this way is paramount to your ability to recognise the position someone holds and to respect it, not from a place of obedience, but through your willingness to contribute. If you cannot contribute because of your emotional and intellectual position or because of another party's behaviour, then ask yourself the question: "Am I ready to begin Living Brave?". If you are, start the process.

APPLYING THE PROCESS

The idea of Living Brave is powerful, it galvanises (I/we want to be Living Brave); it gives a frame of reference (I/we can focus on Living Brave); it brings the challenge of the question (Am I/are we Living Brave?); it leads to the statement (I/we are Living Brave).

Living Brave speaks to our inner need to be connected to something larger than ourselves, i.e. to our Umbrella Beliefs. It gives meaning to the life we lead as individuals and gives purpose to the group enterprise.

We really are at a moment of self-definition:

- in how you want to reinforce or change your approach
- whether there is a motivation big enough to put the work in

My hope is that at this point you have a sense of how the thinking of Living Brave can be something that reinforces the good you already do, brings challenge to the areas that could do with tweaking and catalyses change where there is a need.

As you move forward from this point, the work really begins.

We need a methodology - an approach. There has to be a way for the individual to look at their situation and decide the need to be Living Brave and move forward. It's not enough to have a powerful call to arms if you have no way of moving forward.

The Living Brave Actions process is a way for the individual, the team and the organisation to apply a methodology in the drive to be Living Brave. We have spent a lot of time looking at the methodologies that enable mindsets, the behaviours and the actions that determine a Living Brave approach. Though each part of the thinking in Living Brave works independently, when placed in a process flow it becomes a truly powerful approach. It's time to turn that into an end process.

Recognise the need and ask the question

We have already answered this to some degree; however, the process looks like this:

There has to be a trigger, there has to be something that instigates you or the team's desire to take a frame of approach that is to want to be Living Brave. Why would you want to ask yourself the question? I ask that rhetorically because you and the team want to be able to look in the mirror and at each other with the ability to say "I am Living Brave", "We are Living Brave". That said, there are four triggers for this approach:

4 TRIGGERS TO LIVING BRAVE

1. You want to approach a situation now and in the future with the lens of Living Brave and in doing so set yourself and the team up to succeed

2. You either have something that isn't right to a greater or lesser degree and you recognise that by applying a lens of Living Brave you will be able to course correct and move to a positive outcome or you have something that is working as it should to a certain degree; however, you still want to move it forward

3. You want to apply to the above points a Living Brave frame of reference as you see an inherent value, power, impetus in this way of framing your thoughts and actions

4. You want to apply a Living Brave mindset as you see it as inherently valuable to all frames of reference

The above triggers the question to you or to/from the group that is simply, "Am I/Are we Living Brave?"

LIVING BRAVE ACTIONS

I now want to provide a way to look at your situation, to recognise the need to be Living Brave, and to move forward.

Set 1: To uncover 'negative' impacts

- "Am I/Are we growing and developing in this situation?"
- "Is this situation enabling me/us and those around me/us?"
- "Do I/we feel better for being in this situation?"
- "Do I/we have the momentum to work towards a defined goal?"

If the answers to any of these 4 questions are in the negative, things are probably not healthy for you, the team or the culture and they need to change.

If the answers are mostly in the positive, then you are in a situation where you're probably enacting a Living Brave approach and looking to reinforce and grow your position.

Set 2: To uncover the 'positive' impacts

- "Can I/we do what we are doing better?"
- "Is there any sense that we aren't fulfilling potential?"
- "Would moving this forward be beneficial in terms of growth, contribution or reward?"
- "Would moving this forward enable others, the team and the organisation?"
- "Am I/are we engaged by the thought of doing this?"

Recognising the need for change is no small thing. It says that you recognise that you want to move things to the next step, to aim higher, to occupy the space that belongs to you, to be more, not less and to hold yourself to something bigger. Do not underestimate the potential gap between asking the questions and the endeavour of working through them followed by the cold, hard reality of getting traction and buy-in.

Many great endeavours that everyone agreed could have made a difference remain on the shelf as the truth of what change really means rears its head. Often this triggers doubt and causes those with positional power to pull back from the threatened change as they wrestle with the daily reality of commercial imperatives.

Living Brave sometimes requires some symbolic banner waving to inform the world that change is afoot. However, it can also work quietly in the background helping the individual or team to navigate their own reality and improving things at the local level.

APPLY THE PROCESS

This isn't a tool with a punchy mnemonic I'm afraid. However, it does cover the steps for considering your focus for Living Brave.

- **Step 1** - Context and why?
- **Step 2** - Lay of the land
- **Step 3** - Capture obvious ideas, innovate and sieve for nuggets
- **Step 4** - Risk mitigation
- **Step 5** - Committed action
- **Step 6** - Calibrate to closure

Let's work through the model and see where it takes us. As you explore it, consider how, where, when, with whom, and in what context, you might utilise this approach.

Fig 19: Steps to Living Brave

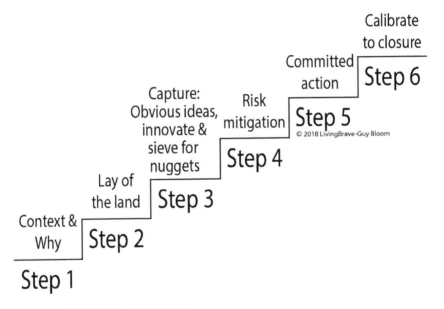

STEP 1 - CONTEXT AND WHY

This a key moment. You are saying, 'Ok, before we get down to action, let's be sure of what we are talking about.'

Setting the context seems so obvious that it's simple to jump past this step. But hold yourself to taking the time to get this right, both for yourself and others. The reason it is so important is that it frames the upcoming effort while working through the model. It sets the direction and galvanises your thinking and that of the individuals or teams you might be working with.

It's very common to speed past this step, especially in group work where there may be impatience and the desire to move on so as to 'not waste time'. Any insight you can bring to yourself and others is by:

Reinforcing   - which enables confidence of focus

Calibrating   - to focus the thinking with greater precision

Changing   - when you or others recognise focus may have been askew

Debating   - if people realise that they are at cross-purposes

Considerations about the above should be kept sharply focused and not attempt to be all-encompassing.

This step should not include multiple focus points. If there are two or more things to focus on, then they should be given individual attention, even though that requires patience and self-control. Think about a specific person, team, project, issue, topic or problem that you want to work on and set yourself on a singular focus.

When it's an issue that is not working in your favour:

- The thing I am/we are wrestling with is…
- It needs to change because…
- If it doesn't change, the impact will likely be…
- With improvement, this will enable…

When it's an issue that is going well and you want to reinforce and/or move forward:

- The thing I/we would like to move forward is…
- The reason it's worth investing in is…
- The benefits that would come from this are…

Here's an example of how this might work in the 'when things are not where they should be' context.

Think about these as 'developmental'.

The template being completed looks like this:

STEP 1 – Context & Why	
What's the context?	What's the 'why it matters'?
(Insert Text)	The thing I am wrestling with is... (Insert Text) It needs to change because... (Insert Text) If it doesn't change, the impact will likely be... (Insert Text) The benefits of this would be to... (Insert Text)

The working example:

Individual Developmental-Step 1: Context & Why

STEP 1 – Context & Why	
What's the context?	What's the 'why it matters'?
Recognition in organisation	The thing I am wrestling with is... I am not getting the recognition that I want in the organisation. It needs to change because... I am losing career credibility and career traction. If it doesn't change, the impact will likely be... that I will stagnate and become disengaged and then either leave or stay and become unfulfilled. The benefits of this would be to... find my motivation, not feel undervalued, and get back on my career track.

Team Developmental-Step 1: Context & Why

STEP 1 – Context & Why	
What's the context?	What's the 'why it matters'?
Relevance as a team	The thing we are wrestling with is... our ability to remain relevant as a team within the organisation. We are losing or can't maintain partner status within key organisation areas. It needs to change because... we will be pigeon-holed as a purely administrative function. If it doesn't change the impact will likely be... that we will be disbanded, performance-managed, restructured. The benefits of this would be to... re-establish credibility, add value to the organisation, cement our roles and not live in constant uncertainty, even fear.

Organisation Developmental-Step 1: Context & Why

STEP 1 – Context & Why	
What's the context?	What's the 'why it matters'?
Innovation capability	**The thing we would like to move forward is...** our innovation capability. **The reason it's worth investing in is...** we are in a constant state of playing catch-up in many areas of the organisation; we follow, we don't lead. **The benefits of this would be to...** attract and retain talent, commercial growth as we take market share, increased consumer brand value.

Now let's look at how this might work when things are on track, but need moving forward.

So, think about these as 'momentum'.

Individual Momentum-Step 1: Context & Why

STEP 1 – Context & Why	
What's the context?	What's the 'why it matters'?
Handling confrontation	**The thing I would like to move forward is...** my ability to handle confrontation with those who are more senior to me inside or outside the organisation. **The reason it's worth investing in is...** I need to be able to hold my place better and have more impact. **The benefits of this would be to...** have increased impact and be seen as even more capable at senior levels.

Team Momentum-Step 1: Context & Why

STEP 1 – Context & Why	
What's the context?	What's the 'why it matters'?
Attracting talent	**The thing we would like to move forward is...** being able to attract talent to the team. **The reason it's worth investing in is...** the reduction in the time it takes to fill gaps and get teams in place. **The benefits of this would be to...** our reputation and the guarantee that we can upscale and deliver on organisational or client need.

STEP 1 – Context & Why	
What's the context?	What's the 'why it matters'?
Accountable behaviours	The thing we would like to move forward is… accountable behaviours within senior management. The reason it's worth investing in is… motivating senior managers to contribute to the success of others outside their own interest. The benefits of this would be to… increased sales opportunities, economies of scale, and increase in shared learning.

Working with the relevant questions will provide great clarity around the context. In essence, it's showing you the reasons why you'd care and commit to action.

When you look at the outputs that this generates, if they don't focus on energy, interest and excitement for you and/or the team, then you're not ready to move on. Instead, you might need to apply crafting, further thought and conversation, or even to start over.

The point is that, once it's agreed in your own mind and the minds of others, there will be clarity around the 'why' of the thing. It provides the reason, point, purpose, the why we care, why you should care, why others should care… It's a rallying cry.

LINE IN THE SAND

This agreement provides a line in the sand, driven by your Umbrella Beliefs. It's a point you can refer back to that says, 'this was the day, the time, the moment when I/we decided where to place my/our energy'. It says that, unless it comes up for review, there is no room for lack of Connection to the focus of my/our energy. It is asking, even demanding, that you commit to the 'Context and the why'.

For teams, in particular, it means being on message with no leaking of personal disagreement or emotional disconnection. It says: 'I am in'. This is crucial to the premise of Living Brave because it demands that the necessary conversations have been held within the thinking process around Step 1: 'context and why'. It says, even if I'm not in 100% agreement, I am 100% committed to the success of the enterprise.

STEP 2 - LAY OF THE LAND

Once we have set the 'context and why', we know where we are focusing and where to direct our energy.

What is needed next is a clear understanding of the landscape. This is a key moment and another one that's especially easy to jump past or speed through, particularly when we're eager to move on or we think we already know what's happening. These things, however, are won at the start, not at the end.

People often shy away from this phase as it seems pointless to repeat what is perceived as already known. You may worry that it will bring up painful feelings around things now passed, or simply that it's all obvious. However, when done properly, this phase brings greater reinforcement, clarity and magnifies Step 1: 'Context and why'.

In Step 2: 'Lay of the land' you gain absolute clarity about what is happening around you. As a team, you get to acknowledge the truth, be it excellent or awful, and to share that truth. It becomes a great way to put things to bed as they are recognised and then become part of this current intent to move forward. This step is key to the overall narrative of the change story. It tells those in and outside the process that history, current truths and potential realities were considered.

Within teams and organisations, I find it's often easier to agree on Step 1: 'Context and Why' than it is to agree on Step 2: 'Lay of the land'. It is the key moment where what is being said or not said has to be Faced Into. Take personal fitness, someone might say 'I want to go to the gym to get healthy and get a six-pack so that I'll feel good about myself, increase my self-respect and energy, and probably live longer'. However, in reality, it's, 'I'm always tired, my other half doesn't like me being at the gym, it's hard to motivate myself and, frankly, I find exercise boring'. That's why you need a sense of what's really going on.

CONTEXT GRID

A sure sign of a person's or a team's capability to think correctly at this step is the ability to home in on what needs to be thought about. That demonstrates that as much as possible has been considered.

In the context of Living Brave, it's about the determination to focus on the sectors that will add value, whilst simultaneously considering the broader realities, known and unknown that might impact on the project.

Fig 20: Context Grid

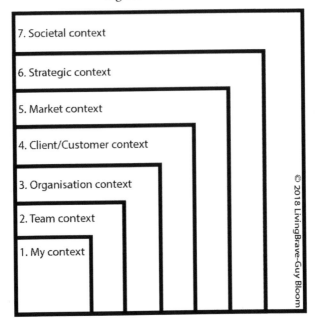

7. Societal context

6. Strategic context

5. Market context

4. Client/Customer context

3. Organisation context

2. Team context

1. My context

© 2018 LivingBrave-Guy Bloom

Do this by looking at the Context Grid in relation to the topic you want to be Living Brave on. We'll be working with the first three examples from Step 1: Context and Why, from pages 226-227.

- For each of these elements, we look at the Context Grid and consider the lay of the land across these seven factors, placing them in the first column of the following grid, with the relevant segment number from the grid. In brackets add succinct notes.
- Next place 'Important' or 'Not Important' in the second column, according to how you rate the impact of that reflection.
- Finally, in brackets, place a Red (know nothing), Amber (some knowledge) or Green (good understanding), to represent the level understanding that you have around the subject.

So, if it's 'important and green' that's good because you need to know about it, and you do, 'Not important and red' is also fine, you don't need to know anything about it and you don't. 'Important and red' is not so good: you are supposed to know about it, but you don't.......You can see how this works.

Note all the examples are working examples, they are not the answers, they are there to demonstrate how the process works.

The template being completed looks like this:

STEP 2 – Lay of the land	
Column 1	Column 2
Part 1: Which number from Context Grid + associated reflection	**Part 2:** 'Important' or 'Not Important'. (Red, Amber or Green)
(Insert Text)	Important (Red)
(Insert Text)	Important (Amber)
(Insert Text)	Important (Green)
(Insert Text)	Not Important (Red)
(Insert Text)	Not Important (Amber)
(Insert Text)	Not Important (Green)

The working example:

Individual Developmental-Step 2: Lay of the land

STEP 2 – Lay of the land	
Column 1	Column 2
Part 1: Which number from Context Grid + associated reflection	**Part 2:** 'Important' or 'Not Important'. (Red, Amber or Green)
1. Key internal stakeholders' thoughts on me (I don't actually know) 5. My overall market knowledge (I'm not that clued up)	Important (Red)
1. My personal impact (I have some insight, but only from friends)	Important (Amber)
2. Team insights on me (very good info, after recent 360)	Important (Green)
7. My impact in the world (right now beyond my ability to focus on)	Not Important (Red)
1. Qualifications for credibility (don't feel it's important, however other senior people have got qualifications that I haven't)	Not Important (Amber)
4. Client strategic focus (Well bedded-in with clients so well-versed here)	Not Important (Green)

Team Developmental-Step 2: Lay of the land

STEP 2 – Lay of the land	
Column 1	Column 2
Part 1: Which number from Context Grid + associated reflection	**Part 2:** 'Important' or 'Not Important'. (Red, Amber or Green)
7. Be knowledgeable in factors outside of the organisation (we don't know much outside of ourselves, so the organisation doesn't perceive expertise) 3. Have a long-term view of our ability to enable the overall organisation strategy (we are currently operating short term) 6. To add value through our efforts beyond our tasks and even beyond company need (how do we connect to a societal value/why?)	Important (Red)
5. Connect our value to the customer experience (our story is an internal resource only, which limits our potential)	Important (Amber)
1. Individuals are disconnected and don't feel engaged (we know they want to be part of something with a purpose, we have to create it) 2. We are losing team cohesiveness (we believe this is interrelated to all other points, but mostly due to not having a 'shared goal'	Important (Green)
4. This doesn't appear to be connected to this topic (we feel confident that there's no focus need here)	Not Important (Green)

Organisation Developmental-Step 2: Lay of the land

STEP 2 – Lay of the land	
Column 1	Column 2
Part 1: Which number from Context Grid + associated reflection	**Part 2:** 'Important' or 'Not Important'. (Red, Amber or Green)
1. Senior manager self-awareness of their individual impact (we know they understand intellectually but are they motivated to care?) 3. We know we are missing opportunities (we don't really know to what extent or the value)	Important (Red)
4. Clients are annoyed by multiple points of contact (we have anecdotal feedback, but need to find more)	Important (Amber)
2. Create enterprise-focused senior management (currently, they don't see a need for anything other than transactional behaviours) 7. This is imperative to our success with future targets (they will require greater insight into potential opportunities)	Important (Green)
5. This doesn't directly impact on customers (there's no obvious link to increased customer value)	Not Important (Red)
6. Not a factor in this process (can't see how this would enable our CSR agenda)	Not Important (Green)

When working with the Context Grid, it's often hard to focus on or even to care, about things that are outside of your span of control. In being Accountable and Connected, and wanting to fulfill your desire to be Living Brave, it's important to learn, to seek out new information, to work at understanding things that aren't easily accessible or directly related to you.

For teams this can be easy as the camaraderie of the process within Step 1: 'Context and Why', which encourages a sharing of knowledge and a commitment to discover and report back. It can also be quite problematic as gaps can be revealed where knowledge should exist, there may be a lack of commitment to learning, to sharing insight and to contributing as you move from the lip service of agreeing on the context to demonstrating real contribution.

There's potential both for it to be plain sailing or for it to be complex.

The factor to success will be gaining a licence to operate from senior stakeholders. If they think that the juice is worth the squeeze, then you're on your way. If they don't, then you could face an uphill struggle because people 'below the line' in Sheep or Wolf behaviour thinking can quickly align with the most prevalent or positionally powerful mindset rather than the one you are working towards.

Step 3 – Capture obvious ideas, innovate and sieve for nuggets

Next comes the consideration of what you know to be true, of what's unlikely, and of what's unknown.

So, get the obvious down on paper first. Then shift your thinking to an innovation space, not just a brain-storming space in order to capture all the thinking of you and the team. Doing this says 'ok, I've captured the obvious things that need doing. Now let's allow the ideas to flow.'

In the end, you'll be left with a cluster of possibilities, although at this stage while striving to consider all options and possibilities, there may be a great many to consider. That's why there is a need to 'sieve' for:

- 'Not Nows' (NN)
- 'Not Evers' (NE)
- 'Move Forward' (MF)

I advise you to record these ratings for if/when you review or find that you need to update this phase. Remembering what you thought about a particular idea is not always possible to recall, but easy to re-read.

This is the template:

STEP 3 – Capture obvious ideas, innovate and sieve for Golden Nuggets	
Part 1: With all that you know from Step 2 – Lay of the land, capture the low-hanging fruit, the 'I just have to do that' thinking	
Capture all ideas (What could you do?)	• (Insert Text)
Part 2: Now let your thinking expand to 'could I......? dare I......? what if I......?'	
Innovate (What COULD you do?)	• (Insert Text)
Part 3: Place the relevant rating 'Not Now (NN)', 'Not Ever (NE)', 'Move Forward (MF)' in brackets next to 'Part 1: Captured and Part 2: Innovated' ideas. Move Forward (MF) are your Golden Nuggets	
Sieve (Give a rating to Part 1 & 2 ideas and innovations) • Not Now (NN) • Not Ever (NE) • Move Forward (MF)	• (Insert Text)
Part 4: Review Part 3: Sieve and select the high-value, high-impact 'Golden Nuggets'. These are the things that excite you and which you believe will make a difference. These are Move Forward (MF)	
Golden Nuggets What are you really going to Move Forward (MF)	• (Insert Text)

Individual Developmental-Step 3: Capture obvious ideas, innovate and sieve for nuggets

STEP 3 – Capture obvious ideas, innovate and sieve for Golden Nuggets	
Part 1: With all that you know from Step 2 – Lay of the land, capture the low-hanging fruit, the 'I just have to do that' thinking	
Capture all ideas (What could you do?)	• Ask colleagues how they see my impact • Read books on this topic • Get an internal coach • Get an external coach

Part 2: Now let your thinking expand to 'could I......? dare I......? what if I......?'	
Innovate (What COULD you do?)	• Join an online forum • Find someone who's navigated this for themselves • Move jobs and reinvent myself at a new employer

Part 3: Place the relevant rating 'Not Now (NN)', 'Not Ever (NE)', 'Move Forward (MF)' in brackets next to 'Part 1: Captured and Part 2: Innovated' ideas. Move Forward (MF) are your Golden Nuggets	
Sieve (Give a rating to Part 1 & 2 ideas and innovations) • Not Now (NN) • Not Ever (NE) • Move Forward (MF)	• Ask colleagues how they see my impact (MF) • Read books on this topic (MF) • Get an internal coach (NE) • Get an external coach (NN) • Join an online forum (NN) • Find someone who's navigated this for themselves (MF) • Move jobs and reinvent myself at a new employer (NN)

Part 4: Review Part 3: Sieve and select the high-value, high-impact 'Golden Nuggets'. These are the things that excite you and which you believe will make a difference. These are Move Forward (MF)	
Golden Nuggets What are you really going to Move Forward (MF)	1. Ask colleagues how they see my impact (MF) 2. Read books on this topic (MF) 3. Find someone who's navigated this for themselves (MF)

Team Developmental-Step 3:
Capture obvious ideas, innovate and sieve for nuggets

STEP 3: – Capture the obvious, innovate and sieve for Golden Nuggets	
Part 1: With all that this team knows from Step 2 – Lay of the land, capture the low-hanging fruit, the 'we just have to do that' thinking	
Capture all ideas (What could we do?)	• Internal stakeholder survey • Seek counsel from internal stakeholders • Team brainstorm, to engage the team and enable thinking • Get a senior stakeholder to sponsor us • Ask senior stakeholders if they have an appetite for the output of our approach

Part 2: Now let the team's thinking expand to 'could we......? dare we......? what if we......?'	
Innovate (What COULD we do?)	• Speak to external teams in other industries to understand how they might have navigated this • Consider relevant books and articles that might enable us • See if a consultant/team coach could help
Part 3: Place the relevant rating 'Not Now (NN)', 'Not Ever (NE)', 'Move Forward (MF)' in brackets next to 'Part 1: Captured and Part 2: Innovated' ideas. Move Forward (MF) are your Golden Nuggets	
Sieve (Give a rating to Part 1 & 2 ideas and innovations) • Not Now (NN) • Not Ever (NE) • Move Forward (MF)	• Internal stakeholder survey (MF) • Seek counsel from internal stake-holders (MF) • Team brainstorm, to engage the team and enable thinking (NN) • Get a senior stakeholder to sponsor us (NN) • Ask senior stakeholders if they have an appetite for the output of our approach (MF) • Speak to external teams in other industries to understand how they might have navigated this (NN) • Consider relevant books and articles that might enable us (MF) • See if a consultant/team coach could help (NE)
Part 4: Review Part 3, Sieve and select the high-value, high-impact 'Golden Nuggets'. These are the things that excite you and you believe will make a difference; these are Move Forward (MF)	
Golden Nuggets What are you really going to Move Forward (MF) on?	1. Internal stakeholder survey (MF) 2. Seek counsel from internal stake-holders (MF) 3. Ask senior stakeholders if they have an appetite for the output of our approach (MF) 4. Consider relevant books and articles that might enable us (MF)

Organisation Developmental-Step 3: Capture obvious ideas, innovate and sieve for nuggets

STEP 3 – Capture the obvious, Innovate and sieve for nuggets	
Part 1: With all that this group knows from Step 2 – Lay of the land, capture what the low-hanging fruit, the 'we just have to do that' thinking	
Capture all ideas (What could we do?)	• External consultancy to do a diagnostic • Internal HR to do a diagnostic • Find examples from other organisations where this has worked • Investigate research on this topic to confirm what we suspect • Get a target audience on board as part of the thinking process
Part 2: Now let the group's thinking expand to 'could we......? dare we......? what if we......?'	
Innovate (What COULD we do?)	• Run an assessment centre to rate individuals • Get them individual coaches
Part 3: Place the relevant rating Not Now (NN), Not Ever (NE), Move Forward (MF) in brackets next to Part 1: Captured and Part 2: Innovated ideas. Move Forward (MF) are your Golden Nuggets	
Sieve (Give a rating to Part 1 & 2 ideas and innovations) • Not Now (NN) • Not Ever (NE) • Move Forward (MF)	• External consultancy to do a diagnostic (MF) • Internal HR to do a diagnostic (NE) • Find examples from other organisations where this has worked (MF) • Investigate research on this topic to evidence, what we suspect (NN) • Get one of the target audience as part of the thinking process (NN) • Run an assessment centre to rate individuals (NE) • Get them individual coaches (NN)
Part 4: Review Part 3: Sieve and select the high value, high impact 'golden nuggets'. These are the things that excite you and you believe will make a difference; these are Move Forward (MF)	
Golden Nuggets What are you really going to Move Forward (MF) on?	1. External consultancy to do a diagnostic (MF) 2. Find examples from other organisations where this has worked (MF)

Think about how prospectors used to pan for gold. You need to sieve and you need to keep watch for what you're looking for. It's easy to let things slip by in your eagerness to get the big one. But remember that a lot of nuggets soon add up!

As you or the team reject something at this point, ask the question: 'is it being rejected because it's not helpful, too difficult or there's no motivation to do it?'. If it is that 'there is no motivation' check that it's not actually the right thing to do, but there's a fear around the workload or fear of it, that is being covered up, it can often be that this is your Golden Nugget.

Step 4 – Risk mitigation

We now have a strong sense of the 'Context and the Why' (Step 1), we're clearer on the 'Lay of the land' and have a deep understanding of the reality around us (Step 2). We've documented ideas and options and we've sieved for the Golden Nuggets (Step 3).

It's time, now, to inspect the Golden Nuggets one at a time and ask: "What can mess this up?" "What are the things that I/we know, or can intelligently assume, will get in the way?" "What are the unknowns?" "How do unknowns become understood?".

In this section we're considering all possible barriers, both:

- (R) = Real
- (P) = Potential

We're saying, as far as it's possible, "This is what we know is true and this is what we can sensibly imagine being possible".

There is a danger here that two things catch you out:

1. Elephants in the Room

Are there any issues that you or others are not brave enough to discuss? Create a moment where people feel motivated, safe and brave enough to say what they are holding back.

2. Daft Factor

I am referring here to when people dismiss anything that's not tangible or immediate as not worth any effort. It takes maturity to look ahead and work on feasibility when you're worried others may see it as daft, unfocused or a flight of fancy.

For hurdles that are (P) = Potential, it's vital you and the team imagine the unknown. You have to give permission for elegant conjecture and turn down the volume on flights of unfocused fancy or scare-mongering.

Follow these four parts:

Part 1: In the first column take the Golden Nuggets from Part 4 of Step 3

Part 2: In the next column, consider all potential barriers and indicate whether they are (R) = Real, an existing barrier, or (P) = Potential, a perceived barrier

Part 3: Next you need to understand the actions that might mitigate these, so document what could/should be done

Part 4: Finally, ask who owns this?

Here is the template:

STEP 4 – Risk Mitigation			
What barriers exist for the Golden Nuggets?			
Column 1	Column 2	Column 3	Column 4
Part 1: Transfer Take Golden Nuggets that you will Move Forward (MF) from Step 3, Part 4. Place here.	**Part 2: Barriers** Think through the barriers that exist for Part 1. Note here, then add (R) = Real (actual barrier) or (P) = Potential (unknown barrier)	**Part 3: Action** What are you going to do that is: Mindset 1: Trusted Mindset 2: Accountable Mindset 3: Brave Mindset 4: Connected	**Part 4: Ownership** Who is the person that owns this? Who's fully Mindset 1: Accountable?
(Insert Golden Nugget)	• (Insert Text)	1. (Insert Text)	(Insert Text)

These are the working examples:

Individual Developmental–Step 4: Risk mitigation

STEP 4 – Risk Mitigation			
What barriers exist for the Golden Nuggets?			
Column 1	Column 2	Column 3	Column 4
Part 1: Transfer Take Golden Nuggets that you will Move Forward (MF) from Step 3, Part 4. Place here.	**Part 2: Barriers** Think through the barriers that exist for Part 1. Note here, then add (R) = Real (actual barrier) or (P) = Potential (unknown barrier)	**Part 3: Action** What are you going to do that is: • Trusted • Accountable • Brave • Connected	**Part 4: Ownership** Who is the person that owns this? Who's fully Mindset 1: Accountable?
1. Ask colleagues how they see my impact (MF)	• Some people may be less than honest to avoid embarrassing me (R) • People don't like giving feedback (P) • People have ulterior motives (P) • Unsure whether I have a licence to do this in the organisation (R)	1. Talk to people personally and allow them time to reflect 2. Get other stake-holders to talk to them to set the scene 3. Guarantee their anonymity 4. Ask for the licence to operate 5. See if anyone else has done this	Me
1. Read books on this topic (MF)	None	None	None
1. Find someone who's navigated this for them-selves (MF)	• I don't know anyone (R)	6. Seek counsel from anyone I know who has a wider network 7. Join an online forum 8. Connect with potential people on social media	Me

Team Developmental-Step 4: Risk mitigation

STEP 4 – Risk Mitigation			
What barriers exist for the Golden Nuggets?			
Column 1	Column 2	Column 3	Column 4
Part 1: Transfer Take Golden Nuggets that you will Move Forward (MF) from Step 3, Part 4. Place here.	**Part 2: Barriers** Think through the barriers that exist for Part 1. Note here, then add (R) = Real (actual barrier) or (P) = Potential (unknown barrier)	**Part 3: Action** What are you going to do that is: • Trusted • Accountable • Brave • Connected	**Part 4: Ownership** Who is the person that owns this? Who's fully Mindset 1: Accountable?
1. Internal stake-holder survey (MF)	• Some will be happy to engage. Others will see this as a waste of time (R)	1. Test the water 2. Seek advice from someone trusted (Jill Smith) 3. Seek external advice	Jack H
2. Seek counsel from internal stakeholders (MF)	• We do not know who these people would be (R) • Some senior players might tell the MD to terminate this process (P)	4. Get out there and ask 5. Brainstorm who is most likely to enable us 6. When we have identified them, ask them	Susan L Jack H
3. Ask senior stakeholders if they have an appetite for the output of our approach, ie do they want it? (MF)	• Some will be happy to engage. Others will see it as a waste of time (R)	7. Speak to our counsel about the approach 8. Test the water with a 'target' and understand the reaction	Tom
4. Consider rele-vant books and articles that might enable us (MF)	None	None	None

Organisation Developmental-Step 4: Risk mitigation

STEP 4 – Risk Mitigation			
What barriers exist for the Golden Nuggets?			
Column 1	Column 2	Column 3	Column 4
Part 1: Transfer Take Golden Nuggets that you will Move Forward (MF) from Step 3, Part 4. Place here.	**Part 2: Barriers** Think through the barriers that exist for Part 1, note here. Then add (R) = Real (actual barrier) or (P) = Potential (unknown barrier)	**Part 3: Action** What are you going to do that is: • Trusted • Accountable • Brave • Connected	**Part 4: Ownership** Who is the person that owns this? Who's fully Mindset 1: Accountable?
1. External consultancy to do a diagnostic (MF)	• No budget (P) • We don't know who to ask (R) • Might be perceived as a waste of money (P)	1. Create a case and bring to Exec Team 2. Ask HR to investigate 3. Ask own contacts 4. Ensure we all believe in its validity and then stand by that	Lucy L Sian M
2. Find examples from other organisations where this has worked (MF)	• We don't know any (R) • Don't have the resources to figure it out (P)	5. Ask own contacts 6. Cost proposal, no more than two slides, keep it simple	Jasper C Charlotte F

When completed there should be a real sense of belief and confidence in the way you are able to Face Into the known and unknown situations ahead. Any movement forward causes a disturbance at some level, as even the most elegant of crafts in the water creates shift as it manoeuvres. Step 4 is about having a sense of readiness and a methodology to follow.

STEP 5: COMMITTED ACTION

Despite trepidation or uncertainty, now is the time for Committed Action. All the planning, thinking, reflecting and speculating in the world is only ever going to give you the best bet as things stand right now, with the information you have right now. There's a great military analogy that says, 'everyone has a plan until the first bullets fly'. It's saying two things:

1. All the planning in the world can go straight out the window when reality plays out
2. Having a plan and a way to plan, keeps the focus when things don't go as you wanted

Many of the people I speak with refer to Committed Action. Mark (Ted) O'Brien, Head of Learning at Fire Service College and previously Head of Incident Command, speaks about knowing when to move to action, "It's easy to plan. You can plan and plan and plan. But there's a time to move, even when you're not sure what the answer is. I believe in planning, success comes from planning; however, when you look back on everything you did, you can always recognise that specific moment when it was time to move, to act, to press on. Ultimately, it's often appropriate to say 'start moving, listen to your training and figure it out as you go'."

Committed Action means moving intelligently to action in a way that allows for constant calibration. Think about people on the playing field. They have to be moving continuously, they require a vision (of being a winning team), they need purpose (to achieve as a team and not through just one person's excellence), a set strategy (of playing within a certain framework) and a plan (rehearsed set pieces and responses to various scenarios).

My personal observation as a martial arts coach is that you can plan and rehearse until you believe you've covered every eventuality. Often it transpires the other person has a plan as well and it is to mess with your plan to mess with their plan. You may not have considered or at least believed their skill set is more advanced than yours. It's at these moments that willingness to adapt is paramount. If what you're doing isn't working, then perhaps a thing you can't imagine working might be the option. If what you're doing is failing, why do you still believe that the 'impossible' option is the wrong one?

It's true that Committed Action requires a fixed focus, a Face Into it attitude; however, it also requires Intelligent Action. This means fully Committed Action coupled with curiosity and speed to adjust. Committed Action is a commitment to the road ahead combined with the understanding, for you or the team, of where the energy must be directed, where the discretionary effort will come in to play and where the mindset and the will to move forward solidifies. The elegance and the craft, remain largely in the learning and the adjustments you make, followed by the drive to move forward again, growing stronger as you go.

DON'T EAT THE RED HERRING

The world is designed to distract you from Committed Action so, now more than ever, there's a sense that things should be easier and that there are distractions that will enhance your life.

Eat some extra food, don't exercise today, avoid that awkward conversation, watch TV, go to a party, don't learn, play instead, just show you are busy and valuable, blame others, lose sight of your personal needs, subjugate yourself to the demands of the workplace, attack or pull away rather than hold your position.

Life will always offer diversions and get-out-of-jail-free cards. It's almost as if you're in a giant, whole-lifetime assessment that's designed to constantly test whether you will do the right thing or wrong thing, to see if you will take the easy road or the one less-travelled. It's as if the assessors are creating constant dilemmas for you. Will you go left instead of right? Take the blue pill or the red one[53]?

Committed Action is for those moments when there has to be movement and it needs the weight of will, motivation, energy and focus. This is for the individual whose need to succeed in the endeavour is paramount. It's for when the team's collective agreement decrees this must happen. It's also when the organisation recognises the value of this behaviour as both a strategic process and a cultural imperative.

Committed Action is accurately described by Major General Paul Nanson, CBE, "There are times when a situation turns on its head and the plan is no longer in play, when the lives of the team, or the people you have responsibility for, are at risk and the situation has to shift and shift now. These are the times when the plan, whether it's well thought through or coming as a reflex response, needs you or the team to not just do it, but to take a form of, in Living Brave parlance, Committed Action."

I like the way Paul speaks about this. It's similar to every high performing leader that I've interviewed or experienced. It starts with their recognition that the situation requires a plan/response and that Living Brave requires an intellectual, emotional and physical commitment.

When he was CEO of the Rugby Football Union, Ian Ritchie said, "When I came to the RFU it had some great things that needed reinforcing and we recognised we should do more of those things. At the other end of the spectrum, there were things that my experience told me had to change. Of course, when you make these decisions you have to factor in the internal politics, the response from external observers and how those in the organisation feel. It goes without saying that only history will tell you if you've got it right, and some things can be drip-fed in. However, some things, perhaps a process, a set of cultural behaviours, an individual's mindset or a strategic direction that no longer works, need to be exorcised quickly because they are damaging. These are the things, in the language of Living Brave, that, once planned for, require Committed Action. They have to happen at pace and with commitment."

Again you can hear that Committed Action is not about unstructured actions, or about diving in headfirst with no care. It's about intelligent, elegant, capable action.

The template to be completed:

STEP 5 - Committed Action
Commitments to making the Step 4 Golden Nugget actions happen (make them real and personalise)
(Insert Text)

The working example:

Individual Developmental-Step 5: Committed Action

STEP 5 - Committed Action
Commitments to making the Step 4 Golden Nugget actions happen (make them real and personalise)
<ul><li>I am not going to give in, this is important to me</li><li>I will reach out to those with more experience, even if this isn't normally my nature</li><li>I have stopped reading books because I find they take too long. But the internet etc and audiobooks means I should be able to digest things faster</li><li>I am going to treat Step 6 as if I was checking in with a coach and being held to account. I need to hold myself to account.</li></ul>

Team Developmental-Step 5: Committed Action

STEP 5 - Committed Action
Commitments to making the Step 4 Golden Nugget actions happen (make them real and personalise)

- We need stakeholders to do the things they promised to do and we will approach them as individuals and as a team to add weight to our requests
- We will commit to regular conversations and set up a project group on our internal discussion board. It can be a closed group but we will stay connected
- We will learn how to Face Into on our fears about getting senior advocacy
- Commit to purchasing the books we need, summarise them for others and move at pace to increase our capability and confidence in this knowledge area

Organisation Developmental-Step 5: Committed Action

STEP 5 - Committed Action
Commitments to making the Step 4 Golden Nugget actions happen (make them real and personalise)

- All contribute to finding the budget
- Lead the way in looking outside of ourselves.
- Demonstrate we have regular streams of new thinking and external input.
- We can stand on the shoulders of others

STEP 6 - CALIBRATE AND CONTINUE

The final step in the process is one of vigilance. It's the commitment to review actions, to make changes, to reinforce the good things that are shining through and to bring challenge where undesirable things are happening.

The activities up to this point are quite easy. They are fundamentally reflective, intellectual exercises and the excitement of the first burst of energy. Be aware they can give a false sense of security around the reality of the work that needs doing.

You know when someone starts a new activity and they are super motivated at the idea of it, the preparation for it, the initial start of it... however when the reality of hard work and commitment start to rear their heads, the whole thing falls apart. You've almost certainly done it over something, you may even do it a lot, you have seen it in others and in the collective of a team or organisation.

CALIBRATION

Think about Calibration as moving in with someone after you have been dating them, it doesn't stop being exciting but it becomes a different experience.

In this step, you really have to take a position of 'this is what defines me', 'this is what defines us'. If you don't see this phase through you are in danger of creating a habit in yourself or the team that is one of non-completion. At an unconscious level, the danger is that you won't develop the bravery and the instinct to 'Face Into' to something you want to change as unconsciously you will know you are unlikely to see it through.

This will be a key element to the stories you create and your Legend. This is about you having 'checkpoints' this is where you make the 'commitment to the commitment' it's the willingness to ask, "How am I really doing?", "How are we really doing?". It's the hunger for feedback, to know:

- Things are working so let's keep going, do more, don't stop
- Our actions are only partly effective, so let's make the changes to hit the mark, let's keep going, don't stop
- This is not working, let's understand why, be brave, Face Into it, keep going, don't stop

Dawn Airey, when CEO at Getty, said: "The reality of making changes in an organisation is a set of component parts. It's listening to people, bringing your own insights, having the debate (where possible), making a decision, moving at pace and then holding yourself and others to account. That 'holding to account' means celebrating the good, the learning from the things that don't work and creating vibrancy and energy around moving closer to the end-game."

Step 6 is about recognising that most things don't go in straight lines, they go in zig-zags. You may enter dark tunnels of uncertainty but being honest and accountable creates an energy around the journey and, most importantly, and I can't stress this enough, you must have a culture that holds people to account yet does not blame and shame. That's not easy, especially when people are inherently fearful of being vulnerable.

The intent in Step 6: Calibrate and Continue, is to ensure that you are on target, it's to check-in and to celebrate success and to challenge where things have not gone well.

It's fair to say that some things do happen outside of your control, but at the same time it's not the 'what happened that we couldn't control' it's the 'what did we do with what we can control' and 'what did we do in response to the things that we cannot control?'

I have used the word 'control' here and it's a word that sometimes has a response "well I can't control that person or that circumstance" and that's true but you can influence those involved in the short to long term and you definitely can control the way in which you and the team react to things that are happening around you.

Remember that this isn't about what happened to you or those around you, the Legend of you and the team is cemented in what you actually did for better or for worse. Whether you develop Trust in yourself, whether others develop Trust in you, or the team will only partially hinge on the success of the endeavour, it will often be affected by the manner of you during the endeavour.

At this step, it's not as simple as "did I/we do it?" It is also very much the "how did I/we deal with the things that happened?"

CELEBRATION VS RECOGNITION

The idea is to 'recognise' the success of an action well done, which needs to be done as per the job role expectation, for your own self-worth and that of the team. However, to also 'celebrate' the actions that came as a result of the known and unknown barriers that presented themselves and how they were dealt with.

The point is that the story of you or your team is not as singular as a tick in the box for something working, it's about the learning, the commitment, the what you had to Face Into things, the bravery and the recognition that success usually happens in a squiggly line, not a straight one.

Understanding that there may be the need to truly dig deep into one's personal makeup and recognise that you may need to reflect on your own behaviour and to make adjustments. That if you cannot find the competence or commitment to do so then in terms of Living Brave, accept that and seek counsel. Who can help? What can help? Read the right book, speak to the right person, get on a forum and ask for support, get a coach.

Do what you must do to make the steps that you have to, this is about intelligent learning, about the recognition that you may well be excellent at moving forward in certain spheres but weak in others, and that is ok.

If necessary, do another Living Brave process for this set of actions. However, recognise that thoughts without action are a self-defeating loop. This is the road of the procrastinator and hiding behind continual planning is a signal to look out for.

Don't be that person, don't be that team, don't be that organisation. If this is truly about Living Brave in relation to the output you want and defining yourself, the team, the organisation as Living Brave then this is another key moment…. Face Into it.

This is where you and team need….BIG PANTS.

WHAT TO DO NEXT

The homeward straight can both galvanise and disengage people. Some see the end and with renewed vigour head for it and in the hurdles along the way they are again energised in the challenge, they Face into it and embody Living Brave. Even at this late stage, those that seem to have been in the race can fall as they are tired, disillusioned or let down by other factors.

This stage is the key moment:

- Have things been achieved?
- Have I/we done what I/we said we would?
- Have I/we Faced into the conversations that needed to be had?
- Have I/we walked the walk or talked the talk?

- Have we adapted?
- What is the quality of the narrative around my/our actions?

Reflect on Step 4: Risk Mitigation, look at Part 3 and give each point a Red, Amber, Green (RAG) rating.

- Those that are Green celebrate, let people know that things are moving forward, take encouragement from small successes to build resilience for the bigger, more difficult challenges.
- Anything that is Amber or Red for whatever reason drops into the next checkpoint and the process keeps on until completion and a final closure statement.

Closure statements are important. They create a way of capturing a journey and the thinking, success, hurdles, barriers, actions and bravery.

This is the template:

STEP 6 – Calibrate to closure	
• Reference Step 4, Column 3, give a Red, Amber, Green (RAG Rating) • Check in at agreed interval to reinforce effort and/or bring a challenge to inaction • Red & Amber items drop through into next checkpoint	
Calibrate each as Red, Amber or Green. Make notes to comment, celebrate and drive forward	
Checkpoint 1: Target 00.00.0000 Actual 00.00.0000	(Insert Text)
Red & Amber items drop through into next checkpoint	
Checkpoint 2: Target 00.00.0000 Actual 00.00.0000	(Insert Text)
As many checkpoints as required	
Closure statement Date: 00.00.0000	(Insert Text)

The working template

Individual Developmental-Step 6: Calibrate to closure

STEP 6 – Calibrate to closure	
<ul><li>Reference Step 4, Column 3, give a Red, Amber, Green (RAG Rating)</li><li>Check in at agreed interval to reinforce effort and/or bring a challenge to inaction</li><li>Red & Amber items drop through into next checkpoint</li></ul>	
Calibrate each as Red, Amber or Green. Make notes to comment, celebrate and drive forward	
Checkpoint 1: Target 11.01.2032 Actual 11.01.2032	1. (Green) This has gone well and I have some useful observations and received commitments to help 2. (Green) Stakeholders were mostly helpful, some not so, but those that were made the difference 3. (Green) Great reactions to this and built real Trust 4. (Amber) Not done yet, have an appointment next Tuesday 5. (Red) Felt like I was too busy and felt a bit embarrassed asking. With reflection, I should have done this and will review for next check-in 6. (Red) Felt like I was too busy and felt a bit embarrassed asking. With reflection, I should have done this and will review for next check-in 7. (Red) Felt like I was too busy and felt a bit embarrassed asking. With reflection, I should have done this and will review for next check-in 8. (Red) Felt like I was too busy and felt a bit embarrassed asking. With reflection, I should have done this and will review for next check-in
Red & Amber items drop through into next checkpoint	
Checkpoint 2: Target 11.03.2032 Actual 02.04.2032	4. (Green) Asked about the licence to operate and was basically told 'yes' so that went well and shows that I am stepping into that more senior space. Pleased with that 5. (Green) Started 'seeking counsel'; thought about where I was on the Accountability Line and what I was fearful of. Thought about the Connections to my Story. Used the 'seeking counsel' mindset which helped me not feel weak. Getting great support and ideas 6. (Amber) I have found this more tricky, I have started to ask those I do know if there is anyone they can introduce me to. Finding that people are keen to help if they buy-in to what I am trying to create and they trust you 7. (Green) I found a few online organisations/forums on LinkedIn etc and they are surprisingly useful and people eager to share

	8. (Green) Meeting a peer from another company, she is working through something similar and we want to see if we can support each other
	As many checkpoints as required
Closure statement Date: 14.06.2032	So, the reading is going well and I'm picking up tips and advice. Getting feedback off people was an eye-opener. Heard some things I liked and some I didn't, however, in doing this I have ended up raising my profile as I have raised my head above the parapet. I'd say with some people I have shifted my brand and the 'story' of me is shifting with a few people (Sandra D and John T in particular). It feels as if they are looking at me to see change. On top of that finding, Jacqui G as a sounding board has been so useful. So glad I didn't let that go. She's really helped me see things from a different perspective. Really surprised that someone is so willing to help someone so much when they are not personally invested. The external conversations have been an eye-opener. Have shown me I'm not alone others' perspectives have shone a light on my actions. In conclusion, It feels as if I have genuine momentum. Things are happening. The trick now is to 'Face Into'. I can say 'I'm Living Brave'!

Team Developmental-Step 6: Calibrate to closure

STEP 6 – Calibrate to closure
• Reference Step 4, Column 3, give a Red, Amber, Green (RAG Rating) • Check in at agreed interval to reinforce effort and/or bring a challenge to inaction • Red & Amber items drop through into next checkpoint
Calibrate each as Red, Amber or Green. Make notes to comment, celebrate and drive forward

Checkpoint 1: Target 09.01.2032 Actual 09.01. 2032	1. (Amber) Not done very well here. We have been a bit half-hearted in who we dealt with. We need help building our confidence to approach some of the more senior stakeholders 2. (Green) Brilliant, she laid it on the line for us and we have to Face Into the fact we still need to develop our confidence and methodology 3. (Green) So again this went well. Some really good conversations had in some other unrelated organisations, via our own Connections. Telling us 'again' that we are not as brave as we need to be. In terms of Living Brave we need to review our Mindset 1: Accountability, accepting we are below the line and recognise we don't have a high Mindset 2: Brave score. We have also recognised that we are talking a good talk but in terms of being Mindset 3: Connected we are very Pull rather than Connected.

	4. (Amber) (Repeat of Point 1) Not done very well here. It's been a bit halfhearted in who we have all gone at. We need help in gaining confidence to approach some of the more senior stakeholders
	5. (Green) All done, we have a great stakeholder map
	6. (Green) Was easy to work out who we should be speaking to
	7. (Green) Gone well, had great advice and showed us the pace and style of approach
	8. (Red) Not done
Red & Amber items drop through into next checkpoint	
Checkpoint 2: Target 11.05.2032 Actual 11.05.2032	1. (Green) We have been talking to people. Going very well and everyone is agreeing to contribute, especially when they found out the Exec team agreed. The story appears to be forming and people see that we are trying to move things forward
	4. (Green) There's a head of steam now. As the interest grows in what we are doing, people are offering to help, guide, counsel. We just need to be careful we don't have too many chiefs trying to steer us and end up in the same submissive place again
	8. (Amber) So we targeted 2 and have done one. The team member who didn't approach their target is unclear as to why they didn't. The rest of the team are disappointed however we hope to enable and support that member
As many checkpoints as required	
Closure statement Date: 14.05.2032	Great strides made. We have approached all stakeholders. We have an active group of advisors and we are learning as individuals and as a team. It feels like a real momentum has been built. We have had to have some really tough conversations with each other and have received some cumulative feedback that hurt our egos, however, the story now is shifting to us not being a group of people interacting, but a group of people working to become a team. The surveys we have done have been hugely insightful and created a real catalyst for us to change. We really must keep the momentum going now as we have created an expectation. We have a strong set of Umbrella Beliefs and these are being constantly reinforced by thinking of the four Living Brave Mindsets of Trust, Accountability, Bravery and Connection

Organisation Developmental-Step 6: Calibrate to closure

STEP 6 – Calibrate to closure	
• Reference Step 4, Column 3, give a Red, Amber, Green (RAG Rating) • Check in at agreed interval to reinforce effort and/or bring a challenge to inaction • Red & Amber items drop through into next checkpoint	
Calibrate each as Red, Amber or Green. Make notes to comment, celebrate and drive forward	
Checkpoint 1: Target 02.01.25 Actual 05.01.2033	1. (Amber) Created but only by a few of us. Some of the team seemed to opt out of the reality of doing the work. We have had to have some very real conversations about Accountability and the focus of some people in terms of Trust. Seems we have pressed the reset button 2. (Green) HR has been excellent, they know good people and have brought forward some great external people for us to consider working with 3. (Amber) Some yes and no here. See first bullet. The same people and same outcome 4. (Amber) See first bullet. The same people and same outcome 5. (Amber) See first bullet. The same people and same outcome 6. (Green) This is done and is a simple and succinct 2 pager/slides. We intend to get a pre-meeting to get the challenge out the way before we get into the room
Red & Amber items drop through into next checkpoint	
Checkpoint 2: Target 11.03.2033 Actual 02.04.2033	1. (Green) All done, we kept it short after the counsel we received. It went well with the cost proposal. Very good team effort on this. Everyone got involved, felt good and the output is strong 3. (Green) We were a bit weak here, but HR nailed it with some great contacts 4. (Green) Feels like a team now, after a false start. We just need to keep the focus 5. (Green) As above after the chat; we have really made strides in this. We have reached out to a lot of high-quality people and got some real insights that we would never have thought of
Red & Amber items drop through into next checkpoint	
Closure statement Date: 13.07.2033	Final note. I think we all feel that we have done well. We didn't gel right at the start, so we had to put our big pants on in order to have those Accountability and Bravery conversations. The proof though is in the pudding. The Exec bought into it immediately. Some great comments about us having seen an issue found solutions and moved them to a point of planned action. So we are now in the process of working with a small but well-regarded consultancy that has a lot of great clients and great testimonials. It's taught us a lot about the power of the team and we are starting to see how Living Brave can really enable us as a team and as leaders of the organisation, not just leaders in the organisation.

PROCESS CONCLUSION

It can be hard work.

Let me change that...it is hard work to put the grind in, to Face Into the challenge of the craft. It's hard work to reflect, create the Umbrella Beliefs, and apply yourself to the thinking that Living Brave suggests as being an approach that will enable you. The templates above are a demonstration of approach, they are there to help you think in a structured way and to show you that nothing good ever came from whimsy, but from hard work.

It's a craft...so Face Into it and get stuck in.

Things to reflect on:

- Am I/Are we prepared to Face Into the work?
- Who could/should I/we involve in the process?
- There are no short cuts

CONCLUSION

This is where we look at

Owning your own space | Living Brave as a shield |
The 'If, Should, Can't Chicken'

CONCLUSION

"Don't fear failure so much that you refuse to try new things. The saddest summary of a life contains three descriptions: could have, might have, and should have."

- Louis E. Boone

Living Brave as a conscious choice to act in a manner of your choosing, it is intentional leadership enabling you to define your own space and the manner in which you want to approach the world. It is also clear that with taking a position comes the reality of taking space and in doing so you are overtly holding a position that others will react to in the positive, curious and the negative. Embrace that. Face Into it.

The thinking, mindset and methodology of Living Brave is the reality of leadership of oneself and the belief that when we are leaders of ourselves, then we are fit to follow and be followed. You may be in a place of positional power or you may not; if you are not you require no permission to adopt the mindset of a leader.

Understand that your place in the world if calibrated elegantly and with integrity will feed your resilience. However, it will require Trust, in the first instance in yourself that you are going to live up to your own expectations of yourself, secondarily in you from others. You will have to constantly reposition and challenge yourself to operate with Accountability to your own Umbrella Beliefs, to be Brave and Connected in pursuing your focus.

It's going to require Umbrella Beliefs that engage and excite, Levers that catalyse, making sure you Face Into things and Big Pants to apply this visioning, pushing forward and focusing on the things that are important enough that you are committed to them in such a way that you see things through, while quietly or loudly Living Brave.

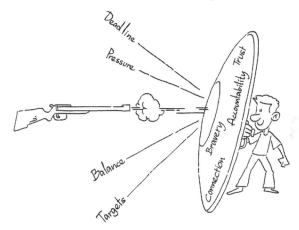

One might say that in Living Brave you are placing yourself into harm's way from time to time and the answer is clearly 'yes' and that's the Living Brave bit, otherwise this would be a book on action planning and diary management.

CALL TO ARMS

Within all this is an undercurrent of helping society, in a time where it truly needs people to be Living Brave. There is a clear focus on ourselves as individuals to improve and calibrate our impact within our own lives and that of others and thus to enable the organisation that we work within. The key perspective is one of 'leader of self', to become leaders of ourselves and not to be passive bystanders. To do this with a recognition that none of these actions requires positional power, because Trust, Accountability, Bravery and Connection are not the domain of the anointed. It's about your ability to grow and develop the human parts of your mindset and actions that create Trust in your way of being that others want to then emulate, that enables them to want the same.

This is the impact on society, this is where organisations should place their focus, on enabling people to understand the mindset and demonstrate the actions that mean their people are vibrant, elegant, resilient participants in society. This is the call to arms.

YOU AREN'T BROKEN... UNLESS YOU DO NOTHING

My strongly held belief is that most of us are Living Brave in many ways, in our everyday realities, let me reiterate, life is not easy, it just isn't. All the power in the world means nothing, all the emotional realities that happen to poor people happen to rich people, the only difference is that a rich person has the experience in more luxurious surroundings.

Believe me, whether someone is wearing a Casio or a Rolex, emotions are the same, the foundations of Living Brave when it comes to Trust, Accountability, Bravery and Connection cut through all the trappings, all the bluff and bravado. Believe me on that.

We all have something now or in our future, that will require the focus of a Living Brave mindset to ensure it is conquered. We all have someone now or in our future that we can enable through this thinking.

These challenges some known and many yet unknown are without question best prepared for with strong Umbrella Beliefs, Trust creation, full Accountability, conscious Bravery and being fully Connected to your own and others context.

As you start on your journey to your own relationship with Living Brave and as you enable others to theirs, it's worth thinking about the If, Should, Can't, Do grid.

Fig 21: If, Should, Can't, Do

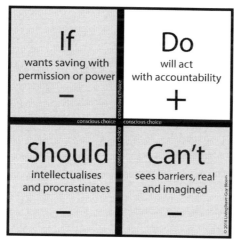

This four-box grid is a simple yet incredibly effective way of asking yourself and others where "am I/are we right now?" If the answer has you, the team, the organisation in any box other than the top right 'Do' box, it's time to start Living Brave, for something that should be changing isn't. And if it stays that way it can create damage to yourself or others around you.

DO	I/we will act, work at it, learn and challenge ourselves to act on that learning
IF	I/we would act if things were different, so I/we are powerless
SHOULD	I/we should act but there are a lot of hurdles and things I/we don't control
CAN'T	I/we can't act and I/we have doubt, anxiety and fear so I/we do nothing

'IF, SHOULD, CAN'T' CHICKEN

Ever heard of the 'if, should, can't chicken'? Thought not, however you know it very well. Think of a chicken in the farmyard and each time they peck you hear 'if' or 'should' or 'can't', now swap that image for a person, who in conversation pecks away at your ability to trust them and the ability of others to trust you via association. As they speak, you can hear "Of course and that would work if, but......", "well yes I know we should, however.....", "hey no argument from me, it's just that we can't do that, so......." There are as many versions of this as you can think of, you hear it in others and you know when you are doing it.

Now let's be clear it's intelligent to recognise the situation you are in, there are barriers, there are things you can't control, there are things you can't change, however, that's not the point.

You are an 'if, should, can't' chicken not for seeing the truth of the situation, not for feeling the emotions that go with that, not even for going into those sections for a few moments.

You are an 'if, should, can't chicken' if you stay there and even worse if you try to get others to agree with you, not on the intellectual level that something isn't right, but at the emotional level getting people to join you below the line of Accountability.

So, operate from 'Do', knowing full well that you may succeed (great, keep going), you may not (learn, Face Into it).

MAKE YOUR OWN KIND OF LIVING BRAVE

This is it, you made it to the end of the book. Well done. I don't know about you, but I was emotional when I finished writing it. Not floods of tears emotional, though there was an element of that for the completion of the 3rd edit. The emotion was a reinforcement and a personal calibration of this is what I am, this is who I am, this is who I am going to be.

Knowing that I often don't get it right but I am clear in my mind what my Umbrella Beliefs are, I want to be Trusted, Accountable, Brave, Connected and I want to enable individuals, teams and organisations to step into their own Living Brave space.

So, you now know what you have to do, find your Levers, Face Into things, put your Big Pants on and don't be an 'if, should, can't' chicken.

You know the question:

"What would you do if you were Living Brave?"

BLANK TEMPLATE

STEP 1 – Context & Why	
What's the context?	What's the 'why it matters'?
(Insert Text)	The thing I am wrestling with is... (Insert Text) **It needs to change because...** (Insert Text) **If it doesn't change, the impact will likely be...** (Insert Text) **The benefits of this would be to...** (Insert Text)

STEP 2 – Lay of the land	
Column 1	Column 2
Part 1: Which number from Context Grid + associated reflection	**Part 2:** 'Important' or 'Not Important'. (Red, Amber or Green)
(Insert Text)	Important (Red)
(Insert Text)	Important (Amber)
(Insert Text)	Important (Green)
(Insert Text)	Not Important (Red)
(Insert Text)	Not Important (Amber)
(Insert Text)	Not Important (Green)

STEP 3 – Capture obvious ideas, innovate and sieve for Golden Nuggets	
Part 1: With all that you know from Step 2 – Lay of the land, capture the low-hanging fruit, the 'I just have to do that' thinking	
Capture all ideas (What could you do?)	• (Insert Text)
Part 2: Now let your thinking expand to 'could I......? dare I......? what if I......?'	
Innovate (What COULD you do?)	• (Insert Text)
Part 3: Place the relevant rating 'Not Now (NN)', 'Not Ever (NE)', 'Move Forward (MF)' in brackets next to 'Part 1: Captured and Part 2: Innovated' ideas. Move Forward (MF) are your Golden Nuggets	
Sieve (Give a rating to Part 1 & 2 ideas and innovations) • Not Now (NN) • Not Ever (NE) • Move Forward (MF)	• (Insert Text)

Part 4: Review Part 3: Sieve and select the high-value, high-impact 'Golden Nuggets'. These are the things that excite you and which you believe will make a difference. These are Move Forward (MF)	
Golden Nuggets What are you really going to Move Forward (MF)	• (Insert Text)

STEP 4 – Risk Mitigation

What barriers exist for the Golden Nuggets?

Column 1	Column 2	Column 3	Column 4
Part 1: Transfer Take Golden Nuggets that you will Move Forward (MF) from Step 3, Part 4. Place here.	**Part 2: Barriers** Think through the barriers that exist for Part 1. Note here, then add (R) = Real (actual barrier) or (P) = Potential (unknown barrier)	**Part 3: Action** What are you going to do that is: Mindset 1: Trusted Mindset 2: Accountable Mindset 3: Brave Mindset 4: Connected	**Part 4: Ownership** Who is the person that owns this? Who's fully Mindset 1: Accountable?
(Insert Golden Nugget)	• (Insert Text)	1. (Insert Text)	(Insert Text)

STEP 5 – Committed Action

Commitments to making the Step 4 Golden Nugget actions happen (make them real and personalise)

(Insert Text)

STEP 6 – Calibrate to closure

- Reference Step 4, Column 3, give a Red, Amber, Green (RAG Rating)
- Check in at agreed interval to reinforce effort and/or bring a challenge to inaction
- Red & Amber items drop through into next checkpoint

Calibrate each as Red, Amber or Green. Make notes to comment, celebrate and drive forward

Checkpoint 1: Target 00.00.0000 Actual 00.00.0000	(Insert Text)

Red & Amber items drop through into next checkpoint	
Checkpoint 2: Target 00.00.0000 Actual 00.00.0000	(Insert Text)
As many checkpoints as required	
Closure statement Date: 00.00.0000	(Insert Text)

INDIVIDUAL DEVELOPMENT
COMPLETED TEMPLATE

STEP 1 – Context & Why	
What's the context?	What's the 'why it matters'?
Recognition in organisation	**The thing I am wrestling with is…** I am not getting the recognition that I want in the organisation. **It needs to change because…** Iam losing career credibility and career traction. **If it doesn't change, the impact will likely be…** that I will stagnate and become disengaged and then either leave or stay and become unfulfilled. **The benefits of this would be to…** find my motivation, not feel undervalued, and get back on my career track.

STEP 2 – Lay of the land	
Column 1	Column 2
Part 1: Which number from Context Grid + associated reflection	Part 2: 'Important' or 'Not Important'. (Red, Amber or Green)
3. Key internal stakeholders' thoughts on me (I don't actually know) 5. My overall market knowledge (I'm not that clued up)	Important (Red)
1. My personal impact (I have some insight, but only from friends)	Important (Amber)
2. Team insights on me (very good info, after recent 360)	Important (Green)
7. My impact in the world (right now beyond my ability to focus on)	Not Important (Red)
1. Qualifications for credibility (don't feel it's important, however other senior people have got qualifications that I haven't)	Not Important (Amber)
4. Client strategic focus (Well bedded-in with clients so well-versed here)	Not Important (Green)

STEP 3 – Capture obvious ideas, innovate and sieve for Golden Nuggets	
Part 1: With all that you know from Step 2 – Lay of the land, capture the low-hanging fruit, the 'I just have to do that' thinking	
Capture all ideas (What could you do?)	• Ask colleagues how they see my impact • Read books on this topic

	• Get an internal coach • Get an external coach
Part 2: Now let your thinking expand to 'could I......? dare I......? what if I......?'	
Innovate (What COULD you do?)	• Join an online forum • Find someone who's navigated this for themselves • Move jobs and reinvent myself at a new employer
Part 3: Place the relevant rating 'Not Now (NN)', 'Not Ever (NE)', 'Move Forward (MF)' in brackets next to 'Part 1: Captured and Part 2: Innovated' ideas. Move Forward (MF) are your Golden Nuggets	
Sieve (Give a rating to Part 1 & 2 ideas and innovations) • Not Now (NN) • Not Ever (NE) • Move Forward (MF)	• Ask colleagues how they see my impact (MF) • Read books on this topic (MF) • Get an internal coach (NE) • Get an external coach (NN) • Join an online forum (NN) • Find someone who's navigated this for themselves (MF) • Move jobs and reinvent myself at a new employer (NN)
Part 4: Review Part 3: Sieve and select the high-value, high-impact 'Golden Nuggets'. These are the things that excite you and which you believe will make a difference. These are Move Forward (MF)	
Golden Nuggets What are you really going to Move Forward (MF)	1. Ask colleagues how they see my impact (MF) 2. Read books on this topic (MF) 3. Find someone who's navigated this for themselves (MF)

STEP 4 – Risk Mitigation

What barriers exist for the Golden Nuggets?

Column 1	Column 2	Column 3	Column 4
Part 1: Transfer Take Golden Nuggets that you will Move Forward (MF) from Step 3, Part 4. Place here.	**Part 2: Barriers** Think through the barriers that exist for Part 1. Note here, then add (R) = Real (actual barrier) or (P) = Potential (unknown barrier)	**Part 3: Action** What are you going to do that is: Mindset 1: Trusted Mindset 2: Accountable Mindset 3: Brave Mindset 4: Connected	**Part 4: Ownership** Who is the person that owns this? Who's fully Mindset 1: Accountable?
1. Ask colleagues how they see my impact (MF)	• Some people may be less than honest to avoid embarrassing me (R) • People don't like giving feedback (P) • People have ulterior motives (P) • Unsure whether I have a licence to do this in the organisation (R)	1. Talk to people personally and allow them time to reflect 2. Get other stakeholders to talk to them to set the scene 3. Guarantee their anonymity 4. Ask for the licence to operate 5. See if anyone else has done this	Me
2. Read books on this topic (MF)	None	None	None
3. Find someone who's navigated this for themselves (MF)	• I don't know anyone (R)	1. Seek counsel from anyone I know who has a wider network 2. Join an online forum 3. Connect with potential people on social media	Me

STEP 5 – Committed Action

Commitments to making the Step 4 Golden Nugget actions happen (make them real and personalise)

- I am not going to give in, this is important to me
- I will reach out to those with more experience, even if this isn't normally my nature
- I have stopped reading books because I find they take too long. But the internet etc and audiobooks means I should be able to digest things faster
- I am going to treat Step 6 as if I was checking in with a coach and being held to account. I need to hold myself to account.

STEP 6 – Calibrate to closure

- Reference Step 4, Column 3, give a Red, Amber, Green (RAG Rating)
- Check in at agreed interval to reinforce effort and/or bring a challenge to inaction
- Red & Amber items drop through into next checkpoint

Calibrate each as Red, Amber or Green. Make notes to comment, celebrate and drive forward

Checkpoint 1: Target 11.01.2032 Actual 11.01.2032	1. (Green) This has gone well and I have some useful observations and received commitments to help 2. (Green) Stakeholders were mostly helpful, some not so, but those that were made the difference 3. (Green) Great reactions to this and built real Trust 4. (Amber) Not done yet, have an appointment next Tuesday 5. (Red) Felt like I was too busy and felt a bit embarrassed asking. With reflection, I should have done this and will review for next check-in 6. (Red) Felt like I was too busy and felt a bit embarrassed asking. With reflection, I should have done this and will review for next check-in 7. (Red) Felt like I was too busy and felt a bit embarrassed asking. With reflection, I should have done this and will review for next check-in 8. (Red) Felt like I was too busy and felt a bit embarrassed asking. With reflection, I should have done this and will review for next check-in
Red & Amber items drop through into next checkpoint	
Checkpoint 2: Target 11.03.2032 Actual 02.04.2032	1. (Green) Asked about the licence to operate and was basically told 'yes' so that went well and shows that I am stepping into that more senior space. Pleased with that 2. (Green) Started 'seeking counsel'; thought about where I was on the Accountability Line and what I was fearful of. Thought about the Connections to my Story. Used the 'seeking counsel' mindset which helped me not feel weak. Getting great support and ideas 3. (Amber) I have found this more tricky, I have started to ask those I do know if there is anyone they can introduce me to. Finding that people are keen to help if they buy-in to what

	you are trying to create and they trust you
	4. (Green) I found a few online organisations/forums on LinkedIn etc and they are surprisingly useful and people eager to share
	5. (Green) Meeting a peer from another company, she is working through something similar and we want to see if we can support each other
As many checkpoints as required	
Closure statement Date: 14.06.2032	So, the reading is going well and I'm picking up tips and advice. Getting feedback off people was an eye-opener. Heard some things I liked and some I didn't, however, in doing this I have ended up raising my profile as I have raised my head above the parapet. I'd say with some people I have shifted my brand and the 'story of me is shifting with a few people (Sandra D and John T in particular). It feels as if they are looking at me to see change. On top of that finding, Jacqui G as a sounding board has been so useful. So glad I didn't let that go. She's really helped me see things from a different perspective. Really surprised that someone is so willing to help someone so much when they are not personally invested. The external conversations have been an eye-opener. Have shown me I'm not alone others' perspectives have shone a light on my actions. In conclusion, It feels as if I have genuine momentum. Things are happening. The trick now is to 'Face Into'. I can say 'I'm Living Brave'!

Team Development
COMPLETED TEMPLATE

STEP 1 – Context & Why	
What's the context?	What's the 'why it matters'?
Relevance as a team	**The thing we are wrestling with is...** our ability to remain relevant as a team within the organisation. We are losing or can't maintain partner status within key organisation areas. **It needs to change because...** we will be pigeon-holed as a purely administrative function. **If it doesn't change the impact will likely be...** that we will be disbanded, performance-managed, restructured. **The benefits of this would be to...** re-establish credibility, add value to the organisation, cement our roles and not live in constant uncertainty, even fear

STEP 2 – Lay of the land	
Column 1	Column 2
Part 1: Which number from Context Grid + associated reflection	**Part 2:** 'Important' or 'Not Important'. (Red, Amber or Green)
7. Be knowledgeable in factors outside of the organisation (we don't know much outside of ourselves, so the organisation doesn't perceive expertise) 3. Have a long-term view of our ability to enable the overall organisation strategy (we are currently operating short term) 6. To add value through our efforts beyond our tasks and even beyond company need (how do we connect to a societal value/why?)	Important (Red)
5. Connect our value to the customer experience (our story is an internal resource only, which limits our potential)	Important (Amber)
1. Individuals are disconnected and don't feel engaged (we know they want to be part of something with a purpose, we have to create it) 2. We are losing team cohesiveness (we believe this is interrelated to all other points, but mostly due to not having a 'shared goal'	Important (Green)

4. This doesn't appear to be connected to this topic (we feel confident that there's no focus need here)	Not Important (Green)

STEP 3 – Capture obvious ideas, innovate and sieve for Golden Nuggets

Part 1: With all that you know from Step 2 – Lay of the land, capture the low-hanging fruit, the 'I just have to do that' thinking

Capture all ideas (What could you do?)	• Internal stakeholder survey • Seek counsel from internal stakeholders • Team brainstorm, to engage the team and enable thinking • Get a senior stakeholder to sponsor us • Ask senior stakeholders if they have an appetite for the output of our approach

Part 2: Now let your thinking expand to 'could I......? dare I......? what if I......?'

Innovate (What COULD you do?)	• Speak to external teams in other industries to understand how they might have navigated this • Consider relevant books and articles that might enable us • See if a consultant/team coach could help

Part 3: Place the relevant rating 'Not Now (NN)', 'Not Ever (NE)', 'Move Forward (MF)' in brackets next to 'Part 1: Captured and Part 2: Innovated' ideas. Move Forward (MF) are your Golden Nuggets

Sieve (Give a rating to Part 1 & 2 ideas and innovations) • Not Now (NN) • Not Ever (NE) • Move Forward (MF)	• Internal stakeholder survey (MF) • Seek counsel from internal stakeholders (MF) • Team brainstorm, to engage the team and enable thinking (NN) • Get a senior stakeholder to sponsor us (NN) • Ask senior stakeholders if they have an appetite for the output of our approach (MF) • Speak to external teams in other industries to understand how they might have navigated this (NN) • Consider relevant books and articles that might enable us (MF) • See if a consultant/team coach could help (NE)

Part 4: Review Part 3: Sieve and select the high-value, high-impact 'Golden Nuggets'. These are the things that excite you and which you believe will make a difference. These are Move Forward (MF)			

Golden Nuggets What are you really going to Move Forward (MF)	1. Internal stakeholder survey (MF) 2. Seek counsel from internal stake-holders (MF) 3. Ask senior stakeholders if they have an appetite for the output of our approach (MF) 4. Consider relevant books and articles that might enable us (MF)

STEP 4 – Risk Mitigation

What barriers exist for the Golden Nuggets?

Column 1	Column 2	Column 3	Column 4
Part 1: Transfer Take Golden Nuggets that you will Move Forward (MF) from Step 3, Part 4. Place here.	**Part 2: Barriers** Think through the barriers that exist for Part 1. Note here, then add (R) = Real (actual barrier) or (P) = Potential (unknown barrier)	**Part 3: Action** What are you going to do that is: Mindset 1: Trusted Mindset 2: Accountable Mindset 3: Brave Mindset 4: Connected	**Part 4: Ownership** Who is the person that owns this? Who's fully Mindset 1: Accountable?
Internal stakeholder survey (MF)	• Some will be happy to engage. Others will see this as a waste of time (R)	1. Test the water 2. Seek advice from someone trusted (Jill Smith) 3. Seek external advice	Jack H
Seek counsel from internal stake-holders (MF)	• We do not know who these people would be (R) • Some senior players might tell the MD to terminate this process (P)	1. Get out there and ask 2. Brainstorm who is most likely to enable us 3. When we have identified them, ask them	Susan L Jack H

Ask senior stake-holders if they have an appetite for the output of our approach, ie do they want it? (MF)	• Some will be happy to engage. Others will see it as a waste of time (R)	1. Speak to our counsel about the approach 2. Test the water with a 'target' and understand the reaction	Tom
Consider relevant books and articles that might enable us (MF)	None	None	None

STEP 5 – Committed Action

Commitments to making the Step 4 Golden Nugget actions happen (make them real and personalise)

- We need stakeholders to do the things they promised to do and we will approach them as individuals and as a team to add weight to our requests
- We will commit to regular conversations and set up a project group on our internal discussion board. It can be a closed group but we will stay connected
- We will learn how to Face Into on our fears about getting senior advocacy
- Commit to purchasing the books we need, summarise them for others and move at pace to increase our capability and confidence in this knowledge area

STEP 6 – Calibrate to closure

- Reference Step 4, Column 3, give a Red, Amber, Green (RAG Rating)
- Check in at agreed interval to reinforce effort and/or bring a challenge to inaction
- Red & Amber items drop through into next checkpoint

Calibrate each as Red, Amber or Green. Make notes to comment, celebrate and drive forward

Checkpoint 1: Target 09.01.2032 Actual 09.01. 2032	1. (Amber) Not done very well here. We have been a bit half-hearted in who we dealt with. We need help building our confidence to approach some of the more senior stakeholders 2. (Green) Brilliant, she laid it on the line for us and we have to Face Into the fact we still need to develop our confidence and methodology 3. (Green) So again this went well. Some really good conversations had in some other unrelated organisations, via our own Connections. Telling us 'again' that we are not as brave as we need to be. In terms of Living Brave we need to review our Mindset 1: Accountability, accepting we are below the line and recognise we don't have a high Mindset 2: Brave score. We have also recognised that we are talking a good talk but in terms of being Mindset 3: Connected we are very Pull rather than Connected.

	4. (Amber) (Repeat of Point 1) Not done very well here. It's been a bit halfhearted in who we have all gone at. We need help in gaining confidence to approach some of the more senior stakeholders 5. (Green) All done, we have a great stakeholder map 6. (Green) Was easy to work out who we should be speaking to 7. (Green) Gone well, had great advice and showed us the pace and style of approach 8. (Red) Not done
Red & Amber items drop through into next checkpoint	
Checkpoint 2: Target 11.05.2032 Actual 11.05.2032	1. (Green) We have been talking to people. Going very well and everyone is agreeing to contribute, especially when they found out the Exec team agreed. The story appears to be forming and people see that we are trying to move things forward 1. (Green) There's a head of steam now. As the interest grows in what we are doing, people are offering to help, guide, counsel. We just need to be careful we don't have too many chiefs trying to steer us and end up in the same submissive place again 8. (Amber) So we targeted 2 and have done one. The team member who didn't approach their target is unclear as to why they didn't. The rest of the team are disappointed however we hope to enable and support that member
As many checkpoints as required	
Closure statement Date: 14.05.2032	Great strides made. We have approached all stakeholders. We have an active group of advisors and we are learning as individuals and as a team. It feels like a real momentum has been built. We have had to have some really tough conversations with each other and have received some cumulative feedback that hurt our egos, however, the story now is shifting to us not being a group of people interacting, but a group of people working to become a team. The surveys we have done have been hugely insightful and created a real catalyst for us to change. We really must keep the momentum going now as we have created an expectation. We have a strong set of Umbrella Beliefs and these are being constantly reinforced by thinking of the four Living Brave Mindsets of Trust, Accountability, Bravery and Connection

ORGANISATION DEVELOPMENT
COMPLETED TEMPLATE

STEP 1 – Context & Why	
What's the context?	What's the 'why it matters'?
Innovation capability	**The thing we would like to move forward is…** our innovation capability. **The reason it's worth investing in is…** we are in a constant state of playing catch-up in many areas of the organisation; we follow, we don't lead. **The benefits of this would be to…** attract and retain talent, commercial growth as we take market share, increased consumer brand value.

STEP 2 – Lay of the land	
Column 1	Column 2
Part 1: Which number from Context Grid + associated reflection	**Part 2:** 'Important' or 'Not Important'. (Red, Amber or Green)
1. Senior manager self-awareness of their individual impact (we know they understand intellectually but are they motivated to care?) 3. We know we are missing opportunities (we don't really know to what extent or the value)	Important (Red)
4. Clients are annoyed by multiple points of contact (we have anecdotal feedback, but need to find more)	Important (Amber)
2. Create enterprise-focused senior management (currently, they don't see a need for anything other than transactional behaviours) 7. This is imperative to our success with future targets (they will require greater insight into potential opportunities)	Important (Green)
5. This doesn't directly impact on customers (there's no obvious link to increased customer value)	Not Important (Red)
6. Not a factor in this process (can't see how this would enable our CSR agenda)	Not Important (Green)

STEP 3 – Capture obvious ideas, innovate and sieve for Golden Nuggets	
Part 1: With all that you know from Step 2 – Lay of the land, capture the low-hanging fruit, the 'I just have to do that' thinking	
Capture all ideas (What could you do?)	• External consultancy to do a diagnostic • Internal HR to do a diagnostic • Find examples from other organisations where this has worked • Investigate research on this topic to confirm what we suspect • Get a target audience on board as part of the thinking process
Part 2: Now let your thinking expand to 'could I......? dare I......? what if I......?'	
Innovate (What COULD you do?)	• Run an assessment centre to rate individuals • Get them individual coaches
Part 3: Place the relevant rating 'Not Now (NN)', 'Not Ever (NE)', 'Move Forward (MF)' in brackets next to 'Part 1: Captured and Part 2: Innovated' ideas. Move Forward (MF) are your Golden Nuggets	
Sieve (Give a rating to Part 1 & 2 ideas and innovations) • Not Now (NN) • Not Ever (NE) • Move Forward (MF)	• External consultancy to do a diagnostic (MF) • Internal HR to do a diagnostic (NE) • Find examples from other organisations where this has worked (MF) • Investigate research on this topic to evidence, what we suspect (NN) • Get one of the target audience as part of the thinking process (NN) • Run an assessment centre to rate individuals (NE) • Get them individual coaches (NN)
Part 4: Review Part 3: Sieve and select the high-value, high-impact 'Golden Nuggets'. These are the things that excite you and which you believe will make a difference. These are Move Forward (MF)	
Golden Nuggets What are you really going to Move Forward (MF)	1. External consultancy to do a diagnostic (MF) 2. Find examples from other organisations where this has worked (MF)

STEP 4 – Risk Mitigation

What barriers exist for the Golden Nuggets?

Column 1	Column 2	Column 3	Column 4
Part 1: Transfer Take Golden Nuggets that you will Move Forward (MF) from Step 3, Part 4. Place here.	**Part 2: Barriers** Think through the barriers that exist for Part 1. Note here, then add (R) = Real (actual barrier) or (P) = Potential (unknown barrier)	**Part 3: Action** What are you going to do that is: Mindset 1: Trusted Mindset 2: Accountable Mindset 3: Brave Mindset 4: Connected	**Part 4: Ownership** Who is the person that owns this? Who's fully Mindset 1: Accountable?
1. External consultancy to do a diagnostic (MF)	• No budget (P) • We don't know who to ask (R) • Might be perceived as a waste of money (P)	1. Create a case and bring to Exec Team 2. Ask HR to investigate 3. Ask own contacts 4. Ensure we all believe in its validity and then stand by that	Lucy L Sian M
2. Find examples from other organisations where this has worked (MF)	• We don't know any (R) • Don't have the resources to figure it out (P)	1. Ask own contacts 2. Cost proposal, no more than two slides, keep it simple	Jasper C Charlotte F

STEP 5 – Committed Action

Commitments to making the Step 4 Golden Nugget actions happen (make them real and personalise)

• All contribute to finding the budget
• Lead the way in looking outside of ourselves.
• Demonstrate we have regular streams of new thinking and external input.
• We can stand on the shoulders of others

STEP 6 – Calibrate to closure	
• Reference Step 4, Column 3, give a Red, Amber, Green (RAG Rating) • Check in at agreed interval to reinforce effort and/or bring a challenge to inaction • Red & Amber items drop through into next checkpoint	
Calibrate each as Red, Amber or Green. Make notes to comment, celebrate and drive forward	
Checkpoint 1: Target 02.01.25 Actual 05.01.2033	1. (Amber) Created but only by a few of us. Some of the team seemed to opt out of the reality of doing the work. We have had to have some very real conversations about Accountability and the focus of some people in terms of Trust. Seems we have pressed the reset button 2. (Green) HR has been excellent, they know good people and have brought forward some great external people for us to consider working with 3. (Amber) Some yes and no here. See first bullet. The same people and same outcome 4. (Amber) See first bullet. The same people and same outcome 5. (Amber) See first bullet. The same people and same outcome 6. (Green) This is done and is a simple and succinct 2 pager/ slides. We intend to get a pre-meeting to get the challenge out the way before we get into the room
Red & Amber items drop through into next checkpoint	
Checkpoint 2: Target 11.03.2033 Actual 02.04.2033	1. (Green) All done, we kept it short after the counsel we received. It went well with the cost proposal. Very good team effort on this. Everyone got involved, felt good and the output is strong 1. (Green) We were a bit weak here, but HR nailed it with some great contacts 2. (Green) Feels like a team now, after a false start. We just need to keep the focus 3. (Green) As above after the chat; we have really made strides in this. We have reached out to a lot of high-quality people and got some real insights that we would never have thought of
As many checkpoints as required	
Closure statement Date: 13.07.2033	Final note. I think we all feel that we have done well. We didn't gel right at the start, so we had to put our big pants on in order to have those Accountability and Bravery conversations. The proof though is in the pudding. The Exec bought into it immediately. Some great comments about us having seen an issue found solutions and moved them to a point of planned action. So we are now in the process of working with a small but well-re

| | garded consultancy that has a lot of great clients and great testimonials. |
| | It's taught us a lot about the power of the team and we are starting to see how Living Brave can really enable us as a team and as leaders of the organisation, not just leaders in the organisation. |

REFERENCES

No.	Link (Correct at time of print)	Page no.	Content
1	http://worldhappiness.report/	10	World Happiness Report
2	https://www.theguardian.com/politics/2010/oct/26/britain-corrupt-mps-expenses-scandal	12	Britain 'seen as more corrupt since MPs' expenses scandal'
3	https://www.theguardian.com/business/2017/jan/18/libor-scandal-the-bankers-who-fixed-the-worlds-most-important-number	13	Libor scandal: the bankers who fixed the world's most important number
4	https://www.afr.com/business/banking-and-finance/citi-rbs-jpmorgan-barclays-ubs-seen-pleading-guilty-to-us-felony-charges-20150514-gh1de4	13	Citi, RBS, JPMorgan, Barclays, UBS seen pleading guilty to US felony charges
5	https://www.theguardian.com/media/2014/jun/26/jimmy-savile-sexual-abuse-timeline	13	Jimmy Savile: timeline of his sexual abuse and its uncovering
6	https://www.vox.com/culture/2017/11/3/16602628/kevin-spacey-sexual-assault-allegations-house-of-cards	13	The sexual assault allegations against Kevin Spacey span decades
7	https://www.bbc.co.uk/news/entertainment-arts-41594672	13	Harvey Weinstein timeline: How the scandal unfolded
8	https://www.bbc.co.uk/news/uk-43091628	13	Ex-Oxfam aid worker tells of sex assaults by colleagues
9	http://appleinsider.com/articles/18/01/05/law-firm-that-extracted-450m-settlement-in-apple-e-books-case-is-going-after-company-for-throttling-iphones	13	Law firm that extracted $450M settlement in Apple e-books case is going after company for throttling iPhones
10	https://www.bbc.co.uk/news/business-46056279	13	German consumer group sues VW over emissions scandal
11	https://www.theguardian.com/commentisfree/2018/feb/17/steven-pinker-media-negative-news	13	The media exaggerates negative news. This distortion has consequences
12	https://www.edelman.co.uk/magazine/posts/edelman-trust-barometer-2017-uk-findings/	13	Edelman Trust Barometer, 2019

13   https://www.edelman.com/news-awards/2019-edelman-trust-barometer-reveals-my-employer-most-trusted-institution   13   Edelman Trust Barometer, 2019

14   http://www.bestyears.com/heroesgone.html   71   Where Have All the Heroes Gone?

15   https://news.sky.com/story/aung-san-suu-kyi-stripped-of-amnesty-award-after-shameful-betrayal-of-values-over-rohingya-11552683   72   Aung San Suu Kyi stripped of Amnesty award after 'shameful betrayal of values' over Rohingya

16   https://en.wikipedia.org/wiki/Dune_(novel)   82   Dune, Frank Herbert

17   https://henrinouwen.org/meditation/hidden-greatness/   83   henrinouwen.org

18   https://www.youtube.com/watch?v=tL-t5rBfNucc   89, 90   Cat on a vacuum cleaner

19   https://ourworldindata.org/child-mortality   89   Child mortality

20   https://en.wikipedia.org/wiki/Alexander_Fleming   89, 90   Penicillin, Alexander Flemming

21   https://en.wikipedia.org/wiki/Spanish_flu   90   Spanish Flu kills 500 million

22   https://en.wikipedia.org/wiki/World_War_II   90   World War 2

23   https://ourworldindata.org/extreme-poverty   90   Poverty figures

24   https://ourworldindata.org/life-expectancy   90   Life expectancy

25   https://ourworldindata.org/war-and-peace   90   Armed conflict death rates reduce

26   https://www.cancer.org/latest-news/facts-and-figures-2019.html   91   Cancer rates on the decline

27   https://www.theguardian.com/global-development-professionals-network/2015/jul/01/global-access-clean-water-sanitation-mapped   91   Access to sanitation increased

28   https://www.pewresearch.org/global/2017/12/05/worldwide-people-divided-on-whether-life-today-is-better-than-in-the-past/   91   Worldwide, People Divided on Whether Life Today Is Better Than in the Past

29	https://conexus.cberdata.org/files/Mfg-Reality.pdf	92	Job losses due to technology
30	https://bits.blogs.nytimes.com/2009/12/09/the-american-diet-34-gigabytes-a-day/	92	Roger Bon, data consumption
31	https://www2.deloitte.com/content/dam/Deloitte/be/Documents/technology-media-telecommunications/global-mobile-consumer-survey-2017_belgian-edition.pdf	92	Consumer usage patterns of the smartphone- Global Mobile Consumer Survey
32	https://en.wikipedia.org/wiki/Lactose_intolerance	93	Lactose intolerance
33	https://www.sciencedaily.com/releases/2012/03/120327124243.htm	94	Cows domesticated 10,500 years
34	https://2www.youtube.com/watch?v=-J54k7WrbfMg	94	Sean Parker, Chamath Palihapitiya - Facebook is 'Ripping Apart Society'
35	https://www.bbc.co.uk/news/world-europe-34818994	94	Paris attacks: What happened on the night
36	https://www.cos-eu.com/en/find-cancer-france-cos/cancer-statistics-france/	94	Cancer statistics in france
37	https://www.washingtonpost.com/news/monkey-cage/wp/2015/11/23/youre-more-likely-to-be-fatally-crushed-by-furniture-than-killed-by-aterrorist/?noredirect=on&utm_term=.cf204e2db18c	94	You're more likely to be fatally crushed by furniture than killed by a terrorist
38	https://www.telegraph.co.uk/news/2018/11/01/work-related-stress-mental-illness-now-accounts-half-work-absences/	95	Work-related stress and mental illness now accounts for over half of work absences
39	https://www.theguardian.com/money/2015/sep/07/america-vacation-workaholic-culture-labor-day	95	Why is America so afraid to take a vacation?
40	https://www.theguardian.com/money/2015/dec/18/britain-private-wealth-owned-by-top-10-of-households	95	Almost half of Britain's private wealth owned by the top 10% of households
41	https://www.edelman.com/research/2017-edelman-trust-barometer	96	2017 Edelman Trust Barometer

42   https://www.theguardian.com/ world/2012/oct/09/taliban-paki- stan-shoot-girl-malala-yousafzai

131   Malala Yousafzai: Pakistan Taliban causes revulsion by shooting a girl who spoke out

43   https://www.jnj.com/credo/

133   Johnson & Johnson, Our Credo

44   https://en.wikipedia.org/wiki/Tim_ Collins_(British_Army_officer)

150   Colonel Tim Collins, known for role in Iraq War in 2003

45   https://en.wikipedia.org/wiki/Kintsugi

153   Kintsugi, Golden repair

46   https://en.wikipedia.org/wiki/Reg_Re- vans

   Reg Revan, Action Learn- ing pioneer

47   https://en.wikipedia.org/wiki/ Moli%C3%A8re

158   Moliere, French playwright

48   https://www.youtube.com/ watch?v=LIL8-f4o0ss

161   Misery, Hobbling scene

49   https://en.wikipedia.org/wiki/Pe- ter_principle

175   The Peter Principle, 1969. 'People rise to own level of incompetence'

50   https://en.wikipedia.org/wiki/Personal- ity_type#Types_vs._traits

207   Trait & Type perspectives

51   https://en.wikipedia.org/wiki/Big_Five_ personality_traits

207   Big Five Personality Traits

52   https://en.wikipedia.org/wiki/Jor- dan_Belfort

214   Jordan Belfort, former stockbroker, Wolf of Wall Street

53   https://www.youtube.com/ watch?v=zE7PKRjrid4

245   Blue Pill or Red Pill – The Matrix

INDEX

Working with

LIVING BRAVE
leadership

KEYNOTE

EXECUTIVE COACHING

TEAM EFFECTIVENESS

LEADERSHIP & MANAGEMENT

DEVELOPMENT

If the thinking and the focus of this book has resonated

and you would like to talk about how we might work together

then please make contact:

Email	**guybloom@livingbrave.com**
Web	**www.livingbrave.com**
LinkedIn	**guybloom**
Instagram	**contactbloom**
Twitter	**@contactbloom**

Printed in Great
Britain
by Amazon

32488220R00179